(THE BEST OF) SHOOTING A DOG THING

by Paul Castle and Friends

Foreword by Paul Cornell,
Introduction by David J. Howe
Afterword by Anneke Wills

HIRST BOOKS

Paul Castle : Shooty Dog Thing

First Published February 2010
by Hirst Books

Hirst Books, Suite 285 Andover House, George Yard, Andover, Hants, SP10 1PB

ISBN 978-0-9557149-4-8

Cover by Lee Thompson

Printed and bound by Good News Press

Paper stock used is natural, recyclable and made from wood grown in
sustainable forests. The manufacturing processes conform to environmental
regulations.

www.hirstbooks.com

(THE BEST OF)
SHOOTY DOG THING
by Paul Castle and...

Jon Arnold, Elizabeth Burak, Lawrence Burton,
Lee Catigen-Cooper, Danielle Ellison, Terry Francis,
James Gent, Angela Giblin, Stephen Gray, James
Hadwen, Tim Hirst, Arfie Mansfield, Iain Martin, Nick
Mellish, Patrick Mulready, Wesley Osam, Richard
Parker, Erik Pollitt, and James Powell.

with thanks to
Lisa Bowerman, Paul Cornell, David J. Howe,
and Anneke Wills.

Cover by Lee Thompson

For Mum & Dad,

and everyone who read the fanzine.

Contents

Foreword	Paul Cornell	7
Introduction	David J. Howe	8
Shooty Dog Thing?	Paul Castle	12
The Accidental Conventioner	Angela Giblin	13
All My Love to Long Ago	Paul Castle	14
Take Five Theory? Nah...	Iain Martin	21
The Seven Stages of Fandom	Paul Castle	23
What's That Coming Out of the Smog?	Iain Martin	27
Doctor in Love	Paul Castle	29
Equal and Opposite Fan Reactions	Paul Castle & Stephen Gray	33
Bernice Summerfield: The Inside Story	Jon Arnold	44
Lisa Bowerman Interview	Paul Castle	47
Benny Accolade	Elizabeth Burak	53
Twenty-Oh-Nine	Paul Castle	57
Craggles Rocked!	Jon Arnold	62
The Twenty-First Century	Patrick Mulready	70
Who Cares!	Tim Hirst	77
Licence Denied	Jon Arnold	79
Nasty, Brutish, and Short	Paul Castle	82
Unmuddying the Waters	Lawrence Burton	93
Going Back to the Beginning	Angela Giblin	97
'And Cut It... Now!'	Jon Arnold	99
We've Got Love for You if You Were Who in the Eighties!	Erik Pollitt	101
The Shooty Review:		103
Timelash	Paul Castle	104
The Two Doctors	James Gent	107
The 'Eighteen Month Hiatus'	Arfie Mansfield	111
The Gift	James Hadwen	113
The Ultimate Adventure	Terry Francis	115
The Stranger	Paul Castle	118
The Age of Chaos	James Hadwen	121
Time of Your Life	Wesley Osam	123

The Holy Terror	James Powell	126
Teach Yourself Ballroom Dancing	Jon Arnold	130
It's All About Unfinished Business	Jon Arnold	134
Do the M.O.N.S.T.E.R.M.A.S.H!	Paul Castle	148
Alien Bodies: The End was Nigh?	Jon Arnold	168
Tune In, Tune Out	Nick Mellish	172
Missing Episodes?	Paul Castle	175
Tennant's Hamlet	Jon Arnold	177
The War Machines of the Daleks	Paul Castle	179
Cy-Fi: The Sixties	Paul Castle	182
The Good, the Bad, and the Ugly!	Paul Castle	199
Iris? Iris? Who the Heck is Iris?	Jon Arnold	205
Missing Pieces	Jon Arnold	207
Doctor What If?	Nick Mellish & Paul Castle	210
Season of Mists	Paul Castle	221
Short Trips: The End of the Road?	Jon Arnold	226
6b Or Not 6b	Paul Castle	230
Who Could Have Been the 456?	Paul Castle	237
Mirror, Mirror, On the Wall...	Lee Catigen-Cooper	240
Iris Wildthyme and the Celestial Omnibus	Jon Arnold	241
Wallowing in the Icecanos of Nostalgia	Paul Castle	244
Suits You Sir!	Paul Castle	246
Dimensions 2009	Richard Parker	247
Afterword	Anneke Wills	250
A Night at the Pictures	Paul Castle & Danielle Ellison	251

FOREWORD
by Paul Cornell

I like a fanzine. I'm glad the internet hasn't completely killed them, that there are still three or four about. You don't get many meaty articles on the internet. And nobody edits it. Ah yes, 'edit', I may have to define that word these days: someone else looks at your work, and tells you that not all of your first draft will be published. That you may have to think about it for a second or two after you've written it. That it might not appear at all, but instead be replaced by the work of someone else. Yes, I know, nothing on the Blogger desktop can prepare you for the sheer ontological shock of all that.

But now I'm scared of sounding so old. So let's look in the other direction. It's good that *Shooty Dog Thing* isn't printed unless it has to be. Because one thing the internet could do, if we let it, is stop us cutting down enormous forests. It's good that a lot of its contributors weren't around for old *Doctor Who*. Sorry, Classic *Doctor Who*. Because we need a whole bunch of *Who* fan writers to fill the ecological niches left by those that went to write for and about the show itself on a professional basis. Because no, we can't be both poachers and gamekeepers. Every few weeks I see a new expression of the prescribed ways in which one can and should be a joyous, happy *Doctor Who* fan, sharing creativity and laughter and Not Taking It Too Seriously, and Drashigs, eh, weren't they a hoot? And I agree, up to a point. It's brilliant we've had a breath of fresh air through our fandom. It's excellent when a fandom has to encounter and deal with the mainstream, and, well, girls. You know I think the new show is as great as people say it is, and I'll always be grateful for having had the chance to work on it. But, damn it, we should value the awkward bastards too. The ones who do Take It Too Seriously. Because I did, back in the day. That's what got me here. So, you in the coat, who believes in something huge and serious and can't make your voice heard over everyone being so damn happy about all this trivial nonsense: don't stop. Write it for a fanzine. If we ever meet, I'll probably find you deeply irritating. But in many ways, that's the point.

So I commend the following collection to you. It includes the funny, the heart warming, the charming, and also the awkward, the arty, the angry. *Doctor Who* fandom has always been a brawling froth of creativity. That continues.

INTRODUCTION
by David J. Howe

Fanzines. I love 'em. But many readers of this book may be wondering what they are. Perhaps they are something which may have been read about on the Internet, or maybe they have been encountered through a passion for football, or perhaps indie music. *Viz* comic started life as a fanzine in 1979, and still retains that anarchic air. There are fanzines available on many subjects, and, once, a long time ago, there were literally hundreds and hundreds of fanzines available on *Doctor Who*.

When I first became interested in *Doctor Who* fandom back in 1976, one of the first things I did was to join the *Doctor Who* Appreciation Society, a group of like-minded individuals who published newsletters and magazines about *Doctor Who*. Their newsletter was (and still is) called *The Celestial Toyroom*, and their magazine was called *TARDIS*. *CT* was an A4 sized publication, stapled in the top left hand corner while *TARDIS* was an A5 sized booklet. Both were the first fanzines that I had ever seen.

The very next year, 1977, I decided to publish my own fanzine. Through the DWAS I had met some fans who lived locally to me and we had formed our own 'Local Group' of the main Society. And we did what many other fans of the time did - we published our own fanzine. The first issue of my first zine had the snappy title of *The Surbiton Doctor Who Appreciation Society Local Group Fanzine* and I photocopied it up at a local shop which had a copier, which were quite hard to find at that time. Copies cost 6 pence per sheet, and there were 6 sheets in the first issue, so the cover price was 36 pence. It was launched at the first ever *Doctor Who* convention, held at the start of August 1977 in Battersea, London, and we sold all the issues I brought with me to the event.

At that first convention there was a single table selling fanzines. There were maybe 5 or so titles there ... the next year, there were about four or five tables which were groaning under the weight of the number of titles. As the years rolled by, so the number of fanzines available seemed to increase exponentially. There were A5 sized ones, A4 sized ones, fanzines hand-written on lined paper pulled from an exercise book, photocopied zines of every flavour, from fiction to articles, interviews to parodies, hand-coloured cartoons to professional quality artwork ... as technology rolled forward and photocopying became more sophisticated and accurate, so the roneo stencil zines of the seventies regenerated into the superbly laid out fanzines of the eighties. Covers became litho, photographic reproduction improved, and soon only colour printing was out of the reach of most fanzine editors, although some of the more successful titles even managed to break through that barrier in time.

The DWAS' newsletter started to take advertisements for fanzines, and before long there were more adverts than there were pages in the newsletter. So a separate publication was created, the *CT Advertiser*, solely to contain all the fanzine adverts there were that many. I collected as many issues of the fanzines as I could, hundreds of titles and tens of issues of many of them. The good ones lasted the longest. Two or three years was a good run, and the zines only stopped when those producing them left school or college, got jobs, girlfriends and boyfriends, and the time needed to edit, publish and distribute them together vanished.

But then, something happened. As the eighties became the nineties, so the number of fanzines slowed, and eventually stopped altogether. They died out, it seems, almost overnight. Many of the talented editors went on to land jobs with publishers, magazines and other companies involved with telefantasy publishing and, of course, *Doctor Who* itself. Gary Russell, one-time editor of *Doctor Who Magazine*, range editor for Big Finish on their *Doctor Who* audio plays, and now script editor for *Doctor Who* on television, started out editing and publishing a fanzine called *Shada*; several of the writers who worked on *SFX* magazine, like Ian Berriman and Steve O'Brien, started out writing for fanzines; Paul Simpson, currently editor of Titan's *Star Trek* magazine worked with me on the early issues of my own zine; novelist and scriptwriter of the acclaimed two-part adventure *Human Nature/The Family of Blood* for David Tennant's Doctor, Paul Cornell, started out writing for fanzines ... many, many talented and creative people honed their writing, editing and artistic skills publishing and contributing to fanzines over the years.

But all the fanzines gradually stopped when this literal hotbed of talent moved onwards and upwards to bring their skills to bear on everything from the BBC's range of DVD releases, to *Doctor Who Magazine*, to the actual show itself. The problem was that there was nothing and no-one to replace them. The culprit was, I feel, technology, and more specifically the Internet. With the Internet, anyone could create a website for free, there was no need to spend your own hard earned cash on photocopying, layout sheets, buying Letraset letters to make the pages look nicer, learning how to lay out words and pictures so they looked nice on the page. If you succeeded then people bought your mag, if you didn't then sales were non-existent and the fanzine folded. With the Internet all of that went. Writers could put their own musings in blogs and on websites where an editor's eye never went near the sometimes incoherent ramblings that were 'published'. All the photos could be borrowed from the BBC website and reproduced in full colour, and even the most illiterate of fans could produce a reasonable looking web page with very little effort and no outlay.

So fanzines died.

Almost.

Because out there were still some people who appreciated the ethos of a fanzine, and of asking people to pay good money for something physical and tangible which you could keep and enjoy and appreciate in a way that ephemeral websites could never hope to replicate. These days, however, the number of print fanzines can be counted on the fingers of one hand. There's *TSV*, a marvellous A5 fanzine produced by Paul Scoones in New Zealand, the marvellous *Enlightenment* produced by Graeme Burk in Canada … but in the UK … next to nothing. Until a zine called *Shooty Dog Thing* appeared, edited by Paul Castle. The interesting thing about *Shooty Dog Thing* was that it was free. Paul had taken the innovative leap of producing the fanzine using the PDF format, which meant that readers could appreciate pages which looked like proper laid out magazine pages. They could be read on-screen, or could be printed out as a double-sided hard-copy to create a proper print magazine format. A brilliant idea, and a great way of maintaining the physical quality of the fanzine while using technology to aid its production.

Celebrating Paul's achievement is this book: a collection of some of the best articles and features from *Shooty Dog Thing*. Talented writers musing on a wide range of subjects, some serious, some less so, but all interesting and all giving the reader something to think about. Fanzines have always been all about trying to present an alternate view, something different from the mainstream, and Paul manages this in the pages of *SDT*. Irreverent, infuriating and perplexing, but always full of ideas and controversy and things that you would never find in the pages of the official *Doctor Who* magazine.

I hope that this collection of some of the work that Paul has presented over the last few years finds favour with fans of the show. Like Paul Cornell's 1997 book *Licence Denied* from Virgin Publishing which presented a selection of fanzine writings from the period, Stephen James Walker's more recent *Talkback* books from Telos Publishing, which present over three volumes many of the best interviews with people involved in the production and making of *Doctor Who*, and the new series of *Time Unincorporated* books published by Mad Norwegian Press celebrating fanzine writing, this book you hold in your hands acts as a sort of historic repository of a fanzine which is almost unique in its time - a free and immaculately presented collection of writings and ideas and opinions which generates a reaction in its readership.

It would be wonderful if more fans of the show could take Paul's model and create their own fanzines, helping their writers to hone their skills, learning how to edit and to be edited, what works and what falls flat, and to create something original inspired by their love of *Doctor Who* and the incredible concepts and visuals which the show presents us with. Who knows ... if this happened, then these young fans could be the magazine editors, cover artists and even script editors, showrunners and writers of *Doctor Who*'s future.

SHOOTY DOG THING?
by Paul Castle

When people encounter *Shooty Dog Thing* the reaction is usually the same. There's a pause, a half smile, and that funny vocalisation made when a question's coming but doesn't quite know how to word itself. Provoking an interest in a complete stranger is a quality that will get any salesman or marketer rubbing their hands with glee and updating their facebook with 'will - this time next year - be a millionaire!'.

But money's not the be all and end all in life: some things have a far greater value. The fanzine *Shooty Dog Thing* came about after a shy young man went to a *Doctor Who* convention called 'Regenerations' in 2006 and lacked the confidence to join in the throng at the bar. He was at the con with some good friends, but they wanted to spend all their time at the guest panels and in the autograph queues, and he'd been there and done all that the previous year. What he wanted to do was join the raucous lot in the overcrowded bar, just didn't really know how. Oh, he knew how to do it online on forums etc: you just jump in with your tuppence worth, but in real life? In real life you've got to be interesting!

So, he created *Shooty Dog Thing*. Most of the time fans recognise the reference - it's how Anthony Stewart Head's character describes K9 in a 2006 episode of *Doctor Who* - and because it's a recognised term it's a meme with a very high fidelity. At 'Regenerations 2007' he had the confidence to simply walk into the bar and talk to people, knowing that his three issues of *Shooty* to date had infiltrated fandom with all the voracity of an STD. He waved hard-copies of the 'zine about and liberally distributed business cards which had all the download details. By the time that shy young man had gotten to bed the next morning, he'd turned into me.

Shooty Dog Thing was created to make an impression in *Doctor Who* fandom, but it far surpassed my wildest expectation. The friends I have made over the past couple of years are worth more to me than that imagined salesman's millions, and the nights I have had drinking in hotel bars until 5am in the morning laughing and joking would never have happened. So, everyone who's ever read *Shooty*, thank you for making life that much more enjoyable.

THE ACCIDENTAL CONVENTIONER
by Angela Giblin
Original material for The Best of Shooty Dog Thing

If you would have told me three weeks ago that by today I would have had breakfast with The Doctor or been kissed by Davros then I would have told you, in no uncertain terms that you were a complete loon who didn't know me at all. And yet… A fortnight ago I did a small and simple favour for a friend and now I find myself in a hotel bar in Swansea drinking with the great and the good of the *Doctor Who* world.

For an event called 'Regenerations 2009' I was expecting to find a room full of the stereotypical sci-fi fan - dirty t-shirt, no discernable social skills, hair cut by his Mum, never spoken to a woman that wasn't selling them something, works in IT and an encyclopaedic knowledge of the cast, crew, plots and characters. 'There won't be anyone like me there' and to a certain extent, I was not disappointed. Don't get me wrong I was thrilled to listen to a gentleman who worked in Asda telling a well respected director of thirty years exactly where he went wrong with episode 3 of season 4. There are definite candidates to prove Sir Derek's quote in *The Times* (which he now emphatically denies when confronted) about fans never having had a wash or a f#@k but there are so many others I was surprised to see. The little boys dressed as their favourite characters in multicoloured jumpers and scarves lovingly copied by dedicated grandmothers was a joy. The wonderfully warm and polite retired actors in the hallways having a 'Thesp off' by quoting Shakespeare at each other were brilliantly funny and the quietly earnest collectors of toys, photos and autographs were all perfectly lovely and what I had considered to be a 'best case scenario'.

What surprised me; caught me off guard and was frankly, staggered by were the amount of people just there to laugh, drink, catch up with friends scattered across the country and generally have a bloody good time surrounded by cool bits of kit you could frighten your friends with from a TV show they really liked. I spent many, many hours sitting with the most welcoming bunch of strangers I have ever met, laughing and joking. Hearing stories of passed conventions, being whisked away every twenty minutes to meet the next person, the next

13

group, the other gang and to take more photos than David Bailey of new friends. What was lovely is that with the female contingent of the weekend being pretty low there was hardly any bitchiness. Obviously there is some - we can't help ourselves - but nowhere near the usual levels and nowhere near as vicious. A tight knit group with a lot of handy information to make the uninitiated feel right at home within minutes.

Onto the celebs: so while I have no idea who most of these actors were, have little idea of anything that was filmed before the new millennium and a new interest in learning, I now know what the bum of a Knight feels like. That there are two ex companions walking around in fashion items taken from my wardrobe (with one of them pretending it's YSL and not Matalan). I have a highly inappropriate and sexually explicit nickname from an ex-Doctor (unearned), and a standing invitation to go to dinner with a supporting actor old enough to be my Dad (unlikely). I never remember falling in to something so easily and so comfortably in all my life and long may it continue.

I was told that Cary Woodward organises the best convention of the year. It's just as well, because nothing will be able to touch this weekend away for fun, new friends and overall presentation. I just can't bring myself to let go now. I'm stalking the Internet for photos of panels I didn't see and stories of wrong rooms and lost trousers in elevators. I'm looking to see where to go next. It may be the best, but it can't be the last.

ALL MY LOVE TO LONG AGO
by Paul Castle
Originally printed in Shooty Dog Thing #4 – Winter 2007

'But in spite of this difference in appearance, the latest Doctor showed many of the qualities of the three who had gone before. The strong will and brilliant scientific brain of the first, the inconsequential humour of the second, the warmth and charm of the third. A strange mixture of contradictory qualities, genius and clown, hero and buffoon, he was well equipped to face the many exciting adventures that lay before him.' From *The Making of Doctor Who*, by Terrance Dicks and Malcolm Hulke, 1976 edition (p22)

I sometimes wonder why it is that us *Doctor Who* fans are so interested in the similarities between the Doctors when it's the *differences* that *differentiate* one from the other. Surely the appeal of regeneration - especially in these last fifteen years or so of *Missing Adventure* novels and Big Finish audio plays which deliver the adventures of the different Doctors in parallel rather than in series - is that it provides a different way of expressing the central character? A different Doctor's reactions to events throw a different slant on a story. I remember when, in 1989, *The Ultimate Adventure* stageplay saw Jon Pertwee bow out and Colin Baker take over, the Doctor's attitude to the Prime Minister (quite clearly Maggie Thatcher, but not explicitly named) changed from charm and deference in the original version to rudeness and disrespect in Colin's stint. This is precisely how it should be - the Doctor isn't simply one man with a different face every few years, he's one man with a totally new personality. Terrance Dicks' approach of writing the character to emphasise the similarities (so much so that when I was reading his novelisations a kid I sometimes didn't know if it was a third Doctor story with Sarah or a fourth Doctor story with Sarah if the cover didn't give it away) just doesn't seem right.

But in the last year or so, I've encountered in passing online comments about something called the 'take five theory'. I don't think there's been anything lengthy written about it, so I hope no-one minds if I nick the idea and run with it here. For those of you who've not come across the term, the 'take five theory' points out that, for all the Doctors from the mid eighties onwards, there's a strong similarity with the incarnation from five regenerations ago. There's nothing conscious about it; I think it's just how it worked out. As the eighth Doctor said, 'I love humans, always seeing patterns in things that aren't there...' though it might be something to do with the fact that since producer John Nathan-Turner's approach to *Doctor Who* in the nineteen eighties, the series has been rather more concerned with what happened in its own history than it ever has before. Wesley Osam commented on this sort of thing in his review this issue, and I think that it's this phenomenon of a more formulaic approach to writing *Doctor Who* that's resulted in the 'take five theory'.

But whatever the origin of this remarkable pattern, it's one which is seductive. It just seems to fit all the facts like a glove, though it's quite conceivable that my seduction with the concept has blinded me to the counter arguments, so I asked occasional *Shooty Dog Thing* contributor Iain Martin to beta read this to temper my approach a bit, but arch-critic such as even he struggled!

Oh, and whilst we're on the subject, this article's not inspired by the recent Children in Need short, but has been knocked back issue after issue since this fanzine began due to me not finding a way to express it. But as Iain said of *Time Crash*'s similarity to the 'take five theory': 'Yes, it was quite blatant, and Tennant's done most of your work for you there!' so if I'm going to write this damned thing at all, it's now or never!

David Tennant & Peter Davison

There are many similarities between these two Doctors, both in front of the camera and beyond it. I think the one that struck me first was that both Peter Davison and David Tennant had quite a task ahead of them when they were announced as the new incarnation of the nation's beloved Time Lord. For them both it was a regeneration that was a make or break for the series in such a way that hadn't been seen since the second Doctor, Patrick Troughton, had the challenge of carrying off the first regeneration convincingly. Both the fifth and tenth Doctors were in a position where the ostensibly target audience of pre-teens would have little or no knowledge of any Doctors before the Doctor they'd just seen vanish in a blaze of light to appear as this strange young bloke. If Peter Davison hadn't succeeded in convincing the youngsters who'd known no-one but Tom as the Doctor, then the series would have whimpered and died before its twentieth anniversary. David Tennant had the same problem - the babies born in the year when *Doctor Who* was last on telly as an ongoing series were now taking their driving tests - and the charismatic and talented actor who'd convinced the world that *Doctor Who* wasn't a joke was bowing out just as the series was getting popular. The naysayers of fandom were proclaiming the end of the world just as the episode of that title was going out on screen. Bless. But David Tennant, like Davison before him, has won his share of the viewers.

Another similarity, whilst we're still outside the box, is that both Davison and Tennant were already household names when they were announced as the Doctor. Peter Davison was well established as young vet'nary Tristan Farnon in *All Creatures Great and Small* (the *Heartbeat* of its day), so much so that a young fan told him on telly (the clip's on one of the DVDs in the *New Beginnings* boxed set, I gather) that he should play the Doctor as Tristan, but brave. And so he did. And David Tennant was a *Radio Times* cover star for his role as Russell T. Davies' version of *Casanova* a few weeks before the return of *Doctor Who* to the screen. And watching that, I thought that he'd make a good Doctor just by being Casanova without the shagging. And so he was, but something must have stuck, for in his first regular episode he was passionately kissed by Billie Piper's character. As the tenth Doctor said, 'still got it then' before going onto find that practically all female co-stars fell for him big time. Quite right too.

I'm labouring the off-screen stuff a little, so I'll breeze through the on-screen stuff. Both the fifth and tenth Doctors have been more youthful than any of their predecessors, and have this wild boundless energy which has them racing about and talking at high speeds as if they need to get the ideas out before they run out of air. They both wear trainers and brainy specs and everything else that TenDoc notes in *Time Crash*, pre-empting this feature somewhat. The only thing the tenth Doctor lacks is the decorative vegetable, the obsession with cricket and, thankfully, the fact that he's not leaving at the end of his third series. Like the fifth, he's *my* Doctor.

Christopher Eccleston & Tom Baker

This is the one match where there's not a lot to say. Both actors really made the role their own and incomparable with other incarnations, so there are more differences than similarities. Though it's got to be said that both Doctors turn on a sixpence from being highly introverted to highly extroverted, and when they're in the room they dominate it the second that they want to. One of the ninth Doctor's most Tom Bakerish moments is in the episode *Aliens of London* where, halfway through a briefing of alien experts in the heart of 10 Downing Street, he suddenly flips from being a totally unnoticed presence in the room to the centre of attention.

One other thing that they share, in my personal opinion, is that they are actors whose Doctor I never rate that highly on those interminable polls we get online, but when actually watching them they are *the* Doctor and you think of none other than them.

Paul McGann & Jon Pertwee

Oh, now this one, *this one* is no mere co-incidence. This is 1996 and one of the most anally retentive eras of the show, where the eighth Doctor was modelled on the *idea* of what the Doctor should be. He was clad in a costume based on the production team's idea of previous Doctors, and looking at the wing collars, cravat and waistcoat this is a clearly smartened up version of Tom Baker's Doctor with a good chunk of William Hartnell, but due to the use of velvet the overall impression one gets is of Jon Pertwee's poncy elegance.

This is reinforced by the adventurous nature of Paul McGann's Doctor, as it's clear from the way he jumps on the police motorcycle and rides like a bat out of hell that if he'd continued as the Doctor in a full series on television he'd have put the third Doctor to shame in terms of vehicles and love of gadgets (the latter indicated by the return of the Sonic Screwdriver) and tinkering with machines (the way he rewires the TARDIS console and shamelessly guts the workings of San Francisco's prized atomic clock for the required spare part).

Other stuff which not only reinforces the impression that producer Phil Segal was a huge fan of Jon Pertwee's *Doctor Who* is the heavy references to Time Lords, the return of the Master as foe, the Doctor's name-dropping, and the *Doctor Who* logo itself, the use of which earned the story the fan title of 'The American TV Movie With The Pertwee Logo'.

Sylvester McCoy & Patrick Troughton

Sylvester McCoy's seventh Doctor's similarity to Patrick Troughton's second has been noted many times before. Both Doctors are of a diminutive stature and are either deadly serious, a little morose, or clown around like a silver age movie comic. Both Doctors wear baggy checked trousers and wear a scruffy jacket in the pockets of which can be found an assortment of junk, and both have a companion they're immediately associated with. The second Doctor has faithful Jamie, and the seventh Doctor has Ace. Both Doctors can barely be imagined without their trademark companion, even though they have a few episodes (six in the case of Troughton, eleven with McCoy) at the start of their run before they've met them. It's funny, but two such similar Doctors, there's not much I can think to write about them! All I can think to say is that if you put season 25's *Silver*

Nemesis at the end of season 4, and transferred season 4's *The Evil of the Daleks* to fill the vacated place in season 25, aside from production values and the like (including different policies regarding number of episodes) you don't have to stretch your imagination too much to see the seventh Doctor and Ace filling their counterpart's shoes, or vice versa.

Colin Baker & William Hartnell

At first glance there's very little to suggest that Colin Baker's sixth Doctor bears the slightest resemblance to William Hartnell's first, but this just means that I have something to write about this section.

Both Doctors started off as something of an unpleasant character, with a spiky temperament and extreme arrogance based on a deep-centred knowledge that they weren't actually very good at controlling the TARDIS, and so over-compensated with bluster and unreasonable arguments. However, get them out of the TARDIS and distract them with a mystery and they're more pleasant company, provided you tread carefully around their egg-shell egos, don't address them as 'Doc' and speak the Queen's English. Oh, and they wear rather similar clothes too, the sixth Doctor merely chooses more refined colours (meaning less likely for mere humans to appreciate) to parade them in.

They both deplore the use of violence, advocating the use of brains to solve problems, but both Doctors have examples where they're seen to act without mercy. In *Vengeance on Varos* (and no, I'm not going to cite that tired old example of the Doctor allegedly pushing two guards into the acid bath - one is knocked into it accidentally by the second guard, who is himself dragged into it by the desperately grasping hand of the first) there are some quite nasty stinging plants which kill instantly - the Doctor and co escape from some decidedly nasty people by tying back stinging creepers of the plant and letting go as the unfortunate baddies pass. This pales in comparison to what the first Doctor was going to do to some poor caveman in order to escape back to the TARDIS in *The Forest of Fear*. His companions were fussing over the man after he'd been mauled by a sabre-toothed tiger when they should have been making clean their escape, so he picks up a nasty looking rock and creeps up with the clear intention of caving the wounded man's skull in. It's only when Ian Chesterton challenges him he quickly thinks up a less violent reason why he should be carrying a jagged rock. The sixth Doctor also guns down the Cyberleader and Cybercontroller with a Cybergun in *Attack of the Cybermen*, which jars with his refusal to accept a weapon earlier in the story, whilst the first Doctor had a tendency to use his walking stick to bash people over the head or across the back. Neither can claim to be perfect, but as the sixth Doctor once exclaims 'I have never said I was perfect!' we can hardly fault him for it.

Peter Davison & 'Junior Doctor Who'

I am so *not* going to elaborate on this, but when applying the 'take five theory' to the fifth Doctor the natural thing to ponder is whether the fifth Doctor is so young is due to his similarity with the young Hartnell incarnation. Some people imagine that Hartnell's Doctor was born (or loomed, or whatever) old, but I prefer to imagine that the first Doctor has actually lived to look like an old man after hundreds of years growing through a childhood, a reckless young adulthood (who the fifth Doctor is doing a 'take five' to), a more adult middle-age and then into the dotage in which we normally tend to picture the Time Lords. The life on Gallifrey that the third Doctor often recalls would come from this Young Hartnellian era.

The Eleventh Doctor & Colin Baker?

Back when I first started working on this article, the newspapers were filled with stories about how James Nesbitt was all set to be cast as the eleventh Doctor. I strongly suspect that the rumours were started in order to give Steven Moffat's new BBC1 series *Hyde* (starring James Nesbitt) some decent publicity. Whilst I've never been keen on the idea, it amused me to note that this would at least have the potential for an eleventh Doctor to resemble the sixth in spirit. Whoever the next Doctor is set to be played by it'd be nice to see the contrast between the fifth and sixth Doctors echoed by the tenth and eleventh.

TAKE FIVE THEORY? NAH...

by Iain Martin

Originally printed in Shooty Dog Thing #4 – Winter 2007

Doctors Ten and Five

The fifth Doctor always seemed faintly unsure of himself, and his actions, as a reaction against his regal fourth incarnation. Whereas the tenth Doctor has become an inescapable singularity of moral absolutism: witness his slaughter of the Racnoss, his cruel charity meted out to the Family of Blood. Also the fifth Doctor was cut from the same cloth as most of previous incarnations: Earth popular culture was so far beneath him it was a safe bet he'd never quote *The Lion King*, or Kylie, or use the expression 'coz' when he meant 'because.' Largely there was a core of tremendous dignity beneath the apparently meek exterior of the fifth Doctor: he never felt the need to harp on about how brilliant he was, or to show off purely for effect: with the possible exception of that cricket match in *Black Orchid*. Similarly, Doc#5 was never patronising (admirable when you look at some of the companions he had) yet number ten can't stop himself...

Doctors Nine and Four

Alien, unknowable, majestic and unstoppable. Not to be confused with the dour media studies lecturer who'd pop out five bodies later. The fourth Doctor was powerful, booming, deranged, larger than life and the centre of his own universe, while the ninth was capable of weakness and desperation (he's prepared to kill the last Dalek with a great big gun.) Yes, both are capable of intense emotional swings, highs and lows, but again the earlier incarnation was fundamentally an alien whereas number nine is trying so hard to be a human. Can you really see the fourth Doctor essaying a mild groove to the opening chords of *Tainted Love*? Reading *Heat* magazine? Finally try to imagine it's Tom in 10 Downing Street facing the Slitheen. He frowns intensely and stares into the camera. 'Would you mind not farting while I'm trying to save the world?' he hisses. It just wouldn't ever happen. Neither was he likely to start doing the jitterbug (or whatever dance it was in *The Doctor Dances*) to woo Romana if he thought she was getting ideas about jumping Adric... Yet the ninth had a jealousy, borne of his aching loneliness, which the fourth Doctor doesn't share.

The fourth Doctor just didn't really give a damn.

Doctors Eight and Three

In the blue corner, a softly-spoken, wild-eyed adventurer, oozing charisma and sex appeal, energy and vitality, constantly excited, surprised and delighted. In the red, an overbearing, pompous, preposterously bouffanted right-wing establishment figure with a nice line in patronising his female friends. Also the eighth Doctor only had ninety minutes on screen, while the third Doctor ponced about for five long years. Number eight didn't blink when he learned Grace was a doctor; number three would have told her to put the kettle on.

Doctors Seven and Two

Again, diametrical opposites. Okay, so these two incarnations both looked short, scruffy, and a bit like pikeys; but one was a dark-sided megalomaniacal manipulator, game-player, springer of traps and eater of worlds, the bringer of darkness, the Ka Faraq Gatri who whittled chess pieces out of bones to trap Fenric. The second Doctor was a jumpy, blundering oaf who called it a good day if he only surrendered once to everyone he met. Imagine a small boy of two ran up to the seventh Doctor and smiled. The seventh would lean over his umbrella and say something to make the child laugh while ruminating darkly about how the boy was destined to die in a horrible battle and it's tough but that's just life. The second Doctor would instinctively throw his arms as high up as they'd go, and make sure everyone else around was surrendering too. The second Doctor was much like the French in that respect. More seriously, while number two blundered, poked about and improvised, the seventh acted carefully and cunningly precisely so as not to have to act like his earlier selves: an undignified bumbler.

Doctors Six and One

Shouty, unbearable, more than usually ready to use violence, it's true there are similarities, but the first Doctor never got close to the warmth occasionally exhibited by the sixth, or the righteous indignation. Also the sixth Doctor never tripped over his lines, ad-libbed desperately or looked around as if trying to remind himself just what the hell was going on. The first Doctor would never have been bullied by a companion into clambering onto an exercise bike, and if he'd landed on Ravolox in his first few adventures, he wouldn't have given a tinker's cuss about uncovering the truth about Earth, he'd have been off sharpish. Also, you have to imagine, had he met Sil, the first Doctor would have put his eyes out with his cane without giving it a second thought.

Masters Thirteen (Delgado) and Eighteen (Simm)

The thirteenth Master had a beard.

Paul Castle's response:

The John Simm Master and the Roger Delgado Master were similar in the way they effortlessly took full advantage of any situation in which they found themselves. In *The Sound of Drums* Simm's Master found the Doctor's TARDIS to be useless to travel freely in, but soon manipulated the two accessible timezones to his advantage before cannibalising the machine to bring victory. This is rather like the Delgado Master finding himself on an island prison in *The Sea Devils* and soon having the governor under his thumb and summoning up creatures from the deep to distract the Doctor. Both Master's plans fell apart spectacularly, but no matter, they always had a way out... Also, they both had a snazzy dress sense - all suits and ties - with a fondness for red velvet lined capes.

THE SEVEN STAGES OF FANDOM
by Paul Castle
Originally printed in Shooty Dog Thing #1 – Spring 2007

'Fan' is a word that people bandy about with no real idea what it means, you hear actors and actresses say on programmes like *Doctor Who Confidential* that they were so glad to be cast in *Doctor Who* because they are such a huge fan of the series. I hold that they were never fans, what they were was something else entirely, and what I want to do here is try and define what - if we're not going to use the word 'fan' - we can call them.

There is a danger when writing stuff like this to come across as a snob, but that is certainly not my intention. Okay, so the people above may not be fans, but they've got fond memories all the same. The poor dears simply have no idea what they're associating themselves with so careless a word. It is, after all, short for 'fanatic' and equally fits 'fantasist'.

I may be a teeny weeny bit rude about some aspects of fandom though, but as with all of my editorial features for *Shooty Dog Thing*, this is my opinion and mine alone. Agree or disagree, you're welcome to post feedback to Braxiatel@yahoo.com. Also remember that if you perceive that I'm being rude about you but you're thinking 'hey, we're mates, aren't we, why are you saying this stuff about me!' you must recall that it's fan types not actual people I'm pigeon holing. Also note that this is slightly tongue in cheek…

1. The Casual Viewer

These are people who just happen to be watching the right side at the right time. They might really enjoy what they watch, or they might not. Either way, there's no way we can call them fans. It's an easy step from that to stage two though…

2. The Slightly Hooked Viewer

These are the people from stage one who have found themselves tuning in week after week. Be careful, it's a slippery slope from here to stage three! This group also includes anyone who remembers it fondly from childhood if they've not automatically jumped in at stage three.

3. The Dedicated Follower of Fashion

You're in good company in this group, I tell you! Her Royal Highness Queen Elizabeth the Second is one of your number. As too are my mum and dad, a couple of mates from work, a cousin I was chatting to at a family funeral the other day and probably the millions of people who don't normally watch BBC1 at 7pm on a Saturday which did during the run of *Doctor Who* - the increase in ratings for *Doctor Who* compared to other programmes in this slot is significant.

Simply put, the 'Dedicated Follower of Fashion' are people who are likely to call themselves a bit of a fan, they think that *Doctor Who* is the best thing on the box in the months it's on telly, and more or less forget about it until it's on again, unless they're prompted by a tabloid story or see it mentioned somewhere. Don't worry too much if you're a Dedicated Follower though, it's a few steps uphill before the next stage...

4. ...Or at least it is if you're a grown-up. **The Newbie Whobies** are normally obsessive, and there's no-one more obsessive than children (apart from maybe scifi fans, who might be a little too cynical for this state). You can bet your cotton socks that the vast majority of *Doctor Who* fans started off as one of these, and their fandom survived both the appeals of other genre honey pots and puberty, because those are the main killers of this stage of fandom, other Fashions to become Dedicated Followers of and the whole growing up thing with all those hormones, interests in the bodies of other people and the effect they have on yours, CDD (Clearasil Dependent Disease), peer pressure and academic achievement. Hell, I still get nightmares about school and university... Anyway, these are all the fankidz you see on *Totally Doctor Who* and chances are, like baby tadpoles you see in garden ponds, most of them will not survive as fans into their adulthood. They stand a good chance of remaining a stage two or three fan though...

5. Fans

Okay, you've survived the perils of puberty and the appeals of other TV series and books, comics, movies and whatnot. You're now a fan. Congratulations! You can either stay where you are and simply enjoy, or more into a more social sphere. There are two ways in which you can go, and this is the bit I warned you about earlier...

But before I lead into the next sections I'd like to quote something from a collection of reminiscences about a public school headmaster called Frederick William Sanderson, who lived between 1857 and 1922. The book is called *Sanderson of Oundle* (pub. 1926) and this particular quote represents his view of education, a far cry from today's stifling world of syllabuses and examcentrisms, but it also fits a certain spirit of fandom I'd like to champion.

'I agree with Nietzsche that "The secret of a joyful life is to live dangerously." A joyful life is an active life - it's not a dull static state of so-called happiness. Full of the burning fire of enthusiasm, anarchic, revolutionary, energetic, daemonic, Dionysian, filled to overflowing with the terrific urge to create - such is the life of the man who risks safety and happiness for the sake of growth and happiness.'

(Ticks box on 'ten things fanzine editors must do' list: 'Be Pretentious.')

6. Fan-bores

There is another quote I have in mind here. It's from J.R.R. Tolkien's prologue to *The Lord of the Rings* (ending the section subtitled *Concerning Hobbits*) and says 'they liked to have books filled with things that they already knew, set out fair and square with no contradictions.' These fans are the people to whom *Doctor Who* is a collection of 796 episodes from the original TV series, the failed 1996 pilot with Paul McGann, plus 28 (and counting) episodes from the new series and nothing else. They are totally telly focused and take delight in claiming that anything else 'isn't canon' (as if we should care) and are boorish when anyone else says anything about the books or audios or comic strips. They are sad, fail to see any humour in *Doctor Who* and are utterly boring and smell :o) Seriously though, these are guys (and yes, I've only encountered male Fanbores) who - until BBC Wales provided new stuff to watch - are totally retrospective, dismissing anything new as unworthy and 'not *Doctor Who*'. This wouldn't be a problem if they let anyone else enjoy the wider universe of *Doctor Who* without butting in - try having a conversation on the newsgroup rec.arts.drwho about the books and you'll see what I mean.

Finally, there's a joke I rather liked which fits here. 'How many *Doctor Who* fans does it take to change a light bulb? None, they all wait for it to come back on.' This type of fan is the unhealthy vocal minority, abhorrent of change and the people who embrace it.

7. Fanboys

This is a non-gender-specific term used for the more creative element of *Doctor Who* fandom and their disciples. This is where it's all happening! When the lightbulb of the TV series went out, they went and got the *New Adventures* series of books to replace it, and when those went there were the BBC Books, then Big Finish audios! Even when the original TV series was still on the air there were hundreds of fans who loved to actively enjoy *Doctor Who*. There were literally countless numbers of fanzines in people's lofts and closets that date back as far as the seventies, and the internet has more or less replaced those with thousands of websites, people like Bill Baggs, Gary Russell and Nicholas Briggs were busy making their own *Doctor Who* adventures on audiotape (and they've gone on to produce the BBV videos, Big Finish audios and voicing Daleks and Cybermen in the new series on telly), and the aforementioned *New* (and *Missing*) *Adventures* and their successors from BBC Books, Big Finish (both audio dramas and books) Telos Publications, and Mad Norwegian Press all come from the fanboys. This is my idea of fandom, it's fun, sociable, and 'full of the burning fire of enthusiasm, anarchic, revolutionary, energetic, daemonic, Dionysian, filled to overflowing with the terrific urge to create'. In my eyes, the ultimate level of fandom is to be a fanboy!

WHAT'S THAT COMING OUT OF THE SMOG?
by Iain Martin
Originally printed in Shooty Dog Thing #2 – Summer 2007

Blimey! I bet you weren't expecting the Macra to pop up. Me neither. Whatever can have inspired Russell T. Davies to write a drama about having monstrous angry crabs in the darkest deepest recesses of polite society? Whatever the reason, it was a lovely nod back to the black and white era of the show, and makes you wonder how great it would be if other c-list *Doctor Who* monsters made a surprise return to the new series. Indeed, let us imagine for a second that series four is devoted entirely to slightly-less-than-great returning foes. How would such a series shape up?

Let's glance into the small, unconvincing screen of the space-time visualiser and have a gander!

1. 'The Re-Awakening' by Russell T. Davies
The Doctor and Martha return to Earth, landing, unusually, at a church near Cardiff. Soon, Martha has discovered the Face of Boe trapped in the wall of the vestry, but the Doctor believes he is instead facing his old enemy the Malus. No-one seems any the wiser 45 minutes later, so to be on the safe side they blow up the church.

2. 'Back in Black' by Russell T. Davies
Professor Rhys Evans' largely pointless 'really dark light' generator attracts the energythirsty attentions of Drathro, who arrives in Cardiff to turn that really dark light a little darker, and a little naffer.

3. 'Goodnight Sweet Heart' by Toby Whithouse
Dr. MandyKan's anti-obesity clinic for children seems to be a roaring success, but who exactly is the sticky-footed MandyKan, and why is he so keen to suck all the Twixes out of Martha and the Doctor?

4. 'Shaft of Doom' by Russell T. Davies
The TARDIS materialises on the outskirts of a large Welsh city and the time travellers become embroiled in a deadly mystery. Are local miners really dying of black death? And what is the secret behind the mysterious owner of the mine, Terry Leptil?

5. 'Bread and Butter and Honey' by Paul Cornell
Can we ever escape the evil in our past and begin life anew? The new proprietor of The Jolly Kiddy's Sandwich Shop, a Mr Bertie Nyder, certainly hopes so...

6. 'Feersum Engin' by Gareth Roberts
The causal nexus is unravelling, threatening the very fabric of the universe, largely because the decrepit, senile and faintly smelly co-ordinator Engin has totally forgotten how to operate his complex exitonic circuitry.

7. 'Escape to Danger!' by Terrance Dicks
A desperate race against time for the Doctor and Martha after the TARDIS breaks down in Wales. Can they race across the country to Llanelli and stop the alien evil of the Rutan in less time than it takes the green blob to climb a reasonably short staircase to the roof of Llanelli Castle? Yes, I'd have thought so. Comfortably.

8. 'Tin Foiled Again' by Mark Gatiss
Martha Jones single-handedly thwarts the Vardan invasion of

Cardiff without even bothering to ask the Doctor for help.

9. 'Direct Sunlight' by Russell T. Davies

The TARDIS materialises at Pip and Jane's Garden Centre in - ahem - Cardiff. The business is a roaring success, despite all the mysterious disappearances - but what is the secret of the new alphacompost? When the Doctor discovers old foes the Vervoids, he realises that when it comes to genocide, once definitely isn't enough!

10. 'Happy Trails' by Helen Raynor

The Doctor has to find some reasonably smart shoes to enter Cardiff's most happening nightspot, Mr Slugg's, where all eyes are on the hottest crew ever to get a residency: MC Mestor and the Gastropods. Will anyone pass the Doctor the sodium chloride in time?

11. 'The Keeper of Tranmere' by Steven Moffat

Football manager Dai Evans is beginning to regret his latest signing, the gormless, immobile stone tosser in goal. Can the Doctor help Ol' Red Eyes regain his winning form and revive the ailing fortunes of Tranmere Rovers?

12. 'The Negligible Menace' by Russell T. Davies

In an honest-to-God jaw-dropper of a season finale, the dreaded Myrka swims through the rift into Cardiff bay where it flails around catastrophically, trying to see where it's going and perpetually banging its head on stuff. With Torchwood leaderless, in disarray, and all getting off with bisexuals from Alpha Centauri, can the Doctor and Martha prevent this appalling spectacle?

DOCTOR IN LOVE
by Paul Castle
Originally printed in Shooty Dog Thing #4 – Winter 2007

By the end of series two finale *Doomsday* I don't think anyone can deny that the Doctor and Rose Tyler were in love, as aside from the whole sob-uncontrollably-into-cushion epilogue he spent half of *The*

Runaway Bride moping over her, and she was never far from his thoughts for the first couple of episodes of the third series. What I'm wondering though, was there something about Rose which was special? Or is it something in the Doctor himself that changed?

Certainly Rose is the first companion for whom there's been any hint of romance with the Doctor, as way back when the series began he was a grandfather / mad uncle figure for the companions, and this is something that never changed right up until the 1996 telly movie, but strictly speaking the girl he snogged in that wasn't a companion, more a fellow doctor cum adventurer, and it's back to being an uncle figure for his non-telly companions Izzy, Sam, and Charley in the comics, books and audios a short time later so it's clear nothing had changed.

It's worth mentioning here the long held fan view that the Doctor and fellow Gallifreyan Romana were at it like rabbits, but I challenge anyone to find me anything about their relationship onscreen that wasn't in any way uncle/niece-like. Admittedly, it's an uncle who's well aware that the niece is far brighter than he ever was so there's a bit of tension there, but in no way can this be ascribed to any 'tween-the-sheets action outside of a bit of sweaty fan fiction channelling fan desires. (Go find a copy of nineties ring-bound fanthology *Warm Gallifreyan Nights* for some eyebrow-raising fan-fic; it's got to be seen to be believed... ;o)

So, is Rose the first girl to catch the Doctor's eye? Obviously not, when you consider that one of the parents of his very first companion, Susan, was once an apple in that eye. But it's an important point, it means that the Doctor once had a family back home, one with cousins and uncles and sons and daughters. And a wife. Now this is where I imprint my own romantic side on the Doctor, I see him as someone who'd remain faithful to a wife even if he was separated from her by light-quillennia of space-time. The character we see on television and in the books, comics and audios, is of a man who loves deeply, but at a step removed. He never considers the possibility of romance; it's just not part of his life. The only time we ever see the Doctor as part of a romantic sub-plot in 'classic' *Doctor Who* is in first season story *The Aztecs*, where he, ignorant of their culture, accidentally proposes marriage to elderly Cameca by making some cocoa. Totally horrified by this, he can barely look her in the eye for the rest of the story as she looks forward to an autumn of blissful union. Watching the story recently I don't think he considers the possibility of marriage to her as a horrible fate, I see it more as the Doctor not knowing how to admit his mistake and let her down gently. Certainly, when she approaches him later, and lets on that she knows the pulley device he's working on will part him from her, he cannot even face her. This is not the action of a man to whom love means nothing, this is a man who is frightened that he might love her back, and showing the slightest sign of this could sacrifice the freedom of his companions - and perhaps the betrayal of his wife - for his own happiness.

It's a telling scene, and one which led me to write this little article, that when everyone else returns any Aztec jewellery to the tomb of Yetaxa, the Doctor turns over the broach which Cameca gave him as an engagement present in his fingers for a few moments before putting it reluctantly on the tomb, and then rushes back to snatch it up and put it in his pocket before hurriedly leaving the planet. He cannot leave the token of her love behind, and one suspects that he never forgot her. This is made explicit in David McIntee's *New Adventure* novel *White Darkness*, when the seventh Doctor starts to wear the broach again, but it changes nothing between him and his wife - the broach is as much a symbol of his devotion to her as it demonstrates his faithfulness.

So who is this wife, who is forever sleeping deep in the Doctor's hearts? And why is Rose such an exception? Two of the books, and *only* two of them out of hundreds to all you telly fans who're rolling your eyes at this juncture, may provide the answer. Lance Parkin's *Cold Fusion* and *The Infinity Doctors* feature a character from the series' prehistory. Nameless in the latter, but called Patience in the former; she's portrayed to eagle-eyed readers as the Doctor's wife from ancient times.

Upon her death in *Cold Fusion*, setting the scene for *The Infinity Doctors*, she's snatched from the timestream by Omega - or Ohm - and lives with him in his immortal fantasy prison (just like the one he lives in up to the events of *The Three Doctors*) waiting for the Doctor. Google the lyrics for Olive's dance classic *You're Not Alone* and you'll get the gist of my fantasy - the Doctor's wife is waiting at the end of time, patiently and with love, and it's her who he remains faithful to

31

all these years.

Well into *The Infinity Doctors*, the Doctor and Patience are finally reunited and live in bliss. But it's one of the archetypes: this world they're living in is false and the Doctor could never be truly happy and so to free him, she returns him to the universe and brings her afterlife to an end, dying in the process. It's tragically sad, but this provides closure and leaves the Doctor to live his life.

And then, Gallifrey is destroyed and all his people are wiped out, and the Doctor's left wandering without a home, without friends and family. And with his lover finally gone, he has nothing to live for. Enter Rose, stage left.

Whether or not Rose is the one for him is not what I'm going to get into here, but she's the person who picked up all the pieces and rebuilt the man, turning a shell-shocked, battle-scarred 'last of the Time Lords' into a person again. He's a man who, from roughly the point of *The Doctor Dances*, realises that he doesn't necessarily have to be alone, but events overtake him and he regenerates. The new Doctor is largely in denial, spending the majority of the second series all but ignoring Rose; witness his ill-fated love affair with Madame de Pompadour. But the return of old companion Sarah in the previous episode and his protestations that he won't simply dump Rose off ('not with you' he says) shows that he thinks of her in a different way to previous travelling companions, but he still won't admit how he feels, not until it's far too late and they're whole universes apart. In *The Impossible Planet*, when it looks like they're stranded, and the Doctor's mulling over the laughable possibility of him getting a mortgage, he ignores Rose's unsubtle hints that they might settle down together. It's almost like his reactions to Cameca in *The Aztecs*, but he feigns ignorance - and it *is* something he has to pretend: see his 'there's something staring me right in the face, but I can't see it' line to Martha in the following series' *The Shakespeare Code* to see ignorance - and the moment passes.

So, with Rose out of the picture, there's no question about whether or not the Doctor can fall in love, it's more a question of whether he will. Given the adventure story nature of the series it's highly unlikely that this will ever happen outside of short-lived affairs in weepies like *The Girl in the Fireplace* and *Human Nature/The Family of Blood* or *Superman II*-like scenarios like we've already encountered in

The Infinity Doctors but the possibility is still there.

Possibility is not the same as probability though, and it's just as likely that, now that his doomed love affair with Rose has captured the hearts of the modern audience, Rose has replaced Patience in the Doctor's hearts, and until there's closure he'll never fall in love again.

So, as we're waiting for the third Christmas special, we have a Doctor who can follow two paths. Will he find love again, or will he never recover from his unrequited love for Rose? If series three is anything to go by, with the Doctor becoming so distant by the time of *The Family of Blood* that his post-restoration reactions to Joan Redfern mirror the notoriously distant manipulator of the seventh Doctor in the *New Adventures*, the only love we'll see from him is towards the universe as a whole.

The more things change, the more things remain the same, eh?

EQUAL AND OPPOSITE FAN REACTIONS
by Paul Castle and Stephen Gray
Originally printed in Shooty Dog Thing #2 – Summer 2007

Introduction
by Paul Castle

Seen from the outside, the history of the television show *Doctor Who* is quite simple. What is now generally known as the Classic Series ran from 23rd November 1963 thru 6th December 1989, with a brief reprise for a one-off American TV Movie on 27th May 1996, before the big comeback in March 2005 restored it as the primary science fiction series on British television today.

But to the fans, it's so much more complicated than that. Rather than marking the end of the series in 1989, the cancellation of the TV series led to something of a renaissance, for in 1991 *Doctor Who* returned as a series of full-length original novels for Virgin Publishing. The *New Adventures* were at the time *the* continuation of the television series, which many of us had by then considered dead and buried. Freed from the constraints of the early evening mainstream TV schedule, and written for a mature audience, the novels took the series to the next level, and many of us consider them to comprise one of the most exciting and innovative eras in the history of *Doctor Who*. However, the 1996 *TV Movie* changed all that, BBC Worldwide realized the financial potential of the *Doctor Who* novels, and instead of renewing Virgin's license the following year, they made *Doctor Who* their flagship range for the fiction department of BBC Books.

The effect this had on the series was profound. Comic strips aside, you could regard the whole of the *Doctor Who* series, from the first TV episode *An Unearthly Child* through to the last *Doctor Who New Adventure*, *The Dying Days*, as occurring in one single continuum without any complications that weren't already present in the TV series. The break in continuity between the Virgin Publishing and the BBC Books ranges were emphasized by some writers, and whilst it was brushed over by others, the arrival of the *Doctor Who* audio range by Big Finish and the emergence of the comics as a continuity event in itself deepened the cracks in the *Doctor Who* universe.

With the arrival of these cracks, fandom set to work, either delighting in the creative potential caused by the crumbling borders of continuity, or using their own creativity to fill in any holes and smooth over the join. In my time I've been on both sides of the debate, but as I'm now a longstanding self-styled 'canon-anarchist' I shall present the case for the fractured continuity, and my friend and fellow resident of Coventry, Stephen Gray, shall present the case for unification. Rather than look at the whole of the continuity, which as Lance Parkin has shown requires a whole book to cover, I have chosen one specific subject to focus on. At the end of the last regular episode of the classic series, the companion Ace continued her travels with the Doctor, and what precisely happened to her after that has proven to be fertile ground for debate: I will argue the case for the different storylines that have built up around her to remain in separate universes, and Stephen will demonstrate how they could be merged into one timeline and why it should be considered.

The Case for Unification
by Stephen Gray

The *New Adventures* - There was a time when Ace's post-TV timeline was rather straightforward. The *NAs* (touted at the time as an official continuation of the TV show) established that after a couple more years travelling with the Doctor, Ace left him during the twenty-sixth century and spent three years in Spacefleet fighting a war against the Daleks. She then rejoined him and new companion Bernice Summerfield before finally leaving the TARDIS to police a time rift in nineteenth century France. Unlike Captain Jack, Ace had a time machine at her disposal, and was referred to as 'Time's Vigilante', a play on the seventh Doctor's mantle of 'Time's Champion'.

Ground Zero: Ace dies? - For the bulk of the *New Adventures* run, *Doctor Who Magazine* tied its comic strips into *NA* continuity. However, at the end of the seventh Doctor strips, the story *Ground Zero* took the decision to contradict Ace's established biography by killing her off. To make matters worse, the Ace seen in *Ground Zero* was clearly the teenaged companion, rather than the older version seen in most of the *NAs*.

There is, however, at least one way to reconcile these two versions. You see, in the *NA Lungbarrow* the Time Lords create a teenaged clone of Ace as a way of interrogating the grown-up version. If *Ground Zero* featured the seventh Doctor teaming up with the Ace clone, rather than the real Ace, then the two versions can happily co-exist. You could even take the line that the story features the real Ace, but then the manipulative seventh Doctor swaps her for the clone shortly before Ace blows herself up. It wouldn't be the only story in which he's gone to great lengths to try and prevent Ace's death.

After *Ground Zero*, and with Virgin books losing the license, there were several sets of stories which seemed to conflict with the original version of Ace's timeline, though to date *Ground Zero* presents the biggest contradiction.

Gale or McShane? - BBC Books's approach to the seventh Doctor was dominated by Robert Perry and Mike Tucker, whose five books featured a plot arc for the seventh Doctor and Ace that conflicted with the *New Adventures* version. The first sign of this was when they gave Ace the surname Gale, when the *NAs* had clearly established her surname to be McShane. Fortunately, another author retconned the mistake, stating that her full name was Dorothy Gale McShane.

However, the biggest problem came when they introduced a

cliffhanger ending in *Prime Time*. In this book, the Doctor discovers Ace's tomb, and finds that she died whilst still a teenager. This plot thread continued in *Loving the Alien*, where they established that the 'real' Ace died, but she was replaced by an almost identical Ace from a parallel universe, who experienced a different version of the story (in particular, she wasn't killed).

This replacement of Ace with a nearly, but not quite, identical character is a significant change to Ace's history, and it's the sort of thing which you would expect to have an impact on Ace's character in subsequent adventures. However, the idea isn't even hinted at in any other stories. Or is it?

You see, the very first *New Adventure*, *Timewyrm: Genesys*, starts with the Doctor accidentally wiping Ace's memories whilst editing his own. He restores them very quickly, but they aren't exactly the same as before (Ace ends up with a memory of some events that happened to Mel). It is, therefore, tempting to place *Loving the Alien* immediately before *Timewyrm: Genesys*. This means that the Doctor's memory-altering antics could be an attempt to give the new Ace the 'correct' memories.

The Hex Problem - Big Finish's approach presents an altogether different problem. In these audios, Ace grows up to be rather more mature than she was in Season 26. This ties in quite nicely with her level of maturity in the earlier *New Adventures*. There is also a new companion, Hex, to whom Ace becomes something of a mentor. On the surface, this doesn't pose much of a continuity problem. As long as he's out of the way by the time Ace and the Doctor part ways in *Love and War*, continuity is left unaffected. However, the later *New Adventure Head Games* established that Mel, Ace, and *New Adventures* companions Benny, Chris, and Roz are the only companions the seventh Doctor has had by that point in his life. So how do we square this circle? The answer probably lies within the text of *Head Games* itself. The list of companions is not given by the narrative, by the Doctor, or by Ace. It is given by the (new) master of the Land of Fiction, Jason, who wants to capture the seventh Doctor's companions. It is entirely plausible that he is completely ignorant of Hex. It is, after all, uncertain how he knew about Mel's existence. Or perhaps Hex died, either whilst travelling with the Doctor or not that long afterwards.

Time Lady? - The webcast *Death Comes to Time* creates more continuity headaches than any other story. Those relevant to this particular article are that the seventh Doctor dies (yes, that's right. Dies, not regenerates), and that Ace, who appears to be the teenaged version, becomes a Time Lord, following the extinction of Time Lords we're familiar with (although the Time Lords seen here aren't exactly the familiar version). The Doctor's (apparent) death raises questions about when this story happens. It could be the final Doctor, who just happens to look and act like the seventh, teaming up with an Ace who has left him, or genuinely the seventh Doctor. If it is the latter, then his characterisation suggests that this is between the *New Adventures* and the *TV Movie*.

If this is the case, then the Ace featured here must be the Time's Vigilante version. She certainly looks older than the TV one. It seems only fitting that a companion who took on the seventh Doctor's role of 'Time's Champion' should become the new inheritor of the Time Lords' mantle. And if she has the kind of powers shown by the Time Lords in this story, it's plausible that she can reverse the Doctor's death.

Why a unified continuity? - What is it that attracts people to Doctor Who rather than another series? Often it's because they have fallen in love with the characters and the universe. Therefore, a story which features an alternative universe version of the Doctor loses much of its appeal. The destructive side of this attitude is the kind of fan who dismisses any set of stories he doesn't like as 'not canon' as an excuse to ignore them. The constructive side, however, is the kind of fan who sees everything as part of one big universe.

Fans like this want the TV series, books, audios, and comic strips to all be about the same Doctor, or at least to be part of the same fictional universe. We want the various different versions to fit together, because otherwise it feels like a different series. As a child, I was a big fan of the (British) *Transformers* comic, but I never cared at all about the cartoon version. Why? Because the two media were unambiguously in different universes from day one. The characters in the cartoon were not the same characters as those I loved in the comic, even though they looked the same and, usually, had the same personality. For many - particularly those fans who came to *Doctor Who* through the books during the mid-nineties - splitting the non-TV stories into separate universes has exactly the same effect. Any attempt to establish this version of reality within the fiction of a story will be interpreted by some as an attack on their favourite stories.

And then there's the matter of references. Most attempts at splitting *Doctor Who* into separate universes group the books, audios, and comics as separate continuities. Yet those of us who are interested in continuity and familiar with the various media will notice many references to stories from one medium in stories told in another. And we tend to give those references more weight than we give any contradictions that arise. Part of the reason for this is that the contradictions within the TV series (UNIT dating, for example) are more severe than the contradictions introduced within, or between, non-TV stories (with the possible exception of *Death Comes to Time*).

And the existence of contradictions leads to another reason for considering the whole thing as one big universe. Many fans enjoy playing the game of being continuity cops. Working out ways in which a contradiction can be resolved is an intellectual challenge which many enjoy. However, in order to do this you have to assume that the stories you are trying to reconcile happen in the same universe. This is particularly true of the slightly insane minority (myself included) who write histories of the *Doctor Who* universe or timelines and biographies of the Doctor. Such projects make no sense if the stories all happen in different timelines or parallel universes.

The Case for Diversification
by Paul Castle

Whilst I can understand the desire to weave together the broken strands of continuity, the result is too much of a patchwork quilt for my liking. The continuity produced by sewing together different cloths and patching with different materials to me is as ungainly as the sixth Doctor's coat. To stretch that analogy, I prefer the tenth Doctor's wardrobe of different suits and shirts to pick and choose between, depending on mood.

I prefer the concept of there being a collection of *Doctor Who* continuities to choose from, a mythos that's structured like the tree of life, with different branches of the tree sprouting from the main trunk. It's an image that's familiar, and the principles can be applied to fictional universes as easily as genealogists and evolutionists apply them to family trees. In this way you can imagine the main trunk that represents the twenty-six years of the TV series (thick and well established) sprouting lineages from the top of the trunk that diverge and follow their own separate paths. I have to add here that as I find the fictional concepts of parallel universes a bit of a cop-out (with Tucker and Perry's alternate reality Ace replacing the dead one from 'our' universe a good example - if lives can be so easily restored, then death loses all meaning), these branches of which I speak are not parallel universes in a fictional sense. Instead, they are constructs made by fans to separate the continuities of different production companies and media. Stephen spoke of his childhood memories of loving the *Transformers* comic as a child, though not caring for the cartoon. I was exactly the same, I adored (and still do) the *Transformers* comic continuity by Bob Budiansky and Simon Furman, but the Animated Movie and *Beast Wars* aside, I have little or no affection for the cartoon series (it's just too simple, whereas the comic's a tad more literate with themes and character development). But, and this is where Stephen and I differ: as the two media were unambiguously in different universes from day one, you can safely disregard the other continuities - the fact that it is a different universe is a *bonus* - it means that comics readers only have to keep up with the comics and the cartoons can get on with telling their own stories. You don't have to worry about conflicts such as the completely different characterisation of Shockwave (in the comic he's ruthlessly ambitious and would stop at nothing to lead the Decepticons, whilst in the cartoon he's just a loyal servant of Megatron), or about how smart the Dinobots are (in the comics they're intelligent, just don't give a fig for the Autobot code and simply go AWOL, in the cartoon they're just stereotypical 'brain the size of a pea' lumbering robot dinosaurs). There's no need to explain anything, not in that kind of way anyway.

Returning to *Doctor Who*, the thing I do is set a 'system restore point' (to use Microsoft Windows terminology) which each offshoot shares with each other, or you could call it the 'most recent common ancestor' of *all* the different universes. Each continuity shares the same history up to this cut-off point, and follows a different route thereafter. This system restore point, the moment at which the continuity can be wiped clean back as far as and re-written as a fresh and totally different story, is undisputedly the last regular episode of the classic TV series. You can have myriad discrepancies between the *New Adventures*, the Big Finish audios, the comic strips and countless other continuations of the classic series without having to worry about how they all fit together. That leaves you free to enjoy stories with the Irregular Auxiliary version of Ace without having to worry about how she even exists when a different version of the character was killed in a comic produced by a different company at an earlier point in her life.

So, how many different universes do we have featuring Ace? I worked it out to be four when I had the original idea for this article, but Stephen reminded me of the Perry/Tucker novels from BBC Books These novels I'd not read - one consequence of the split in the book ranges back in 1997 was that instead of the two monthly ranges of *Doctor Who* books to keep up with, featuring alternating past Doctors in one and the eighth Doctor in t'other, we now had a third range that continued after the *New Adventures* lost the character of the Doctor but retained the hugely popular ex-companion Bernice Summerfield in the lead role. The consequence was that one range had to be dropped, and so I stopped buying the past Doctor range - which I regarded as the weakest of the three. Of course, you learn as the years pass which ones are worth picking up later. Right, where was I? Oh yes, I'd worked out that as there were four distinct versions of Ace, I laid them out as the Ace of Hearts, Spades, Diamonds, and Clubs. When Stephen pointed out that the Perry/Tucker books constituted a fifth, I called that the Joker.

Ace of Hearts - This is the Ace from the *New Adventures*. She grew steadily disillusioned with the seventh Doctor's manipulations throughout the early *NAs*, and left the Doctor in Paul Cornell's *Love and War* after the Doctor used the people she'd grown close to as pawns in his game to save the day. That didn't save the people she loved, so she left the Doctor in the twenty-sixth century (just as he acquired archaeologist Bernice Summerfield as a companion) to find a life for herself without living in the Doctor's shadow. Returning a few books (and several years later on her personal timescale) in Peter

Darvill-Evans' *Deceit*, she was now a hardened warrior with a commission with one of the most dangerous arms of the military - the Irregular Auxiliaries - who specialized in fighting Daleks on the front line. Rejoining the Doctor and Benny, she retained her distance from the Doctor, but they clearly showed a lot of affection for each other during more relaxed times aboard the TARDIS. She eventually left the Doctor back in the Paris of the nineteenth century, where she lived as Dorotheé McShane, and had limited time travel capabilities in order to keep her eye on a space-time rift as a jokingly self-styled 'Time's Vigilante'. One wonders if she was involved in the early days of Torchwood, and if it's the same rift as the one in Cardiff, but that's neither here nor there. I called her the Ace of Hearts because this is the version of the character that's closest to my heart, unrepentant *New Adventures* fan that I am, and she's the one who fell in love and was Sorin's grandmother, her sweetheart from *The Curse of Fenric*.

The problem some people have with the soldier Ace from the *New Adventures* is how they cannot see the Ace from the TV series end up as a solder fighting Daleks. Forgive me for pointing out the obvious, but the Ace of the TV series beat up a Dalek with a baseball bat, wiped out half a squadron of Cybermen with a catapult and loved all things that went BOOM! If *you* were a girl in your late teens with *those* qualifications stuck in deep space in the middle of the Earth Empire during the third Dalek war, wouldn't *you* become a Dalek Killer? Heh, I've just noticed how similar this Ace is to Alan Moore's title character from *2000AD*'s *The Ballad of Halo Jones*. Co-incidence?

Incidentally, I was discussing this Ace with a guy on the Outpost Gallifrey forum a few months ago, and he didn't like the idea that Ace would become a soldier so much that he couldn't stomach reading *any* of the *NAs* (even those without Ace in them). I suggested to him that as in the same book we meet the soldier Ace, we see her fighting alongside a clone of legendary Dalek Killer Abslom Daak, it's possible that the soldier Ace is a clone, programmed to become a soldier, with the original donating her body-print in return for some cold hard cash with which she could use to set up a life in the twenty-sixth century. He was happy with that and more willing to read the books. Just shows how much this stuff matters to us fans, and how easy it is to come up with solutions off the cuff.

Ace of Spades - This is the Ace who features in the *DWM* comic strip, *Ground Zero*. She sacrifices her life to save the whole of humanity's collective unconsciousness from some insectlike aliens called the Lobri, getting blown away by a can of Nitro-9. I remember the ever-enthusiastic Sophie Aldred saying in interviews that she thinks that Ace should die in a huge explosion saving the world, and bless him, this is the end Scott Gray wrote for her in *DWM* #241 back in the summer of '96. She's not got much of an existence beyond this one comic strip, as earlier comics saw her in her *New Adventures* persona alongside Benny and the Doctor, but you could say that she's from the same fictional universe as all her pre-Benny comics strips in *DWM* (that is, every issue from her first appearance in 163's *Fellow Travellers* thru 192's *Cat Litter*, returning only to die in issue 238's *Ground Zero*). I call her the Ace of Spades because I have something of a black sense of humour...

The problem people have with the self-sacrificial Ace is that she cannot - by definition - live to fight another day, and this is fair enough. I like Ace of Spades because I think *DWM* writing her out in a manner Sophie always wanted is sweet, and she saves humanity into the bargain. That puts her alongside Pete Tyler (deceased) in the hall of unknown heroes who humanity owes their lives to. To say - as some fans I've talked about this with online have theorized - that her injuries weren't as severe as the Doctor had initially thought not only undermines the story, it also makes the Doctor look a bit of an idiot.

Ace of Diamonds - This is the Ace that Sophie Aldred is currently playing in Big Finish's range of *Doctor Who* audio plays. There's no special reason to say that she's not the character who went on to fight Daleks in the twenty-sixth century, or eventually become a Time Lady (she is, however, clearly too old to later die in the comics) but as the Big Finish audios are a going concern, I regard it as too limiting to impose a future on her beyond the next audio. Let her find her own destiny with the seventh Doctor and Hex. I call her the Ace of Diamonds because that's what she is to Hex: she's his rock - hard as diamond and just as beautiful.

Ace of Clubs - This is the mature Ace as seen in 2002's online webcast *Death Comes to Time*. In the story she becomes a Time Lady, something which was supposedly planned for the cancelled twenty-seventh season in 1990. I can't really paint much of a picture as to precisely *why* she should be separate from the other versions of Ace, but as everything else about the story makes the production an outcast from the rest of any other *Doctor Who* continuity (rather different Time Lords to any seen elsewhere, the Doctor dying, etc) I'm not going to worry about that too much. I call her the Ace of Clubs because she's joining the ranks of the Time Lords; I wonder if there's a quarterly newsletter? People don't tend to have much of a problem with her, as it's not generally seen as part of any particular *Doctor Who* continuity anyway. It's a one-off, unrelated to anything else before or since, to be enjoyed (or not) on its merits alone.

The Joker - Tucker and Perry's BBC Books version of Ace. I've not read all of them, mainly because I've not been overly impressed by the ones I did read, and not been convinced by anything anyone's said about them. There's nothing I recall about any of the other BBC Books to feature Ace which means they can't fit in with the very early *New Adventures*, so I'm just calling on my reader's prerogative to ignore the Tucker/Perry books here. They're shunted away as the Joker card as far as I'm concerned and I see no reason to drag the BBC Ace books by other writers down with them. Think I'm being unfair? Well, you've every right not to have a problem with parallel versions of Ace who exist for no good reason other than allowing her to be killed and brought back easily, just for the shock value, but I do. So ignore it or place it wherever in the continuity you like - Stephen's made a few suggestions how it can fit in before the *New Adventures* - I leave it up to you.

Conclusion
by Paul Castle

I don't think either of our cases are conclusive, but even if one or the other were, Stephen and I would probably both agree to differ regardless. We just have our own way of viewing the worlds of *Doctor Who*, and neither of us has the right to enforce our views on the other. And that means that none of you have any right either. There was a huge debate about canon on Outpost Gallifrey back in February, where someone in the forum was insisting that because Paul Cornell had adapted his *New Adventure Human Nature* for the TV series, it meant that all the *NAs* were invalidated from 'the canon' as stories cannot happen twice in the same continuity. (<cough>*The Daleks / Planet of the Daleks* </cough>). This led to lots of fans arguing the case for various continuities and what canon is or should be. Paul Cornell picked up on something I said in the forum and quoted me as the starting point in his blog on the inherent problems of shared universes and canon, so it's worth me saying it again here: if anything can get *Doctor Who* fans at each other's throats, canon can.

So please, follow our example here, and accept that there are different ways of enjoying *Doctor Who*. Whilst it is fertile ground for discussion, it's not worth fighting over.

BERNICE SUMMERFIELD:
THE INSIDE STORY
reviewed by Jon Arnold
Original material for The Best of Shooty Dog Thing

My wife doesn't know it, but I'm in love with another woman. And I've been in love with her for seventeen years now. She's been with me pissed and sober, loved up and cursing what love does to us, ecstatic and despairing. And yeah, she's been married to other men too, shagged a fair number of aliens, saved the universe once or twice, and been to the past and future. I've seen her at her best and worst, she's seen me in similar. And we don't care, because we know the universe is not a perfect place and somebody has to do the tidying up afterwards and take the bins out. I know she'll always be there for me, just as she'll always be there for all the other fans of my generation. All I've got to do is open a book, or slip a CD into the player and there she is. And after all those made up love letters to her that we've come up with over the years, she's finally getting a real one, the type of adoring yet utterly honest one she deserves. It's been four years in the crafting, but then you'd want no less for such one of the most remarkable woman in the universe.

I was always irresistibly reminded of the title of the greatest hits by the ever pretentious punk pop pretension the Manics when it came to *The Inside Story* - 'Forever Delayed'. Big Finish had tantalised us with the volume Benny deserved for five years, dating back to a trailer on the 2004 *Doctor Who* audio *The Axis of Insanity*. Over those years, for various very good reasons (chronicled in the book itself), it seemed to be turning into the *Doctor Who* equivalent of Harlan Ellison's infamous *The Last Dangerous Visions*, almost ready to publish but never quite actually published. I was beginning to think that Benny's very own *Down Among the Dead Men* would come out before we'd finally get *The Inside Story*. As it turned out we only had to wait five years for *The Inside Story*, Ellison's readership is at 38 years and counting, and looks like they're the ones who'll end up waiting past 2566. Instead, despite her devoted fanbase waiting for an announcement, we were almost caught when Simon Guerrier announced in April 2009 on The *Doctor Who* Forum that the book would be published in the summer, and not only that, it would include extra material on events in Benny's life in the intervening years. Finally, after five years of waiting we had our reward.

And it's some reward, like being enforcedly celibate for five years and then meeting the partner who connects with you on mental and physical levels. It's a gorgeous looking book, which always helps put the reader in the right frame of mind. It comes wrapped in a glossy Adrian Salmon dustjacket, pleasantly reminding me that his artwork's become my definitive mental template for Benny, no mean feat given how long Lee Sullivan's initial picture stuck in my head and the strong impression made by Lisa Bowerman. And the internal design work by Alex Mallinson is gorgeous too, while there's a faintly ridiculous amount of text crammed in, obviously meaning a small font, the book's still got a sense of space. Just a quick flick through will give you the sense that the placing of every boxout, pull quote and illustration's been carefully considered, and placed to enhance the content.

And the content's undoubtedly worthy of that treatment. Fittingly bookended by affectionate and honest tributes from Benny's twin creators, Paul Cornell and Lisa Bowerman, it's very much in the spirit of Big Finish's previous *Inside Story*, Ben Cook's treatise on the first fifty Big Finish audios. It tracks Benny's history, from her conception to future plans, through prose, comic strip and sound, forensically recording and spotlighting every appearance and what seems like every mention there's ever been of her anywhere. We even get pictures and some details of a fan production involving Benny from the Sci-Fi Sea Cruise, her only onscreen appearance with the Doctor. It wouldn't surprise me if Simon had tracked down and read every single word written about her and tried to find a way to include it. The detail's so great, there's even an interview with the chef who catered for the Benny cast and crew for a couple of years. It's that thorough. There's some lovely gems deservedly tracked down and preserved in book form - I'd quite forgotten Matt Jones' lump in the throat beautiful tribute from DWM #245 for instance. We get the introductory article from DWM #192, background notes for the Braxiatel Collection, candid photos, speculative proposals for a potential Benny computer game, the Benny 'movie' and unmade scripts and a reminder of the short lived Benny 'shop'. That last one caused me to curse being too skint to take advantage of it whilst it was running.

As well as thoroughness, it also echoes the honesty from everyone involved that was probably the most impressive feature of Cook's book. Decisions and scripts that didn't work out are looked at and discussed - extremely useful when it comes to contentious issues such as why Jim Mortimore's 'Last of the Drop Dead Divas' was never produced. It can't have been easy for Guerrier, writing a great deal of this when he was still involved in producing the range, to find an objective viewpoint, but a lack of ego means he pulls this off. He somehow finds the perfect balance between fan, professional and chronicler, the talented bastard.

But the greatest feat of this book is that it reminds you why you fell in love with the character in the first place, and continue to love her. Even at a distance of going on for twenty years it's astonishing to note exactly how strong and fully formed a character Benny is simply from the initial outline, and how much potential she carries. It reminds you of how she fitted into the novels in precisely the way Ace, designed for TV and with her story nearly played out onscreen, didn't. It made me ponder whether Paul Cornell's greatest contribution to *Doctor Who* fiction was opening it up the way he did in *Timewyrm: Revelation*, or if it's actually Benny. And it's a salient reminder than the *New Adventures* wouldn't have been half the range it

46

was without Benny, the right companion in the right place at the right time, the first companion to really question the Doctor's actions and keeping him from becoming a monster. It's one of the more obvious *New Adventures* influences on Russell T. Davies' revival of *Doctor Who*, she's a prototype for the post-Rose companions. It gladdened my fanboy heart to see all the creative people in the book enthusing about her, and finding fresh takes on the character.

Really, when you think about it from a purely logical viewpoint it's utterly insane that a niche character, a spin-off of a spin-off, should attract a lavish tribute which has clearly taken such time and effort. But you know, it's a reminder of how bloody wonderful the world can be sometimes that someone cares enough to make that effort. I've been wanting to read this love letter to the other woman of my dreams for five years. It's a pleasure to discover that someone at least equally as worth of her loves her as much as me. There are some things worth waiting years for.

LISA BOWERMAN INTERVIEW
by Paul Castle
Originally printed in Shooty Dog Thing #3 – Autumn 2007

Hi Lisa! Next summer will be your tenth anniversary in the role. Did you ever imagine a decade back you'd still be playing the same role today? And what was it like filling the boots of a character who'd already been in a list of books as long as your arm?

It's very hard to believe I'll have been doing Benny for a decade next year. It's not until I see the photos taken during the first few recordings that the truth is all too evident!!! I'll be honest and tell you I didn't know a thing about Bernice, and just how popular she was - until I actually got the job. It's been quite well documented that it wasn't until I talked to Stephen Fewell (just after I'd got the audition for Bernice) - that he informed me she was 'an icon'! - So, no pressure there then!!

Is it a role you particularly enjoy playing, or are you just shamelessly in it for the money? ;o)

Money? What money?!!

It's extremely rare for an actress to find any sort of challenging role in this profession - and I'm so lucky to have stumbled across one of the most enduring and fun characters to play! Writers instinctively know how to portray her - Paul Cornell created such a distinctive character that they all hook onto her strengths and weaknesses(!) - although sometimes with varying levels of success. So much has been thrown at her in the last 9 years (in audio form at least) - that the part has never been less than enjoyable to play!

I see from the Big Finish website that the plays are recorded in a day. Is it a gruelling non-stop 9 to 5 schedule to cram everything in, or is there room to breathe and enjoy yourself aswell?

It sounds perverse - but I enjoy doing them so much, that even if it's a long day (and occasionally writers have put her in EVERY scene) - I enjoy every minute. There have been a couple of 'Benny lite' scripts though - and that always gives you a good opportunity to have a gossip with the other cast - and sample the delights of the Moat Studios hot and cold running snacks (lethal!)

It's normally the scripts that have a lot of 'running' and shrieking that knacker you the most though - the Draconian one was hard work! I also seem to remember that, that was recorded on the same day as *The Silver Lining* (which was a short for *DWM*) - so - yes, that was a gruelling day!!

With Bernice appearing in both the audios and the books, do you feel sometimes like there's this other Benny out there having all the fun with a huge cast at the Braxiatel Collection? How often do you actually get to see people like Harry Myers, Stephen Fewell, Miles Richardson, Louise Faulkner and Steve Wickham?

Sometimes things come up in the script that have directly related to storylines introduced in the books - which can be a bit of a surprise. I think it might have been *Skymines of Karthos*, when I started reading it and thought... hang around a minute - at exactly what point did I become PREGNANT?!!! Then of course it was all explained - which frankly made it even MORE confusing (for those of your readers who might not know what I'm talking about - I refer them to *The Squire's*

Crystal - which will reveal all so I'm told!).

It is frustrating sometimes that the budget doesn't stretch to a slightly more expansive cast. Smaller casts are great though, when the writing is tight. The drama can be a lot more concentrated. I wouldn't mind the odd 'epic' here and there though - just for a change!

I actually see quite a lot of the others. Both Steves, Louise and Miles have been friends for a long time now - even before the Bennys started. Like most actors we all pick up again very quickly even if we haven't seen each other for a few months.

And is it off down the pub for a quick pint after recording?

You might think that - I couldn't POSSIBLY comment!

Have things changed over the years? People have (as happens in any line of work) moved on and others come up. Do you feel like you're slipping into a favourite pair of shoes every time to return to the studio?

Actually it's been the same team pretty much from the beginning.

Over the 9 years we've worked in 4 or 5 different studios... but the longest serving of those is Moat Studios run by the estimable Toby Robinson - which have been located in both Stockwell and now near Notting Hill. The atmosphere there is great. We all have our little booths - and it feels like home. (Don't worry I've yet to decorate it with cushions and rugs!)

I've also been involved with quite a few other BF audios (including *The Tomorrow People* and *Sapphire and Steel...* shameless plug!) - and now as I'm also directing, the control room is feeling quite cosy as well!

Simon's just told me not to be scared of asking you about what you think of him, Gary and Eddie as producers. I understand that you've just recorded your first one with Eddie?

Gosh - onto my third producer?!

I've adored them all! Gary was great - let's face it, he employed me, saw Bernice through for seven and a half years as well as all his *Doctor Who* duties, and fought my corner when BF got the *Doctor Who* gig - without him Benny would not have been around today.

Simon? Oh - he's rubbish! (joke)!

Simon had a lot to do when he arrived. A lot of story arcs had been set in motion, and I think he saw it as his duty to try and tie them all up. My God - he's done a magnificent job! The stories set on the Braxiatel Collection are great - and the 'regulars' have proved hugely popular.

What scored him a lot of brownie points though, is that he kept me informed of plans from the very outset. I never used to be quite sure what was going on from one moment to the other - but I felt Simon really included me in the decision making. As an actor you can feel a bit powerless at times; you tend to take what's thrown at you - even if you're not sure about it. Mind you - I blanched a bit when *The Summer of Love* was presented to me!!

Eddie has Bernice Summerfield running right through him! In fact as a pimply, wet behind the ears youth he was actually there on my very first day of recording nine years ago, interviewing me for a fanzine! *[The fanzine was Oh Yes It Is!, edited by Will Howells - Paul]*

There's nothing about her he doesn't know - which is great if you come up against some reference that you don't understand in a script! I've no doubt she's in safe hands - and he has just as many plans to push things forward, as Simon had - hooray!

With the Big Finish recordings taking just a day every few weeks, what else do you do? I've heard Harry Myers on BBC7 a couple of times, do you do other radio work yourself? Or are things mainly on the stage?

I'd just like to get one thing straight - to the readers. Actors are actors - not 'TV actors', not 'Stage actors' or even just 'radio actors'. We do the lot!! Who'll ever employ us - we'll do it!

Actually I've been quite lucky recently as I've had a little flurry of acting work. I did a stage play back in June (with Julian Glover - who some of you might know) - then I've done episodes of *Spooks*, *Doctors* and *Casualty* in the last few months. The last was a bit odd, as I was killed off as a regular character in that - 20 years ago! It was a bit like going back to your old school!

Also, as I've said - I've been doing a bit of directing for BF - which I really enjoy.

Alas, all my contacts in BBC Radio (who I used to do a lot for many moon ago), have either retired, died, given up or are teaching - so haven't done 'legit' radio for a long time!

I've had a quick google and found your 'LB Photography' website which helps provide actors with a photographic portfolio. How did that come to fruition? Was it a niche in desperate need of filling?

Ah - my 'daytime' job! However busy you are as an actor - it simply doesn't pay the bills - most actors 'do something else'! I'll try to pot the history! - Started taking Spotlight photos at drama school (as I was sick of seeing people ripped off for really bad shots) - kept it up as a hobby once I'd left college (only took people I knew, or had worked with). Hit a bit of a brick wall acting wise about six and a half years in, and set up my photo business in 1990.

Luckily I've been around so long I'm pretty well established on that front now - with about 50 odd agents who use me regularly for photographing their clients, as well as most of the drama schools.

I've also done quite a lot of stage production photos, and a few magazine shoots, and even the shots for the 30th Anniversary book of *Emmerdale* (thank you very much Lance Parkin!).

I changed my title to LB Photography about 7 years ago, on the request of an agent (who never took me on!) - as a lot of people had assumed I'd given up acting!

I understand you're also a trustee of Denville Hall, a Retirement Home for actors. My knee-jerk imagined Morecambe & Wise *joke aside, that sounds like a wonderful cause and would be interested in hearing more about the home and how you came to be involved.*

The person who got me involved with that was Lalla Ward - who was then Chairman of the committee at Denville. It's pretty famous within the profession, as it's the only single occupation retirement home for actors in the country (not to be mixed up with Brinsworth House - which provides care for the variety profession!).

I've been involved with the house for 6 years now, and took over as Chairman from Lalla about 18 months ago. She then went onto become joint chairman (with Geraldine James) of our sister charity TACT (The Actors' Charitable Trust) - of which I'm also a trustee, and is a grant giving charity to help support the children of actors who have special needs either financially or medically.

Denville is really a great place. More like a 5 star hotel than your average image of an old people's home! We completed a big rebuild a couple of years ago, and have also added a 15 bed dementia wing. I've had the opportunity to get to know some really extraordinary actors from a generation I never thought I'd ever have the privilege of meeting.

All donations gratefully received - plug over!! *(you can find out more at* www.denvillehall.org *and* www.tactactors.org - *Paul)*

Looking back at your early work, before the Doctor Who *episodes (which look nightmarish, running around a sandpit in the middle of a heatwave encased head to toe in a 'Cheetah Person' costume) you had a role in the early years of* Casualty. *Was there a feeling at the time that the show would be a major big thing for the BBC over the next two decades?*

Casualty was actually my first ever TV job. I was young, and naive, and knew bugger all about TV acting. I was SO lucky to be in a cast of amazingly experienced actors. (I played the paramedic Sandra Mute by the way!)

I think the programme was a very different beast to the one we know now. It was much bleaker and more issue led - and a whole lot grittier than the sanitized soap it's become.

I think we all knew it had the potential for going on further - but it looked pretty certain that it was going to be scrapped after series two - which in many ways prompted my decision to be killed off (doh!). Mind you there is a theory (though a very loose one) - that my decision to go effectively saved the programme, as my last episode went in over ten million in the viewing figures - and that made them 're-evaluate' - actually I'm not convinced by that - but the writing was certainly improving - so in many ways I think that was the reason.

Can I be honest? I think it's well past its sell by date. We made a series of fourteen episodes in those days - they're now making forty odd - go figure!! (I think it's called the law of diminishing returns!)

And finally, the big fanboy question. If there was an opportunity for Benny to rejoin the Doctor Who *fold as a guest down at BBC Wales for an episode, how would you feel about that? Or would you prefer playing a new character?*

I'd LOVE to - but it's not going to happen. Believe me - the question has been asked - many times!

So I'll just have to resign myself to being the Bob Holness of *Doctor Who* (... he played James Bond on radio - a favourite Trivial Pursuit question!) - as by the time they ever DO decide to go down that route I'd probably be better casting for Benny's granny!

I'll let you in on a secret - I was actually offered the part of 'Wirey Woman' in *Utopia* - for those of you who saw it - you'll understand why my answer was 'not today thanks'! Still - we live in hope. There do seem to be a lot of cats turning up - so if all else fails I'll be back in the fur!

Thank you Lisa!

BENNY ACCOLADE
by Elizabeth Burak
Originally printed in Eye Of Orion #4 – Summer 1999
Reprinted in Shooty Dog Thing #3 – Autumn 2007

My adulation of Bernice started in 1998. Before that, I hadn't even heard of her. In fact, I was almost completely unaware of the current, huge *Doctor Who* Universe or of the *New Adventures*, having not kept up with the *Doctor Who* part for some considerable time. The role playing scenario in which I had become embroiled (a queer amalgam of Storm Constantine and *Doctor Who*) led to my first encounter with *Oh No It Isn't!* and Bernice Summerfield. The GM arranged for a large group of us to get together and made us role-play most of the *Oh No!* story (which none of us in the game knew anything about) and I was cast in the unenviable role of playing the good professor. Unenviable because in this story, she played as anything but like her usual self!

I must confess that, although I had role-played with dwarves, Middle Earth and all that ilk before, the collection of pantomime characters which the GM made us encounter was different, and startling enough to be engaging, as well as funny. Believe me, after only a few glasses of Chilean red, the pantomime jokes and characterisations we all indulged in started to get hysterically out of hand. At one point I had to control ten shivering feet of savagely out-of-control songsheet while getting the eclectic collection of gamers in front of me to sing, 'Row, row, row your boat.' Believe me, it is only when you try to get a group of a dozen or so players, reclusive and seriously weird bachelors to a man, in their late thirties/early forties to sing that you thank all the angels around that you are not a teacher!

When the gaming concluded, I was lent the audiotape and the book and on the trip home in Gabriel (my beautiful Saab 900) I played out the tape. I grinned a lot and laughed out loud at the Grel. The book was enjoyable too, but the tape rather made it for me.

But it was Benny that really took off in my imagination. Feisty, hard drinking, a scientist, vulnerable, thirty-mumble years old, prone to the odd sassy comment, I identified with her enormously. Yes, I have to admit that she has the annoying sporadic habit of doing that motherly thing that us thirty-mumble-year olds are randomly prone to. However, if I were stuck in a tight corner, enemy coming at me from all directions, armed with only a frying pan and my trust Maine Coon cat, I wouldn't mind having Benny at my back.

I won't spoil the plot for any of you who have not, as yet, read this story but I was particularly taken with the fact that the universe colluded to make Benny forget her persona as strong, capable and gritty. Instead, it started to make her enjoy her gender-bending confusion of roles as her pantomime characters. 'Bother' and 'Golly' were the strongest words she was able to use, although she did use them with aplomb! A word of caution here, though, might be appropriate. If you hate, I mean really hate, pantomime then this piece of Cornell magic will really not ring your bell. If you're not sure, I can heartily recommend the audio tape over the book. The Grel will win your hearts, along with Benny of course!

I have since also listened to the audiotapes of *Beyond the Sun* and *Walking to Babylon*. It has only strengthened my admiration of Benny's character. It is uncommon in TV fiction to get a female character that is convincing, not prone to doing that screaming thing in which the *Doctor Who* females were often forced to indulge, married, and involved in the very thick of plot lines which, to date, have rarely run out of breath. Her ambiguous feelings for Jason, her ex-husband as she markedly underlines on several occasions, come through as being rather believable. Jason himself is not made into some enormous bugbear for us to hate but a rather irritating rogue. He claims to only look after Number One but his deep-seated concern for Benny's welfare gives lie to this. He is also irrationally jealous of even the most tentative approaches by other males towards her although, for me, it is only this that lies uneasily with my perceptions of Benny and the choices of men she makes on the path of her life. I wouldn't have pegged her as having much truck with such juvenile behaviour in the first place, but then love is irrational and strikes where you least expect it!

Otherwise, her encounters with friends, colleagues and lovers are very true-to-life and, to me, illuminate the inner bit of Benny that falls sweetly and warmly in love. Her gruff and self-deprecating exterior is easy to empathise with, and with it her sassy putdowns combine to make a great picture. It is a delight to see a female character making choices without being constrained into the options of shrinking virgin or gaspingly desperate husband-seeker. She is not afraid of her relationships, even when they do not work out, as in the case of Jason. She is also allowed to break the female stereotype in other ways, one of the sweetest for me being when she is delicately seduced by one of her students - delicious! She reaches out and grasps warmth, affection and love with both hands while still acknowledging it might be difficult. This does not seem to deter her and I enjoy that facet of her character too, as most of us poor mortals are condemned to draw back in fear of committing some sort of non-existent *faux pas* when presented with the opportunity for love. She cares for herself enough to know that, if she lets her romantic possibilities be clouded by self-doubt, love will pass her by and it is clear that this is one thing she does not intend to let happen.

She also cares for others, and cares deeply. She seems to quietly acknowledge the privilege of friendship that her colleagues around her provide yet can humorously send up other senior members of St. Oscar's. The wild romantic in me is delighted to find her blessed with so much love in her life. She feels herself honour bound to protect those who she considers her extended 'family' and, whether they like it or not, they find themselves warming to this rambling, kind hearted misfit, as I have done.

She also exhibits that unusual combination in a fictional character of simultaneously being brave while scared of what will happen to her. Yet even in these situations, she will do what she is aware of as the right thing, even if metaphorically she drags herself, kicking and screaming, to do it. In a lot of fiction, when females are not screeching in the background (please, spare us!), they are portrayed as Valkyrie-types who stalk, gung-ho, through the blood and gore. Neither comes close. Of course fiction is just that - fiction. But it does help to have characters with which you can identify as exhibiting characteristics that are recognisable in yourself, or in the people around you.

One of the things I have found missing in her characterisation so far is any display of real passion for her chosen subject - archaeology. Many scientific types in the real world, particularly in the more pure sciences, show ardour and fire for their chosen subject and get to spout on with contagious enthusiasm to any captive audience that has shown even some interest in their given subject. This has not happened so far, although I am waiting for Santa to send me some of the forthcoming audio CDs that have been promised by Big Finish Productions and I may find that this aspect of her character gets fleshed out some more.

That aside, Benny shows that she is damned smart (you don't get a professorial position in archaeology for being kind to cats) and yet appallingly disorganised (witness her loathing of writing up reports). Both of these features I noisily applaud. I hate this Barbie-doll approach to female teachers that dictates that they must be prim and neat and not too clever. It cheers me unreasonably that she has a healthy disrespect for her publishers, cares very much for her students and enjoys a pint of good beer or a drop of fine spirit. I am delighted at her ability to put it away, neither getting mawkish nor descending into an attack of female conniptions. She also cares deeply about other worlds and civilisations but is not averse to showing illogical favouritism when the baddies are really bad. After all, it would sit oddly if a character started spouting some sort of political correctness about how we should all live in harmony while the bad dudes are priming their wicked-looking guns, having already ravaged the planet of most of its sentient and sapient life. Most people have a sneaking empathy for the underdog. It is human nature after all, and it is a character's very humanity that is important to have as an unwavering bass line in a fictional situation. Benny's character, showing the character strengths and flaws that make her much more than a one-dimensional cartoon drawing, fulfils this last criterion admirably and for that reason will continue to make me want to listen to stories about her. Way to go, Benny!

TWENTY-OH-NINE
by Paul Castle
Originally printed in Shooty Dog Thing #4 – Winter 2007

Some fans take the news that there's not going to be a full series in 2009, just three specials, as a portent of doom, recalling the so-called 'eighteen month hiatus' of the mid eighties (which, in reality was just a deferral from a Spring 1986 showing to the Autumn - rather akin to *Torchwood*'s second series moving from Autumn 2007 to Spring 2008 and no-one's making an issue out of that) but fans tend to think like that. The plain and simple fact of this is that (a) modern telly does this sort of thing all the time and (b) the break's allowing David Tennant to tour the country doing Shakespeare, so you can go out and linger by the stage door and possibly meet the guy, and (c) we've still got three specials to look forward to before (d) a guaranteed full fifth series for 2010.

I'm not the sort of fan who panics at such news, nor am I one who keeps eyes peeled for all scraps of information about what may or may not happen in 2009, I'm of a third kind. I like to take what little information we have (the more minimal the better), look back over what's happened in the past, and formulate some wild theory which just *sounds good*. To be or not to be? Well, what do you think?

So, for the 2009 Specials, I'm going to propose adaptations of three books, just as was done with *Human Nature*, and the only facts I'm going to work on is that David Tennant is in it for the whole sequence and Billie Piper is returning.

The Infinity Doctors
Adapted from the 1998 novel by Lance Parkin
Showing May Day Bank Holiday 2009
'Sing about the past again, and sing that same old song. Tell me what

you know, so I can tell you that you're wrong'

The Doctor is a much respected member of the High Council of the Time Lords, one who's laboured to make Gallifrey more involved in the affairs of the universe, to use their powers to make space-time a better place. As his friend the Master of Ceremonies (played by John Simm) remarks, 'a cosmos without the Doctor scarcely bears thinking about.'

The story opens with the arrival of the war fleets of the Sontarans and the Rutans over Gallifrey, two species that have been at war for millions of years. The Time Lords have agreed to host peace talks between the two species with a great deal of trepidation, but the Doctor's agreed to single-handedly host the talks. The troubles start immediately as both delegations arrive at opposite sides of the Capitol at the same time and both would be highly insulted if not personally met by the Doctor.

Getting around the problem by breaking all rules in the book (the Doctor pops back in time after welcoming one side, and is therefore able to be in two places at once) both delegations are welcomed and the talks begin.

Meanwhile, the Time Lords have witnessed a new phenomenon, which they called The Effect. This 'Effect' causes great concern as it's essentially a probe that 'picked up every atom of matter in the universe, examined it and put it back' and originated from the very end of the universe. Gallifrey's supposed to be shielded from all eyes, existing in a dimensional fold outside of normal space-time, but the Effect scanned them as easily as it did the encircling fleets of ships. But what's worrying the Time Lords is: what if the Effect can do more than merely examine?

Back in the conference rooms things are not going at all well, the Doctor's sitting back in his chair, arms folded, as the Rutans and Sontarans shout at each other, looking set to drag up every detail of every crime the other side has committed. When he hears of the Effect from an aide, the Doctor stands up and roars for silence, before berating the two leaders of the galactic empires for their behaviour like they were hatchlings. He orders the two delegations to sit and be quiet, as something important has cropped up. Before leaving the room, he keys in a command at his chair computer and the room shimmers for a second, without either delegation noticing. We see him emerging from a blue Police Box: the conference is being held inside his own Ship, for everyone's protection.

The High Council have decided to send the Master to the end of the universe with a small team of specialists, and the Doctor somehow manages to get invited along for the ride instead of continuing with his duties. Whilst the High Council are indignant at being left to baby-sit the highly volatile situation of two war-fleets ready to obliterate each other at the first sign of trouble, the Master supports the Doctor's decision as it was the Doctor who instructed the team of specialists in the first place and therefore in the perfect position to go instead of them.

Just as the Doctor and the Master leave for the origin of the Effect, the first signs of trouble break out in the conference chamber: the Sontarans and the Rutans have started to fight, and bits of Sontaran and Rutan flesh litter the floor. And if that wasn't enough, the fleets both contact the High Council demanding a situation report. The Castellan (Geoffrey Palmer) and President (Judi Dench) look at each other and wonder what on Gallifrey they were going to do...

Meanwhile, hundreds of billions of years in the future, a TARDIS arrives and burns itself out from the strain of the journey. From within emerges a second TARDIS, which falls into a decaying orbit around a black hole. It's only a decade or so before the end of the universe, and this is the last black hole with matter left to consume: all the others are quiet, sated, undead. There are no stars in the sky: the void is black and silent.

The black hole is pinned by a needle, which is an artificial construct a light year from end to end, and is slowly being consumed. The Needle is the last refuge of life in the cosmos, but aside from one pitifully erratically powered dome on the vast surface with minimal lifesigns, all is dead: evidence of vast planet-sized cities and dried oceans pepper the surface. The Doctor and the Master head for the last bastion of life, located within a region just about to pass the event horizon.

They find three very old and frail men, huddled inside a library and burning books on a fire in order to stay warm, all the time arguing which of the classics currently burning will be missed the most ('should we burn the Wyndham before or after the Moorcock', 'we really should have saved the Dickens for later': that sort of thing). The

Master and the Doctor are invited to join them around the fire, but they need to trace the source of the Effect. They're pointed towards the door at the rear of the chamber, through which they pass into a realm of anti-matter. They find themselves in the presence of Omega, greatest hero of Gallifreyan history and the man who died whilst founding the Time Lord race. Omega is mad with hatred for the Time Lords, who he feels betrayed and abandoned him. He plans to entrap the Doctor and the Master in his universe of antimatter whilst he returned to be the God of the Time Lords and wage war on the universe. The Doctor however has an antimatter converter on his person (confiscated from the Rutan leader at the start of the story) and in the split second as Omega gives them equal power to himself and departs, the Doctor and Master hug, one matter and one anti matter. The explosion destroys the Needle, the black hole, and the departing Omega, possibly kickstarting the next Big Bang in the process. The Doctor and the Master send themselves back in time on a mental impulse, but are caught up in the backlash of the explosion, visions of alternate realities and histories as space-time is warped out of shape by the power of the Effect re-writing history. We see the Master's history distorting, his good deeds turned to evil.

The Doctor ends up on the floor of his TARDIS, wearing his more familiar (to us) brown pin-striped suit, and finds himself amongst the delegations of Sontarans and Rutans. Everything is quiet, everything is calm. The scanner screen shows what's left of Gallifrey: all is dead, the Effect destroyed the Doctor's entire timeline, and he now remembers the Time War and the Daleks. The Sontarans and the Rutans, having been trapped within the Doctor's TARDIS and held within the confines of the Temporal Grace (meaning that no matter how much they killed each other, the effects always reversed and they came back to life) they'd settled their differences and bore witness to the Effect and the Time War and the destruction of Gallifrey and their warfleets. They agreed to differ, having witnessed how small and petty their conflict was, and how alike they really were.

The Doctor takes them home to their own worlds, and is left alone in his TARDIS. He decides to scuttle his ship in the ruins of the Homeworld, but upon doing so to great special effects and emotional orchestral music, he wakes up on the floor of a very English looking study. He's helped to his feet by someone played by Sean Connery.

The Doctor is speechless, unable to say anything but 'what?!'

The man smiles at the Doctor, saying, 'welcome home son...'

Unnatural History

Adapted from the 1999 novel by Jonathan Blum and Kate Orman

Showing August Bank Holiday 2009

The Doctor's father, Daniel Joyce, is the leader of the San Franciscan division of Torchwood, set up after the creation of another Rift following the events of New Year's Eve 1999 (with the planet being pulled inside out through the TARDIS and then *not* in the events at the start of the Doctor's eighth incarnation). Until the Doctor's arrival the new Rift was relatively quiet, but his TARDIS was drawn into the space-time fracture following his suicide dive into the heart of the fractured realm of space-time that used be called Gallifrey and stuck fast, opening the divide. The Doctor was thrown free, to be caught by some device of Joyce's. There's a fair bit of family reunion stuff (though no sign of Mum, presumably being human she's long gone) and it turns out that the events of *The Infinity Doctors* scattered a few surviving Time Lords and Gallifreyans across the cosmos.

The Rift has claimed the attention of The Unnaturalist, a pan-dimensional explorer who collects impossible creatures and temporal deviations, and the half-human Doctor has just been added to his list. Also on his list is one Rose Tyler, a Goth druggie living on the streets of San Francisco. The Doctor saves her, but 'Dark Rose' has no memory of him and hasn't lived in London for years, not since running away to America at the age of fourteen with her mum's lottery winnings. Other anomalies include a vast Kraken in the bay, unicorns in Golden Gate Park, vampires lurking in the shadows at night, and families of Mandelbrots wandering the streets.

Joyce and the Doctor have to work out how to free the TARDIS from the Rift before the timeship rips the Rift fully and irreversibly open and the West Coast is flooded with mythological creatures from other dimensions.

The Doctor also has to work out how to save Rose (there's evidence of some very clumsy temporal editing in her biodata: one of Joyce's interests is biodata - and the mapping of individual timelines - but she's determined not to be saved and the audience is manipulated into siding with her), how to stop the Unnaturalist collecting his specimens, saving San Francisco from the Kraken, and tracing the temporal manipulation back to its source: Christmas 1976 in Cardiff.

No Future

Adapted from the 1993 novel by Paul Cornell

Showing Christmas Day 2009

Christmas 1976, and it's Anarchy in the UK: history's been changed and all hell's breaking loose.

The Doctor teams up with Captain Jack and his team of *Life on Mars* rejects as they fight the invasion of the Robot Santas and Robot Snowmen whilst punk rock rioters trash the cities. Behind it all is the Meddling Monk, one of the Time Lords who survived the destruction of Gallifrey in *The Infinity Doctors*, and who went on to engineer the events of *Unnatural History* and the editing of Rose's history. The Meddling Monk is drawing power from the spirit of Omega, who's trapped in the Cardiff Rift, but he's just as incompetent as before and if the Doctor and Jack can't prevent his mad schemes of revenge, the planet will be destroyed at midnight on Christmas Day!

CRAGGLES ROCKED!

by Jon Arnold

Originally printed in Shooty Dog Thing #4 – Winter 2007

He couldn't have known it at the time but Craig Hinton's contribution to *Doctor Who* has been overshadowed by a throwaway line early in his *Doctor Who Magazine* reviewing career.

In the long term few will remember him for his stint as *Doctor Who* Appreciation Society coordinator, one who worked hard to help restore the organisation's reputation in the eighties. A few more will remember him as an insightful contributor to 80s zines such as *DWB*, a few more again will recall him as Gary Russell's successor as *DWM* reviewer. And some of us will remember him as always witty and engaging company, ready with a bitchy yet hilarious quip or anecdote. Of course, there's also his literary and audio contribution to the ongoing *Doctor Who* story, of which more later.

Nope, Craig will be more widely remembered for the one word he gave initially to the *Doctor Who* fan community and thence to the wider world of genre fandom: Fanwank.

Since that initial article fanwank's become something of a cheap insult, a judgmental insinuation that a work lacks creativity, relying on old continuity references in place of any real interest. Often, it's used as lazy shorthand for a fan not liking the way authors have used references to continuity - the focus on the self gratification insinuation of the term. Yet, as initially coined it didn't have such negative connotations, being rather a statement of fact - 'Some of the amazingly obscure continuity references demonstrate a perfect example of fanwank'.

Craig became further associated with the word through his literary output revelled in his status as 'Fanwank God', to the point of proudly emblazoning the phrase on a t-shirt at the Gallifrey 2005 convention. Going through Craig's work for this article it struck me that calling most of his work fanwank in the currently understood context is hugely off beam. While, as he admitted of his first book, *The Crystal Bucephalus*, taking out the continuity references wouldn't damage the story in the slightest, their presence in his stories actually improves and strengthens the story. Because while a lot of the writers of *Doctor Who* fiction saw continuity as something of a burden and hindrance to the stories they wanted to tell, Craig saw it as one of *Doctor Who*'s greatest strengths, that sense of a shared universe where an imaginative kiss to the past can strengthen the reader's enjoyment of a story. After all, if you're not interested in the *Doctor Who* aspect why have you bothered buying a *Doctor Who* book? As a consequence of this very few, if any, of Craig's kisses to the past are random. Even with his most deliberately fanwanky book, *The Quantum Archangel*, the continuity references are well researched and judiciously chosen. When asked about what makes a good *Who* story in the first *I, Who* reference book he emphasises 'strong villains, a central, moral theme and a simple storyline with dialogue polished to perfection' and as a result of his sticking to his own guideline, despite the reputation for fanwank, Craig's work is some of the most enjoyable and accessible in the range. And while it's stuffed with references, fanwank on his own terms, his work rarely tries to merely emulate televised stories but instead tells stories which could have fitted in during the eras they're set in.

The Crystal Bucephalus, originally submitted as a *New Adventure*, bubbles with the *joie de vivre* of someone achieving a lifetime ambition and loving it. It's deliberately sprawling and epic, ranging in scope from 17th century France to the eponymous 108th century time travelling restaurant, and establishes what became Craig's trademarks quickly - a mixture of soap, high camp, OTT dialogue, great gobs of fanwank, something nasty happening to the TARDIS and what I assume to be accurate theoretical physics put into literary practice. If it isn't accurate then at least it's consistent, influenced no doubt by Craig's then main career as a technical writer. It's not quite perfect, with the regulars often being given actions and lines more in keeping with the *New Adventures* cast and the soapy interactions of the guest cast verging on the parodic but the sheer energy Craig obviously put in is more than enough to overcome those faults. It's also worth going through for being the most trenchant, interesting and often funny critique of organised religion in the *Who* novel range. Oh, and it has the best last line of any *Who* novel. If you want a flavour of the original *NA* version then try and track down a copy of the *Perfect Timing 2* fanthology, which has a brief but interesting extract which proves Craig's contention that Rebecca Levene's suggestions improved the book immensely. There's also another unofficial follow up short story. Despite suffering the 'curse of Kamelion' after finishing the book, Craig bravely returned to write for the robot in the fanthology *Perfect Timing*, a story called *One Perfect Twilight*. It's a bold attempt to strengthen a relatively unpopular companion, using the events of *The Crystal Bucephalus* as a background to turn Kamelion into a lonely tragic figure while explaining his absence for the better part of the televised Season 21.

Craig's second novel also featured one of the less popular companions. After Big Finish's sterling efforts to rehabilitate both the sixth Doctor and Bonnie Langford's Mel it's difficult to remember quite how brave *Millennial Rites* seemed at the time of its publication. Here we get a character who's recognisably the sixth Doctor but far more sympathetic and likable than in any TV story (and, as a bonus, never in his technicolour nightmare coat) plus a strong Mel who's closer to her original character outline than the default position of Bonnie Langford's public persona. Finally, the sixth Doctor becomes a character who's actually fun to read about. Oh, and it's the story which finds an interesting way to employ the Valeyard, no mean feat after the way the character's backstory was muddled at the end of *The Trial of a Time Lord*. *Millennial Rites* doesn't just succeed on character work alone though. At the time of publication, October 1995, the Colin Baker era was still a memory much of fandom seemed to be trying to forget, an era some fans characterised as so bad that one eighties fanzine ran an infamous 'JNT Must Die!' front page. *Millennial Rites* not only revitalised the Doctor and Mel, it gave them the gripping tale they'd lacked on television, placing them at the heart of a storyline based on the X- Men's *Inferno* saga, much as *The Also People* was based on Iain M Banks' Culture (not content with that nod to his beloved American comics, there's also lawyer dodging cameos from John Constantine and Doctor Strange and elements derived from DC's *The Books of Magic*). Craig then adds elements from the Troughton Yeti stories, a sly play on the then current Millennium Bug fears and, refreshingly after the *New Adventures* overkill of ancient evils from beyond the dawn of time, a villain from the universe after ours. It's clear Craig had great fun in using this set up to turn London into a hi-tech fantasyland replete with mystic rulers and the Doctor as saviour/destroyer. Instead of turning into the self indulgent mess it could have become in lesser hands these elements all coalesce into something that rivals *Managra* or Gareth Roberts' comedies as the pinnacle of the *Missing Adventures*.

There's more lawyer dodging in Craig's only *New Adventure*, this one dodging the legal eagles from Terry Nation's estate. The Daleks barely appear but they're a looming presence in the novel much as the Doctor was in *Birthright* and that scheming background presence is the most effective use of them in the novel range, only rivalled by Simon Clark's *The Dalek Factor*. Despite that, *GodEngine* isn't half as much fun as Craig's two previous *Missing Adventures* although it's nowhere near as bad as its cheap nickname 'GodAwful' might lead you to expect. Again, it's born of an idea to poke around in the backwaters of continuity, this time what might be happening in the rest of the solar system during *The Dalek Invasion of Earth*, the fate of the Transit network and what happened to the Ice Warriors after *The Seeds of Death*. Oh, and as you might expect there are plenty of references to every race that thought about going near Mars. As a novel it fleshes the Ice Warrior culture out much as *Star Trek: The Next Generation* fleshed out Klingon culture - actually, with all the militarism, traditions and honour on display here it makes them extremely similar cultures. Now in the *New Adventures* there's one character perfect as a guide to the Ice Warrior culture. Unfortunately, and evidently to Craig's chagrin, Benny departed as a regular in the previous novel so all the cultural asides aren't quite as smoothly delivered as they might have been. We see the first real hints of darkness in Craig's work, despite an ostensible victory there's a downbeat epilogue to the action which suggests Hartnell was right in *The Aztecs* about the inability to change history, even one single line. Yes it's depressing and, in places, a little confusing but the sterling work expanding in Ice Warrior culture make this worth a look. Craig returned to write for the Daleks - well, one Dalek - in the *Lifedeath* fanthology. *A Meeting of Minds* is essentially a conversation between the Dalek Emperor and the TARDIS and brings a tragic element to what was very much a one-dimensional villain.

If you've survived so far you'll be ready for Craig's ultimate continuityfest, *The Quantum Archangel*. This sequel to *The Time Monster* is literally dripping with fanwank and the one that Craig admitted in an interview with the *Shockeye's Kitchen* fanzine had 'burnt out his fanwank circuits'. I'd go so far as to say that the Millennium War sequence is the single fanwankiest sequence in *Doctor Who* history, twenty four different references in just under two pages. Even there, the densest mass of continuity references ever seen, the references are anything but gratuitous, immaculately researched to see which races might have been able to participate in a battle 150 million years ago. Again, the sense of a shared universe is reinforced, even where throwing in unfamiliar but evocative names in a Robert Holmes or Russell T. Davies style could have worked just as well. After reading this you might even want to go back and watch *The Time Monster* again, convinced by the background work Craig does that it's not that bad. Where it falls down a little though is the complex physics, which might be consistent but to a relative layman like myself is fairly impenetrable, particularly given that this is a brave attempt to make sense of the weird and wonderful physics of the *Doctor Who* universe.

For fans of RTD's version of *Doctor Who*, *Synthespians*™ is probably the best place to start as it gives a familiar *Doctor Who* villain a 21st century makeover – almost literally. Actually, it's a more interesting use of the Autons than that seen in *Rose*. Unusually though, Craig writes the sixth Doctor and Peri fairly conventionally, both seeming particularly at home in a world based on the brash camp of eighties America, right down to a villain seemingly based on razor magnate Victor Kiam. *Synthespians™* is relatively low on continuity, with the rather obvious exception of the adversaries. The central concept, the Nestene Consciousness using plastic surgery as an invasion tool, is so obvious you'll wonder why no one thought of doing it before. Craig isn't afraid to pursue the idea to horrifically camp extremes either, getting away with a pair of exploding Auton breasts but, in a rare outbreak of good taste, not including a proposed Auton condom scene. The structure's reminiscent of *Revelation of the Daleks* with the first half exploring the colony (complete with spoof shows such as 'Dusty The Fearless Monster Killer') and the second half being a payoff of that build up. What we get is a simultaneous satire and celebration of plastic eighties glamour, particularly that seen in Craig's beloved American glam soaps. As a result it's a light, shallow read that might not linger too long in the memory after you've finished but is slyly inventive enough to entertain for a few hours.

Craig's work wasn't all about fanwank though. *Excelis Decays*, his only *Doctor Who* audio, contains no references outside the previous *Excelis* plays and is an unremittingly bleak conclusion to the *Excelis* trilogy including elements based on Orwell's *1984* and Huxley's *Brave New World*. In other words it's the most atypical story Craig ever wrote, the dystopian setting not lending itself to his more usual lightweight fare. Craig's inexperience in writing scripts shows in that there's a lot of talk but relatively little action (summed up by the character of Commander Sallis who does little but sit behind his desk) but it ends up being a satisfyingly bleak conclusion to the *Doctor Who* storyline of the trilogy. For Craig it had the added bonus of inspiring his friend Ian Collier to return to acting after a long time out of the profession.

Uranus, Craig's last published *Doctor Who* work (in Big Finish's *Short Trips: The Solar System*), is very much a return to the type of SF soap first seen in *The Crystal Bucephalus*, It's a sequel of sorts to *The Daleks' Masterplan*, working in continuity references to emphasise that this is the *Doctor Who* universe. It's inessential but if you're looking for a taster to give you an idea if you might like Craig's work it's ideal, combining as it does soap, fanwank and a solid SF rationale. It's part of Craig's best *Who* related work but didn't feature the Doctor, nor any fanwank references. He himself thought his Iris Wildthyme short story, *Came to Believe*, was the best thing he'd ever written. Unlike his similar pronouncement regarding *Excelis Decays* it's also true. That a respected literary figure such as Paul Magrs might ask Craig to contribute to an anthology might surprise those who couldn't see beyond the self deprecating Fanwank God reputation. Stripped of the *Doctor Who* setting and elements which provided him with a literary comfort zone, Craig falls back on personal experience to provide a story of how Iris redeems a raging alcoholic author to ensure he writes her favourite book. The portrayal of alcoholism is unflinching and realistic, the black humour of the protagonist adding a depth and poignancy missing from the usual harrowing scenarios presented in fiction. Like most of Iris' own tall tales, it covers the same ground as a *Doctor Who* tale, in this case Steven Moffat's *Continuity Errors* (from *Decalog 3: Consequences*), but it's more emotionally true than that. The toughest thing with these stories of redemption is to have the subject earn that privilege but it's something Craig pulls off with aplomb, never taking the easy route of preachiness regarding abstinence or potentially easy cures. This is a story that Craig could never have told within the confines of *Doctor Who* but fits perfectly as an Iris tale, and excellent as other stories in the collection are, it's worth the cover price of *Wildthyme on Top* alone.

If you're looking for some of Craig's critical work on *Doctor Who*, aside from tracking down *DWM* issues from the mid 90s, your best bets are two volumes from Telos Publishing, *The Television Companion*, which contains reviews Craig wrote for *DWM*, and Shaun Lyon's guide to the second season of the 2005 revival, *Second Flight*, with Craig as one of the guest reviewers. His enthusiasm for the 21st century revival is evident in his words.

Although his output was cut short by his tragically early death in December 2006 it's a mark of the impression Craig left on fandom that a tribute fanthology, *Shelf Life*, is currently due for publication in May 2008 and a friend of his, Chris McKeon, is completing *Time's Champion*, his proposed regeneration story for the sixth Doctor. They're appropriate memorials to a man who had supportive words for many fan authors, his Outpost Gallifrey memorial thread being marked by several posters remarking how he'd been supportive of their fictional efforts. Craig's contribution to *Doctor Who* may not be as groundbreaking as the likes of Paul Cornell or Lawrence Miles (although both could be every inch Craig's equal in the fanwank stakes) but for sheer entertainment value there's very few authors that come close.

Brax's bit:

It hardly seems like 12 months since I received a text from a mutual friend regarding Craig's death a few hours before. I was just doing a spot of shopping in Morrisons after my nightshift at B&Q, and spent the next few minutes wandering aimlessly around the store with my basket. It was like being drunk without the pleasantness, I knew I was in the store for a reason, just the whole place was too bright and too noisy and one-step removed, like being underwater. I gave up and left without buying anything. Once home, I logged onto OG and spent the morning quietly reading the tribute thread before retiring to bed. I can't claim to have been a great or a close friend, but he's the sort of bloke who'd be quite happy to put you up overnight if you had nowhere to stay. The first time I met him, in 2000 after just a couple of months posting to the same yahoogroup, I was warmly invited into his home in Walthamstow where his chef-by-trade boyfriend had cooked some delicious pasta. Over the course of the emails arranging this he even sent me the word document of his forthcoming novel *The Quantum Archangel*, knowing that I'd buy the book regardless of having read it. He was ever so proud of his work and wanted people to read it so much he couldn't wait for the publication day. A pleasant evening followed where lots of red wine was drunk, gossip was laughed over and *The Five Doctors* was watched on DVD. He put me and my girlfriend up a few months later when we met up in the Tav, and the drive back to his from Central London was spent vaguely planning a future meet up in Hyde Park for some classical music event, where we'd dress up, us men in Tuxs. Never happened though, shame.

When I first stated my intention online to move to Coventry (which turned out to have been Craig's old hometown) he offered his old empty house as my new accommodation. It wasn't to be though, as the place had turned out to have become uninhabitable in his absence, but the thought and spirit of generosity was there. As my missus put it, he was a lovely bloke. I wish I'd stayed in touch over his last four or five years. We got on well, and enjoyed the odd phone call and email. And when in the summer of 2006 I started thinking about *Shooty Dog Thing* one of the people I was writing for was Craig, as this was the sort of thing he would have enjoyed. I lost touch with many many people when I dropped out of online fandom a few years back, and this fanzine's my device to get back into the scene. But with Craig I left it too late. Same old story, eh? We should make the effort to stay in touch with our friends. Craig's missed by everyone who knew him and everyone who enjoyed his glorious novels.

Oh, and we both loved the Quarks - those adorably crap tinpot terrors from *The Dominators*!

Craig Hinton 7th May 1964 to 3rd December 2006

'THE TWENTY-FIRST CENTURY IS WHEN IT'S ALL GONNA CHANGE...'
by Patrick Mulready
Originally printed in Shooty Dog Thing #5 – Spring 2008

One of the best things about the science fiction genre is its ability to look introspectively at the future: How the present often subtly drives the direction in which history is moving. William Shakespeare called death 'the undiscovered country, a country destined to be forever unmapped; mysterious; unknowable.' and to all intents and purposes the same applies to the time after we're gone: the future of the world we leave behind. The concept of the future is one which is both tantalizing and terrifying in equal measure. We know it's coming, and it can't be stopped. We know that our children will be a part of it, and we worry about the shape of what we're creating in the here and now. This makes it prime territory for speculative fiction. And future speculation happens to be a specialty of one particular television series - *Doctor Who*.

When Captain Jack Harkness states in the opening credits to spin-off series *Torchwood*, 'it's all gonna change, and you gotta be ready', it serves as a pronouncement; perhaps a warning. But for our purposes it serves best as a springboard for an overview of the parent series' depiction of that, then, 'undiscovered country': the twenty-first century. How much relevance do the object lessons of these previous visits to the future still have for us, now that we've arrived in that oft-imagined era ourselves? And most importantly, what do these tales of times yet to come - which have paradoxically now arrived - tell us about the era in which they were first shown? Time to put a mirror up to reflect the times.

Let's set to one side what we know about the twenty-first century from the first three seasons of *Doctor Who* since it returned to us in 2005. No Adam and the Dalek, no Battle of Canary Wharf/'Cybermen in Every Home', no Slitheen or the Master in Downing Street, Sycorax over London or 'Judoon Platoon on the Moon'. Those would show the twenty-first century as the *present*, rather than as the *future*. Let's see how Classic *Doctor Who* envisioned the myriad changes of the coming century.

In strict chronological order, these are the stories in which 20th Century *Doctor Who* has shown us their unique (to each era) imaginative projections of what *might* come to pass within the undiscovered country of the 21st:

The Enemy of the World (Patrick Troughton - Broadcast 23rd December 1967 - 27th January 1968. Set in the year 2017.)

The Power of the Daleks (Patrick Troughton - Broadcast 5th November - 10th December 1966. 'Allegedly' set in the year 2020.)

The Seeds of Death (Patrick Troughton - Broadcast 25th January - 1st March 1969. Set in the year 2044.)

The Wheel in Space (Patrick Troughton - Broadcast 27th April - 1st June 1968. Set in the year 2068.)

The Moonbase (Patrick Troughton - Broadcast 11th February - 4th March 1967. Set in the year 2070)

Warriors of the Deep (Peter Davison - Broadcast 5th - 13th January 1984. Set in the year 2084)

Paradise Towers (Sylvester McCoy - Broadcast 5th - 26th October 1987. Set in the year 2100)

[editor's note: the dates come from Lance Parkin's *A History of the Universe* (1996 edition) and are often subject to debate.]

What's that you say? You're noticing a preponderance of Patrick Troughton on that list of twenty-first century visitations by the Doctor? Well spotted! There's a reason for that, which has a lot to do with the message *Doctor Who* has sent over the years. As a genre, science fiction is influenced by its own times. *Doctor Who* - a byproduct of that genre - is naturally is no different. For Great Britain in the late nineteen sixties, it was a period of tremendous influence worldwide, culturally, socially, stylistically, thematically. A period of confidence and forward-thinking, and *Doctor Who* in the late sixties reflected that.

What got transmitted on television to depict 'The Century Yet To Come' was a direct product of what the age thought of itself. A mirror reflecting the hopes, dreams, and aspirations of the day. In these stories, Earth was - admittedly somewhat simplistically - shown to be a place where nationalistic and political differences mattered less than the goal of humanity working together in common purpose. Technological progress trumped ideology. Humanity is shown to be basically the same; but wears (debatably) cooler, hipper clothes, and travels around the world (or even beyond) with fantastic ease. These are the Troughton-infused twenty-first century years of *Doctor Who* - the swinging sixties clad in a form-fitting silver jumpsuit.

So what did we see? Short answer to the question, we saw exactly what we were to see in every decade of Classic *Who*: the normal flow of commerce and human congress interrupted repeatedly by Daleks (*The Power of the Daleks*), Ice Warriors (*The Seeds of Death*), and Cybermen (*The Wheel in Space, The Moonbase*.) Our slick, cool, sub-cinematic future was sent into repeated chaos when its orderly systems, our ingenious inventions like transmatting, controlling the weather, or tentative exploration of other worlds were interfered with - and each time, it brought the world to the brink of disaster.

But why would it do that? Is the future so unprepared for alien tampering in our affairs? The answer, naturally enough is *yes*. The dictates of drama and the need for a weekly diet of thrilling action/adventure saw to it that humanity - whatever the era, however technologically advanced - would always be at a disadvantage. Always teetering on the brink but for the timely intervention a certain cosmic hobo, who would impose himself into the situation and convince the monsters their schemes were doomed to failure. Twenty-first century Earth might be a technological near-utopia - but in reality it was the same old damsel-in-distress awaiting rescue it had ever been.

Well, that was the formula for a story, at least. In much of the Troughton era, stories involving this century were cut from that mould. But two tales which deviate slightly from this are *The Power of the Daleks* and *The Enemy of the World*. In the case of the latter, the extraordinary hero is mirrored by the dangerous doppelganger of the extraordinary villain Salamander: a mere human. A dangerous man whose ambitions threaten to wreck our rose-tinted future by taking over the world using the very technological wonders we created. His method of terrorism is manufactured natural disasters that can hit anywhere. And worse, he was as adept at impersonating the Extraordinary Hero as our hero was at playing him.

Even with the different focus on who the nature of the threat in *The Enemy of the World* - the steeping out into the unfamiliar framework of the then highly popular, spy/espionage genre - to distinguish it from all those alien invasion stories, this 2017 tale still depicted a future where technology basically ran smoothly. Technology had made many things possible (not all of them good) and the whole world was a knit unit of purpose - perhaps even misdirected purpose.

The other entry in this break-the-mould format is *The Power of the Daleks*. This story, which by the available evidence, is set in the year 2020, posits the possibility that humans have colonized distant space - which is a bit of a contraction to the established timeline of events (after all, that setting would put it only three years after *The Enemy of the World*). Interestingly, it also reveals that the future isn't quite as sparkling clean and politically free of strife as we might expect. Rebel colonists trying to overthrow the Colony's Governor? A Chief Scientist who is either unaware or unwilling to acknowledge what the Daleks are capable of? Perhaps this can be attributed to the fact that this was the first story featuring the 'new' Doctor, and the personality of the show hadn't yet developed into what we see of the twenty-first century in the later Troughton episodes. Perhaps it's also possible that the setting of this story was meant to actually be farther into the future. Or more likely, it simply shows us the future through the slightly differently angled mirror of a production team (and a series itself) in a state of transition. Either way, its apparent contradictions don't seriously distract from the on-going theme of our interest.

Setting aside *The Power of the Daleks*, the message from the Troughton years about the century that is to come was an optimistic one: no need to worry, we've seen the future, and it's brilliant, save for the odd alien attempt to destroy us. But this was not the case when eighties *Doctor Who* paid a couple of calls on the twenty-first century.

Between *The Seeds of Death* and *Warriors of the Deep* fifteen years of real time had elapsed for audiences. And what a decade and a half it was. The energy crisis came upon us in the early nineteen seventies. Our western confidences were shaken by years of unemployment and inflation. We'd seen such a change in the economy that trusted industries like manufacturing left us to find cheaper places to set up shop. We'd seen corruption and scandal in political high office, undermining our trust in government and other institutions. And after shaking all that off, we arrived in the nineteen eighties with a renewed resurgence in the painfully slowly dying Cold War.

Welcome to the dawn of post-modernism. An age where established institutions aren't necessarily to be trusted or taken at face value, people who might have been portrayed as heroes in a different time (police, the military, government, even institutions of faith) can be as menacing as the actual bad guy, if not the story's outright villain, and help can come from the most unlikely and unexpected places. But I digress a bit.

When the early eighties, with Margaret Thatcher and Ronald Reagan as world leaders, set a goal of defeating communism around the world, people got nervous. This, they said, is taking the Cuban Missile Crisis of the early sixties and exponentially increasing the danger. This, they said, is begging for nuclear holocaust to destroy mankind. Times changed and *Doctor Who* changed with them. We - and the series - bade a worried goodbye to our hopelessly optimistic, nineteen sixties view of the future. With dedicated anti-communist, anti-totalitarianism Reagan and Thatcher in power, the West was almost certain to precipitate the very war that left us with no future - certainly no future anyone would be eager to actually experience. Science fiction at the time became all about the post-apocalyptic experience. And the only alternative to idea of a nuclear holocaust was a permanent cold war stalemate.

It was that permanent cold war stalemate idea that serves as the underlying assumptive logic for *Warriors of the Deep*. When the nineteen eighties held up the mirror to itself, a cold war was still being waged a hundred years from now. East and West continued to be power blocks dividing up the planet, and neither side could be really happy until the other was driven out of existence. It was markedly different to the Troughton era depiction of the twenty-first century. It was...*Now*.

Enter into this cold-war-without-end scenario a threat neither side saw coming. More than that, a rare threat that for once didn't originate on Skaro or Telos, Mondas or Mars. No, this threat was domestic in a strict 'native to planet Earth' sense, and yet just as seemingly alien as a chorus of pepper-pots screaming '*Ex-Ter-Mi-Nate!*'. And being native to Earth, these Silurians and Sea Devils had once again decided that the posturing apes had to go. You have to hand it to their sense of timing: after a reptile age that ended sixty five million years ago, what better time to remove humanity than when it's at its most paranoid and eager to engage in fighting among itself. Just insert yourself, stir the pot a bit for both sides, and let their own weapons take care of them for you.

This was a marked contrast from the Troughton era stories - there never was a sense that the Earth was poised to destroy itself the moment the Cold War went hot. By the time of *Warriors of the Deep, we* were providing the 'aliens' with the means to destroy us. And *they* were only too happy to exploit our paranoia, suspicion and wariness. The mirror reflecting our own times is revealing a few imperfections.

When Peter Davison's Doctor ends the story by observing all the death that's happened, human upon human, Eocene upon human, and human upon Eocene, and how close all of this came to consuming billions of people on the Earth, his words 'There should have been another way' are far more telling in terms of how the nineteen eighties viewed the future. There should be another way: we shouldn't be a divided planet, a dangerous, ever present gulf of economic and political ideology between us.

The irony, if we look at a post-script to this, is that five years after this story aired, the Berlin Wall came down. Another 18 months after that, the Soviet Union collapsed of its own inertia.

Communism in the West was dead. The Cold War - always a disturbingly artificial construct to begin with - was over. And as a result, *Warriors of the Deep* openly contradicts the Troughton years' vision of the twenty-first century (these things are inevitable in show spanning more than twenty years - and that's part of its rich appeal).

Finally, near the end of the series' original twenty-six year run was *Paradise Towers*. Set at the very end of the twenty-first century. Indeed, one could convincingly argue that *Paradise Towers* is more of a twenty-second century setting. I include it here because of a personal belief that years which end in a zero mark the tenth and final year of any particular decade, rather than the first year of a new one. After all, we start counting with 'one' not with 'zero'. Thus, *Paradise Towers* is set in the tenth and final year of the final decade of the twenty-first century.

And what we get with *Paradise Towers* is a dystrophic breakdown of social interactions. Dystopias are nothing new in science fiction, or indeed in *Doctor Who*. Even the Troughton years dealt with dystopian realities in stories such as *The Krotons*, for example.

But for this seventh Doctor story, what we see is the breakdown of a civilization set within the microcosm of a single building. An interesting, highly imaginative use of the near omniscient mirror reflecting our own present. But peeling away the next layer of the story, we find that the reason for this social chaos is that it was imposed by the very architect who designed the building, because he couldn't stand the notion that people would actually inhabit his marvellous creation. (I wonder if the Doctor ever met Frank Lloyd Wright, or read *The Fountainhead*.) What our reflective mirror shows us here is an uneasy metaphor for the lurking fear that our governments are more concerned with building the perfect functioning model of their rule, rather than ruling for the good of those they're supposed to exist to serve. The result is residents who descend upon each other, gangs (after a fashion) battling for turf, and a bureaucratic enforcers of the law too hamstrung by their own rules to do anything about the situation. In short - the total and utter breakdown of civilization. Hardly the technological wonderland like we've been introduced to in the past - and rightfully so. Times, once again, they were a changin'.

So, with these snapshots of the Doctor's previous stops throughout the century that is to come, what message is there to take from this? What is it that we've got to be ready for, as Captain Jack would have us believe? Judging by what we've seen, the twenty-first century is an era of fantastic technological change, an era where (if you set aside *Warriors of the Deep*) humanity comes together in common purpose: a veritable utopia threatened only by enemies - both internal and external - waiting for us, as always, out there in the dark...

As Captain Jack Harkness has already cautioned us - 'it's all gonna change, and you gotta be ready'. We stride forward into the twenty-first century forearmed with the cautionary visions *Doctor Who* has provided of what *might be* / *what could be* for the times to come.

WHO CARES! GEEKS IN DOCTOR WHO RESIGNATION CRISIS!
by Tim Hirst
Originally printed in Shooty Dog Thing #5 - Spring 2008

An orchestrated campaign to force the resignation of *Doctor Who* producer Russell T. Davies is gathering speed on the internet. Geeks from all over the world are demanding that the respected producer, 44, steps down immediately. 'He's ruined our show!', whined one nerd, from the comfort of his single bedroom yesterday. He continued, 'Just four years ago *Doctor Who* was a joke among the public, and kids had never heard of it! Now, it's the most popular thing on telly! It's outrageous!'. Another dweeb, 31 year old Davros Apple Mackintosh, added 'It's just not fair. We liked it when the only time *Doctor Who* was on TV was a clip of the Myrka on *Room 101*, or a clip of Martin Clunes looking like a tit. Now we are forced to watch 13 episodes a year, a Christmas special, two spin offs, two companion documentary series and an animated adventure - it's sickening! RTD should go now!'

The show's new found popularity has caused controversy among long-term fans of the smash hit time travelling show, with many disappointed that the new series didn't die on its arse, like the ill-fated 1996 movie starring Joe McGann. One alleged fan, named only as 'Krynoid' said 'Back in 2005 we had every confidence that it would fail. It seemed almost guaranteed, what with a northern Doctor and a silly pop star and no wacky costume - we didn't even need to see the first episode to know it would be crap.' Krynoid choked back tears as he stroked a battered old paperback called 'Lungbarrow'.

Davies - dubbed 'The Big Bastard' by Whovians, as they like to be known - has been voted one of the most influential people in television, and is one of the most sought after TV producers of recent times - and while most *Doctor Who* fans are proud to have him at the helm of the series, a vocal minority is insisting that he resigns, citing the fact that the latest episode got 12 million viewers. 'It's not fair!' wailed a man in a greasy anorak, 'In 1988 we were getting 4 or 5 million - tops! Why can't we go back to the good old days? I want my mummy!'

Loyal members of the public were quick to defend the hit show. Maureen Puffbiscuit, 46, of Leatherhead fumed 'These geeks are trying to ruin our favourite programme! My kids love *Doctor Who* and so do all their friends!' Barry Thruntwhistle, 35, of Droitwich agrees, 'I suppose they want the wobbly sets back and the crap effects - well I want Spangles and Tonka Toys back but life moves on!'. The army of Whovians remained defiant however. A woman spod - apparently the only one - said, 'The general public know nothing - they like *Eastenders* and *Big Brother*, for Tom's sake!'.

A BBC Wales insider said yesterday, 'Yes, it's true - *Doctor Who* is pants these days. We don't seem to attract decent actors anymore, the toys don't sell, the *Radio Times* isn't interested and we can't win an award for love nor money! Maybe Russell should go and live in a cave and think about what he's done!'. Old telly god Michael Grade had a suggestion - 'A hiatus - that's what these so-called fans really want - take it off the air for a couple of years and bring it back a shadow of its former self - that's what I'd do if I was at the Beeb'.

The Chief Geek yesterday claimed he was confident about the campaign. 'I'm confident about the campaign', he mumbled. 'We demand that Russell resigns immediately and that no further attempts are made to make *Doctor Who* popular or likeable. After all, we've been watching telly all our lives, and we know best. Fact!' And with that, he picked up his thermos flask, tucked his trousers into his socks and walked off, one leg going slightly faster than the other.

The campaign reached a high yesterday as a charity single - originally released in 1985 - was remixed and re-released. 'Doctor in Distress 2008' is the brainchild of 'Styre' - one of the founders of the Whovian Collective. Smelling slightly of sour milk, he wears all black, except for a baseball cap with the show's 1980s logo and a badge bearing the sinister slogan 'I am a Target Reader'. Other fans have taken to wearing t-shirts emblazoned with the legend 'It's Our Show - Leave it alone!', while others still wear their greying 'Smoke Me a Kipper' T-shirts from 1992.

Readers wishing to download the song, or buy one of their exclusive 'Who Gives a Toss' car stickers, or even those just wanting a good laugh, can log onto www.weareallexperts.com

LICENCE DENIED - MORE THAN 10 YEARS OUTSIDE THE TARDIS
by Jon Arnold
Originally printed in Shooty Dog Thing #5 – Spring 2007

Doctor Who fandom always had a bad press, at least until March 2005 when, all of a sudden, what seemed like the whole country suddenly realised we'd been right all along and dammit, it is the single best idea for a series in the history of British television. Hell, even in the early nineties, when *Star Trek: The Next Generation* and *The X Files* inspired a shift in pop culture that made sci-fi shows as close to cool as they're ever going to get, we were vastly below even the previously untouchable *Trek* fans on the Anorak Scale, condemned to follow a seemingly dead series. We'd become something of an outsider subculture, a refuge for those seen as freaks, geeks and other assorted outsiders. A subculture that was developed enough to take over when the BBC didn't seem to be interested in the show any more, continuing the show in our own way. We wrote the new stories, the new books, audios and videos, turned *Doctor Who Magazine* into a professional fanzine, we filled the hole where a TV series wasn't with intelligent writing, new perspectives on old stories and even on *Doctor Who* fandom itself. Much as I love the Cartmel and Holmes eras, my late 70s/early 80s childhood *Who* and the current Welsh reincarnation, the nineties is by far my favourite 'era' of the show, when it was all being written by fans like me for fans like me. *Licence Denied* is a guidebook and a tribute to where that creative urge began: the scabrous, libellous, intelligent, creative and witty world of the fanzine. You'll learn a hell of a lot more about the mindset and attitudes of British *Doctor Who* fandom from this book than any number of dry academic studies and be a lot more entertained along the way.

Licence Denied was Virgin's inspired two-fingered salute to the BBC taking the book licence back after twenty-four years in 1997. In a situation where you could excuse the publishers for feeling fairly bitter given the BBC's previous attitude towards the Who fiction licence, it would've been easy to go down the Boxtree cash-in route of hiring Adrian Rigelsford or Peter Haining, telling them to fill a couple of hundred pages and bunging out the results whilst maximising profits by skimping on fact checking or proof reading. Yes, *Licence Denied* was almost certainly cheap and is, to an extent, a cash-in, but being from the Virgin stable of *Who* books it's clearly been a labour of love. If nothing else illustrates how much better Virgin understood the *Doctor Who* book buyers than BBC Books at the time, it's that Virgin were publishing this while the BBC put out *Doctor Who: A Book of Lists*, which did exactly what it said on the tin and reprinted a lot of *Who* facts anyone who cared enough to buy such a book knew anyway - the type of cheap cash-in your well-meaning gran, who knows you're interested in *Doctor Who*, is conned into buying by the logo to fill your Christmas stocking. That *Licence Denied* rises so far above the status of the largely undistinguished and ill-researched volumes is entirely down to the inspired editorship of Paul Cornell.

Paul's one of those rare types who's just as passionate about fandom as the shows and books that begat it. And he's never less than enthusiastic and evangelical about those passions, persuasive to the point where a Cornell eulogy could almost sell *Star Trek* to the most blinkered *Who* fans. It's similar, on a smaller scale, to Sir David Attenborough's informed and infectious passion for wildlife, a passion that draws in people who would normally hold no interest in the subject. While *Licence Denied* could easily have turned into the fanzine equivalent of all those 'I ♥ 80s' clip shows that cropped up around the turn of the millennium, Cornell always steers it away from cheap, shallow nostalgia and instead comes up with the tribute that the era deserves.

This isn't necessarily an attempt to present a 'best of', more an attempt to capture the zeitgeist of the British fanzine heyday. Each chapter presents a strand of what was going on from Ness Bishop's wide-eyed enthusiasm, expressed mainly through poetry, through literate analysis from the likes of Thomas Noonan, to the scathing wit of John Molyneux and Ian Berriman and pretty much every conceivable type of article in between. The collection's personal nature means that only the most catholic of tastes could love every word but conversely only the most narrow-minded couldn't find a few articles to enjoy. While I wasn't overly keen on Nick Cooper's long convention review (reading about someone else's good time isn't as fun as being there), it's more than made up for by Molyneux's 'DIY Guide to Convention Invitations', Jan Vincent Rudski's infamous incineration of *The Deadly Assassin*, or any of Gareth Roberts' myriad contributions. Even the fan poetry's got a certain charm to it. You can probably tell a lot about what sort of a fan you are by which articles you enjoy. The only downside is that there's always an article or two you wish had been included - something from DWIN's *Enlightenment*, some other representation of US fandom, or Tat Wood's astonishing analysis of the effect rapid growth would have on an ordinary frog as seen in *The Claws of Axos*. It's a minor quibble though; the fact that it's such a personal selection is the book's major strength.

Sadly, these days fanzines aren't anywhere near as prominent as they were, particularly in print form - we've got message boards and blogs to argue or post new fiction in now. Some of us have even got BBC Books or Big Finish for that. *Licence Denied* is therefore as much of an early eulogy for a dying era as a tribute to fandom's creativity. But even if it's the dying art I think it is, at least it's inspired a last gasp of glory. Usually a review of a book like *Licence Denied* would be beyond the remit of *Shooty Dog Thing* - the point is usually to introduce new fans to the old series, or give old style fans a different perspective on old stories. But on *Shooty Dog Thing*'s first birthday it's appropriate to give a tribute to the inspiration behind the fanzine - on one fateful trip out, the esteemed editor of this very 'zine was short of some reading material. So he grabbed the first book that came to hand and after remembering exactly what he loved about fanzines, and following encouragement from his significant other, channelled his (previously frustrated) creativity into a 'zine that captured the spirit of the era presented in *Licence Denied*. And it's through *Shooty Dog Thing* that I ended up spending an extremely pleasant afternoon over a pint with the editor chatting about life, the universe and everything and all points in between. Yes, even including *Doctor Who*. As *Licence Denied* makes clear, fandom's a community bound by a shared love but that's only a starting point to meet new friends with common interests outside fandom. *Doctor Who*'s just the social glue that holds a community with massively diverse interests together, the same sort of function as the other communities with a strong fanzine background, football and music. Nine years ahead of Russell T. Davies saying precisely the same thing with his series two episode *Love & Monsters*, Paul Cornell made it clear exactly why fandom should be cherished.

I like to think that Paul would be delighted to know that *Licence Denied* was the direct creative inspiration for *Shooty Dog Thing*, continuing the fanzine tradition. It's exactly the response this unfairly neglected treasure deserves - aside from a second volume.

NASTY, BRUTISH, AND SHORT
by Paul Castle
Originally printed in Shooty Dog Thing #5 - Spring 2008

There aren't as many returning monsters or villains in *Doctor Who* as people seem to imagine, so it's no real surprise to see the Sontarans cropping up in 2008's series. I am in no doubt that before long all the recurring concepts or characters will reappear. The first year gave us the Daleks and Autons, as well as the idea of *Doctor Who* itself, the second brought us the Cybermen and the original entity Sutekh the Destroyer was a mere echo of, and last year we encountered the Master and the Macra. That's essentially a pattern of well known recurring foe with a minor (or relatively minor) support act cropping up each year. It's a bit like having Elton John at your concert, with Chesney Hawkes as a warm up. One wonders what the minor returnees will be in 2008: could it be (my educated guess) the Sensorites? The Ogrons? Yartek Leader of the Alien Voord? Personally I'm hoping for a Wirrrn vs Foreign Hazard Duty story, but don't rate my chances highly.

But anyway, it's no big deal really and I'm only really mentioning it because I can't think of much to say about the Sontarans by way of an introduction to them. You see, I've never found them all that interesting, and whether you're familiar with them or not the only introduction you need will be in the episode when they return. To me they're really nothing more than yet another group of warmongering aliens that stomp around with big guns and shout a lot. Imagine the Klingons with baked potatoes as their heads instead of being crowned with Cornish pasties and you're pretty much there. They're fighting an endless war with their spacefaring-jellyfish-like Rutan foes, and can mass-produce themselves through cloning in order to prevent their conflict's humungous casualty rate from being a problem.

So, right, what more can I say about them then? Not much aside from challenging you to name all the Sontaran stories in *Doctor Who*. The average fan will be able to list off *The Time Warrior*, *The Sontaran Experiment*, *The Invasion of Time*, *The Two Doctors* and be wondering if they could get a bonus point for mentioning *Horror of Fang Rock* (where we meet the Rutans) before you could write your own name, but I'm willing to bet that no-one will be able to confidently list off *every* story in *all* media featuring them. There's something of a thing in fandom of regarding one medium of fiction as being more real than any other: only the TV series 'counts'. That is what I've got to say in this and every other issue of *Shooty Dog Thing*: there's more to *Doctor Who* than just the telly series. Forget canon and continuity and all those other post-pubescent fanboy obsessions and get back to why you liked *Doctor Who* in the first place: the wide variety of stories.

The Time Warrior

BBC1, 4 x 25 minute episodes (15th Dec 1973 - 5th Jan 1974)
by Robert Holmes (writer), Alan Bromly (director)
Linx the Sontaran is stranded in medieval England, but using some rather crude time travel equipment he kidnaps scientists from the 'present' day (possibly also snatching the odd greengrocer judging by the presence of potatoes in the pre-Walter Raleigh castle kitchens) to help him fix his ship. All this doesn't go unnoticed, and both the third Doctor and a nosy little journo by the name of Sarah Jane Smith set out to find out what's become of the missing scientists.

Hugely enjoyable, and undeniably the best of the televised Sontaran stories to date. I loved this as a kid when it was released as a movie edit on VHS, and now it's out on DVD I look forward to watching it again (I always wait for the sales at Christmas and let mum know which ones would make a cheap present for me - I'm in no hurry!).

The Sontaran Experiment

BBC1, 2 x 25 minute episodes (22nd Feb - 1st Mar 1975)
by Bob Baker & Dave Martin (writer), Rodney Bennett (director)

Styre the Sontaran is performing experiments on humans in order to assess their physical and mental vulnerabilities before invading Earth.

Quite why he's doing this isn't clear, as this is hundreds of thousand years in the future, the whole planet (by implication) looks like Dartmoor and is totally deserted aside from the few humans he lured there in the first place (oh, and also the fourth Doctor, Sarah and Harry, who turned up just in time to put a spanner in the works). Whilst it does have a tendency to drag, it's beautifully shot: the escape from the studio for two whole episodes more than makes up for any slow patches.

The Invasion of Time

BBC1, 6 x 25 minute episodes (4th Feb - 11th Mar 1978)
by David Agnew (writer), Gerald Blake (director)
It's the end of the fourth episode of the adventure, and the Doctor's been oh so clever and trapped the Vardans who were attempting to take control of Gallifrey. In doing so he laid the planet wide open for attack, but was in full control of the situation and all's well that ends well. Except... where did those Sontarans spring from?!

This is the best way to utilise the six episode format: tell a four part tale and wrap things up nicely just in time for a huge 'to be continued...' twist at the end.

The Final Quest

Doctor Who Weekly, 4 pages in #8 (5th Dec 1979)
by Steve Moore (writer), Paul Neary (artist)
Katsu the Sontaran, the cruellest of his race, hides a terrible secret that haunts his dreams at night: he once fled from a fight. His quest therefore is to find the ultimate weapon that will never let him be defeated again, but when he finds it on a peaceful world with no other defences he's led on a chase to a nearby lifeless planet where - you guessed it - the ultimate weapon is biological and kills him and the brave pacifist.

A simple little tale told effectively across the four pages, it's an enjoyable 2 minute distraction.

The Outsider

Doctor Who Weekly, 8 pages in #25 & 26 (2nd - 9th Apr 1980)

by Steve Moore (writer), David Lloyd (artist)
Skrant the Sontaran lands on the planet Braktilis to subjugate the populous and set the world up as another stronghold in the fight against the Rutans. He meets local astrologer Demimom, who does a Gaius Baltar and joins forces with Skrant in order to save his neck and perhaps profit.

Not bad, it's got a couple of good morals: don't be too restrictive of your daughter, don't pay much attention to your horoscope, and don't team up with any invading Sontarans (who in turn should be a little less obvious about their Achilles heel). And yes, it's David Lloyd as in the Alan Moore comic book *V for Vendetta*. The *Doctor Who* comics have had their share of the greats.

Dragon's Claw
Doctor Who Weekly/Monthly, 34 pages in #39-45 (10th Jul - Oct 1980)
by Steve Moore (writer), Dave Gibbons (artist)
Deep within the ancient Shaolin monastery lurk the Eighteen Bronze Men, who bestow great powers of combat on the monks. When the fourth Doctor, Sharon and K9 investigate they find that the Bronze Men are actually stranded Sontarans who are attempting to...

...well, I'll let you discover for yourself as it's rather fine and a shame to spoil the story. All the fourth Doctor *DWW/M* strips are available in two collections: *The Iron Legion* and *Dragon's Claw*. I'll let you work out which collection this story's in for yourself. The majority of these strips are drawn by the superb Dave Gibbons (who, like David Lloyd above, went onto draw for Alan Moore, giving us the genre-defining *Watchmen*). I recommend you pick up these *DWM* strip collections from Panini: you can get them for a good price from Amazon.

The Gods Walk Among Us
Doctor Who Monthly, 4 pages in #59 (December 1981)
by John Peel (writer), David Lloyd (artist)
Styx the Sontaran lands in ancient Egypt to find a willing slave workforce who hailed him as the toad god, until Tothmes overhears his log entry outlining plans to use the planet as a place from which to strike against the Rutans (and get destroyed in the retaliation). When Styx lies down in his new base deep within the pyramid to recharge,

Tothmes tells his superiors that the god is dead and should be honoured as befits his kind. Five and a half thousand years later, the tomb is excavated and the Sontaran is freed!

That makes it sound so crap though - it's not, honest. This is mildly amusing stuff that uses its four pages incredibly well. I hope that Panini release these back-up strips someday, as they're really far better than the strips for *Doctor Who Adventures* and *Battles in Time*.

The Two Doctors
BBC1, 3 x 45 minute episodes (16th Feb - 2nd Mar 1985)
by Robert Holmes (writer), Peter Moffatt (director)
Stike the Sontaran contributes a bit of muscle to aid Dastari and Chessene the augmented Androgum continue their illegal experiments into time travel in return for shared knowledge of the technology that would turn the tide of the eternal war against the Rutans. They're dispatched by their allies before they can get the chance to pre-emptively return the favour.

An enjoyable story, but the story doesn't really do the Sontarans any favours. The actors chosen aren't stocky enough to carry off the costumes (the head and neck area looks like it's balanced on top of the shoulders rather than growing up from the chest area) and they're not given much to do. The story could have used Cybermen or Ogrons to the same effect, or the Voord or Zygons or Terileptils or the Melkur or-

In a Fix with Sontarans
BBC1, part of Jim'll Fix It, (23rd Feb 1985)
by Eric Saward (writer), Marcus Mortimer (director)
Nathan the Sontaran is hunting the sixth Doctor within the TARDIS, but the Time Lord has doubled back to the console room and is trying to battle the intruders from there. He somehow manages to activate the teleport and old companion Tegan Jovanka is beamed up, followed shortly after by eight-year-old Gareth Jenkins who's been Jim'll Fixed into the adventure. He helps the Doctor and Tegan defeat the invading Sontarans just before a hideous face materializes on the monitor screen...

...but it's only Jimmy Saville. I cringed at this when I was a teen (it showed up on the *Colin Baker Years* video) but watching this on *The*

Two Doctors DVD I found it rather sweet and charming. Adds nothing to Sontaran lore, but who cares!

Pureblood

Doctor Who Magazine, 28 pages in #193-196 (25th Nov 1992 - 17th Feb 1993)

by Dan Abnett (writer), Colin Andrew (artist)

The Rutans have encountered a long-lost race of Sontarans, a colony who lost touch with their brethren long before the war, before the species took to cloning. The Rutan, seeing the opportunity to get past Sontaran defences, inflamed hatred in the 'pureblood' Sontarans for their 'weak and decadent' cloned kin. The resultant army passed straight through the defences of Sontarr (sic) and the planet was destroyed. A single ship carrying the Racepool escaped, and made it to a human genetics space station where the Doctor and Bernice Summerfield had just arrived. Much to everyone's surprise, the Doctor agrees to aid the Sontarans save their people. Only trouble is, a Rutan spy is on board and it's not long before the purebloods arrive...

Well, as James Hadwen noted in issue 3, this story is not exactly a great comics introduction for Benny's character, but I think it's a fantastic comic strip for the Sontarans themselves. It adds so much to the mythos, and it's a shame that it's all too often overlooked.

Shakedown - Return of the Sontarans

Dreamwatch Media, 50 minute video (Oct 1994)

by Terrance Dicks (writer), Kevin Davies (director)

Steg the Sontaran and his squad are on the tail of an escaping Rutan spy, and have tracked it to Space Station Beta. The Sontarans are boarding all ships that have recently docked at the station, hunting for their enemy. One of these ships is the Tiger Moth, a solar sail conversion job on a shakedown cruise to prepare a team of super rich VIPs for a high-profile solar sail race. Captain Lisa Deranne and rich ex-smuggler Kurt assist the Sontarans in the search for the Rutan, who is on board and killing the crew, whilst preparing for a double cross by the Sontarans.

Same concept as *Alien Vs Predator*, with humans caught between two warring species of aliens and trying not to get diced in the crossfire, this direct-to-video spin-off starring familiar faces in unfamiliar roles is one of the finest Sontaran stories produced, and certainly the best of all the direct-to-video *Doctor Who* spin-offs which were abundant in the nineties. Terrance Dicks unashamedly recycles old dialogue (some of Linx's stuff from *The Time Warrior* regarding male/female differences, and Steg echoes the Cyberleader's assurance to his Lieutenant in *The Five Doctors* about how promises to aliens have no validity) but this is done well. Oh, and the Sontarans have had a nineties makeover: they're still recognisable, but are an enormous improvement on previous designs. Recommended.

Lords of the Storm
Virgin Publishing (Dec 1995)
by David A. McIntee

The Sontarans are infecting the population of a human colony with a retrovirus that would make the world look like a Sontaran occupied planet to Rutan deep-space sensors. Their plan is to draw the fire of the Rutans' big guns whilst they counter-attack. Onboard the Sontaran fleet, however, is a deep cover Rutan spy who discovers that the Sontarans know all about a direct subspace link to the Rutan Throneworld which had been set up as an escape route. The Rutan breaks cover and escapes.

One of two connected books from Virgin's *Doctor Who* range, this features the fifth Doctor and Turlough. It's been well over a decade since I read this, so memories are vague, but I recall enjoying it: lots of Rutan/Sontaran fanwank (in a good way). Leads directly into *Shakedown*.

Shakedown
Virgin Publishing (Dec 1995)
by Terrance Dicks

The Sontarans track the Rutan spy from *Lords of the Storm* to Space Station Beta, where it's also being tracked by the seventh Doctor's companions Cwej and Forrester. The Rutan smuggles aboard the Tiger Moth solar ship and is discovered and killed by the Sontarans, with more than a little help from ship's captain Lisa Deranne. But the story doesn't stop there...

Terrance Dicks goes the extra mile when novelising his direct-to-video smash, instead of a straight adaptation of the script he makes the video the middle third of a much longer *New Adventure*, which was the current ongoing series of *Doctor Who* at the time. I can't honestly recall much more about the book though, for the same reasons as McIntee's *Missing Adventure*: too many years since reading.

The Eight Doctors
BBC Books (Jun 1997)
by Terrance Dicks

A squad of Sontarans is sliced and diced by a Raston Warrior Robot.

This is a book of greatest hits, but one sung by cover-version artists. Here the Sontarans are cut and pasted into that memorable scene from *The Five Doctors*, taking the place of the hapless Cybermen. In an entry for a book full of cameos, it's an opportunity to note that there are many Sontaran cameos in the books, comics, and audios (a single panel in Alan Moore's *Black Legacy*, a reference in Paul Cornell's *Love and War*, a 'walk-on' in BBV's *Infidel's Comet* by Simon Gerard and Colin Hill - there are dozens). It's only here though, where hundreds of cameos and references are brought together, something is created that's far less than the sum of its parts. Avoid *The Eight Doctors* at all costs.

Mindgame
Reeltime Pictures, 30 minute video (Sep 1998)
by Terrance Dicks (writer), Keith Barnfather (director)

Tharg the Sontaran has been captured, teleported from his current battlefield, and placed in a cell alongside a Draconian and a human by a mysterious alien who wants to determine which is the stronger race. Can they put aside their differences in order to escape, or will they tear each other to pieces?

Whilst not a bad production, it's rather staged and talky. *Mindgame* would have benefited from being one of the audio CD dramas that BBV were just starting to produce at the time. The Sontaran makes up for his lack of intelligence with nothing but bluster and yet more observations on female thorax construction, and comes a poor third alongside Miles Richardson's Draconian and Sophie Aldred's mercenary. This is a shame as the Sontarans have been written far better than this in the BBV audios.

The Infinity Doctors
BBC Books (Nov 1998)
by Lance Parkin

The Doctor has invited the Sontarans and the Rutans to Gallifrey in an attempt to negotiate a peace settlement, only just as soon as the delegates arrive, the Homeworld is hit by the biggest crisis in its history.

Forget *The Eight Doctors*, this is how continuity-fests should be done. You'll gather from last issue that I'm a fan of this novel: it's an exploration of what *Doctor Who* is by showing us what it wasn't whilst simultaneously being quintessential *Who*. Rather than chuck in loads of Doctors and monsters without any idea of how to use them, here we have the Sontarans and Rutans used to good effect. They're only one of the sub-plots we return to now and again throughout the main story, but it's got a satisfactory set-up and conclusion. I can't recommend this book highly enough.

Unnatural Born Killers
Doctor Who Magazine, 7 pages in #277 (5th May 1999)
by Adrian Salmon (writer & artist)

A Sontaran colonisation squad has landed on a planet where they're planning on wiping out the humanoid population in a refreshing little war after their journey. The locals are peaceful though, so the Sontarans are just starting to settle for the second-best option of a massacre when the village champion wakes up. Kroton, 'the Cyberman with a Soul' from way back in the *Doctor Who Weekly* back-up strips easily fights them off, destroys their colonisation ship and walks off into the sunset as the locals celebrate. This lovely little strip kicks arse, the art is superb and the laid-back 'voice-over' by Junior Cyberleader Kroton as he dispatches Sontaran after Sontaran oozes supercool. This is *Buffy the Vampire Slayer*'s Angel meets Spiderman meets Darth Maul. He's got the moves of Maul, the wit of Spidey, and the tortured soul of Angel. The Sontarans are just there to get their butts kicked, but as they look so amazing when Adrian Salmon draws them you can forgive this. Have a look in Panini's *The Glorious Dead* collection of eighth Doctor *DWM* comic strips to read this. I highly recommend this and all the other *DWM* graphic novels: they collect a criminally under-rated aspect of *Doctor Who* at a bargain price.

Mindgame Trilogy - Battlefield
Reeltime Pictures, 15 minute video (May 1999)
by Terrance Dicks (writer), Keith Barnfather (director)
After the events of *Mindgame*, Tharg the Sontaran finds himself back in his war, but when shot down almost immediately by a long range Rutan sniper he's left to die in the mud. Making a report on his recent capture, he reflects on the heretical discovery that not all non-Sontarans are inferior.

Like the original Mindgame, this would benefit enormously from being a CD release, but I have to grudgingly admit after ten minutes or so of checking Facebook status updates and stuff whilst watching, I did start to get into it. Shame it's only just over fifteen minutes long, but it's a promising sign that the rest of the trilogy will entertain when I get back to it later.

Silent Warrior
BBV Audio Adventures In Time & Space, 60 minutes (Dec 1999)
by Peter Grehan (writer), Tim Saward (director)
Starn the Sontaran is smuggling an army through human space in order to strike the Rutans from behind; can Sylvia and mysterious traveller Alex prevent the human species becoming the Sontaran's next target by saving the Rutans from destruction?

A laid back but enjoyable story, one which sums up what I loved about the Doctorless BBV audios. This one has a bit of a blatant Doctor-substitute to save the day, but don't let that put you off.

Old Soldiers
BBV Audio Adventures In Time & Space (February 2000)
by Colin Hill & Simon Gerard (writer), John Wadmore (director)
Brak the Sontaran crash-landed in Europe in the midst of World War One. 80 years later UNIT's Captain Alice Wells is led to a top secret safe-house where she interrogates Brak about his involvement in a series of deaths during a British weapons-testing program decades previously.

Superb. Essentially a two-hander between John Wadmore and Sally Faulkner, it's a discussion about war and morality and honour. This is the best of the 'old monsters' BBV CDs.

Conduct Unbecoming

BBV Audio Adventures In Time & Space (September 2000)
by Gareth Preston (writer), John Wadmore (director)
Bestok is one of the greatest Sontaran generals, one of the finest in an increasingly stagnant race. Summoned back to Sontar, he learns from the High Command that the Sontaran racepool is sickening; the genetic information from General Sontar is degrading rapidly and a new genetic template must be found before the entire species is corrupted beyond hope of recovery. Bestok is one of the shortlisted suitable candidates, but others might find his conduct unbecoming of a Sontaran...

This reminds me of the series three *Doctor Who* story *Evolution of the Daleks*, where Dalek Sec is aware of the need to change in order for the Daleks to flourish once more, but in doing so he stops being a Dalek and is dealt with accordingly. This would be a contender for being the finest of the BBV audios, but ends so suddenly you don't so much think 'what?' as 'oh, was that the end?' and you end up playing the last track again (a distraction which breaks the tension).

Faction Paradox: The Eleven Day Empire & The Shadow Play

BBV Audio Adventures In Time & Space (both October 2001)
by Lawrence Miles (writer), Nigel Fairs (director)
Sontaran military might is used here by the Great Houses to invade the Eleven Day Empire of Faction Paradox.

The story is all about Faction Paradox Vs the other Houses during the War, and doesn't really concern our toad-faced chums much, who seem to just be the mercenary army, but all that post Eighth Doctor Adventures stuff is well worth a look (even if the tone's not quite right for the Loa cultists in these early Faction audios).

The Betrothal of Sontar

Doctor Who Magazine, 28 pages in #265-267 (1st Feb - 29th Mar 2006)
by John Tomlinson and Nick Abadzis (writers), Mike Collins (artist)
Colonel Snathe is in charge of Sontaran Mining Rig 'The Betrothal of Sontar', an installation on the planet Serac crewed by the genetic detritus of the cloned species: everyone not worthy to fight for the empire. When the tenth Doctor and Rose arrive, the insane Snathe is on the verge of discovering the ancient secret doomsday weapon of

Thanatos, which he believes will restore him to glory. Whilst he and the Doctor investigate the Ventrux Massif, Commander Lerox (a pacifist Sontaran, or as close to one as you're ever going to see: he believes you should only kill the enemy, not everyone in sight) takes Rose under his protection as he investigates his superior.

Anyway, this 28 page strip has enough plot for a telly episode, I recommend you dig it out again. It's not a strip I rated highly on my original read, but consumed in full in one sitting it's enjoyable stuff.

The Sontaran Stratagem

...is the next Sontaran story, and will be on telly before the next issue of *Shooty Dog Thing* comes out. I hope you've enjoyed this little journey through Sontaran history, personally I've found reading all the comic strips and replaying all the CDs (and watching the odd one or three on the box) has changed my *ho-hum* attitude to them a bit and I've whetted my appetite for their return. One of the things I didn't appreciate before is that just because they're clones doesn't mean that they're all the same; those of us who are friends with a pair of identical twins know that they don't share the same personality, and the same thing applies here. Despite their heritage the Sontarans aren't just another race of aliens like the Cybermen or Daleks who act the same; they may share a common goal but their identical genes don't make them robots, they're individuals and that allows for a bit more personality and therefore a more enjoyable story.

UNMUDDYING THE WATERS
by Lawrence Burton
Originally printed in Shooty Dog Thing #5 - Spring 2008

As something of a pedant where Postclassic Central Mexican culture is concerned, I am often forced to apply my boot to the TV screen when some supposedly authoritative documentary fails to make the distinction between Zacatenco and Tlatilco pottery phases or tries to pass off postconquest folklore as legitimate pre-conquest mythic history (I'm looking at *you*, Michael Wood).

What seems particularly galling is that with such an impressive body of academic study now available, even in 2008 your average television presenter is still apparently unable to achieve the high standard of what is essentially a 1960s kids programme. I'm referring of course to John Lucarotti's *Doctor Who* story *The Aztecs*.

The Aztecs is set in the Central Mexican city of Tenochtitlan in the year 1507 (and absolutely *not* 1430 as has been erroneously suggested) at the height of a culture speaking the language we know as Nahuatl. Inevitably *The Aztecs* is not perfect - the people in question were called Mexica rather than Aztecs (it's a long story); some aspects of set design favour Teotihuacano and Tilantongo styles over those of Tenochtitlan; a few minor theological points are fumbled; and the Nahuatl *x* is pronounced *sh* (as in *sherry*), so names like Yetaxa and Tlotoxl should be pronounced *Yetasha* and *Tlotoshl* - but given that the Mexica would hardly have been speaking pseudo-Shakespearean English in the first place, it's probably not worth writing to your MP about this last point.

However, these quibbles are easily ignored given the limitations of anthropological and archaeological knowledge in 1964, the restrictions of the BBC budget, and not least the fact that John Lucarotti's script revealed a genuinely sympathetic understanding of its setting. The otherwise mighty Kate Orman reintroduced the Doctor to Mexico in her novel *The Left-Handed Hummingbird*, and whilst her writing was evidently inspired by a wealth of thorough research, I feel this was somewhat undermined by a less objective take on the subject, particularly with regard to her portrayal of Huitzilopochtli (the much revered God and culture hero) as a sort of nuclear-powered Freddy Kruger. John Lucarotti's tale on the other hand presents an inordinately complex moral argument without recourse to easy solutions, and as such remains the more satisfying story to my mind.

When writing *The Aztecs*, John Lucarotti's only moment of weakness remains his puzzling decision to give his characters names which just sort of 'sound a bit Aztecy' without bearing anything beyond a passing resemblance to true Nahuatl linguistics. Which finally brings me to the point of this article, namely seeing if it's possible to shoehorn the titles of Lucarotti's characters into something conducive to translation...

AUTLOC (Muddy Waters) - Alleged High Priest of Knowledge whose general dress and conduct suggest affiliation to the Quetzalcoatl cult, although more as a senior religious instructor than a fully qualified man of the cloth. *Autloc* appears to be a vague phonetic anagram of *Tlaloc*, the rain God whose name is sometimes loosely translated as *Pulp of the Earth* from *tlal-li* (*earth* or *land*) and *-oc* (suffix denoting *on* or *adjacent to*) - although this interpretation is no less contested than any others that have been offered. If we take *au-* to be synonymous with the *a-* of *a-tl* (*water*), this being the only realistic available stem (*auh* is the particle *and, then, well,* or *but*, none of which would carry any meaning in this context) we seem to get something equivalent to *Pulp of the Earth and Water* which immediately brings to mind the legendary blues artist. Well, perhaps not immediately but if you've got any better ideas then I sure would like to hear them.

CAMECA (Holes) - Regal Lady with a more than passing interest in William Hartnell's buns. Try as I might, I'm unable to find anything within Frances Karttunen's *Analytical Dictionary of Nahuatl* which might allow for a less weird translation. Unfortunately this leads me to conclude that it can only be *Holes*, extrapolating this from the name of *Amecameca* (a town at the southern end of the Valley of Mexico) meaning *Water Holes* by virtue of the prefix *am-* pertaining to water.

CHAPAL (Grasshopper) - Architect and designer of the garden in which William Hartnell delivers an impressive *oh shit!* face having unwittingly accepted Cameca's proposal of marriage. Although only mentioned in passing, Chapal is ironically one of the few characters sporting an unambiguously credible Nahuatl name. Whilst John Lucarotti spells it *Chapal* in his novelisation, it is difficult to take this for anything other than *Chapul* meaning *Grasshopper*. A pedant might question such an interpretation based on the lack of the customary absolutive suffix *-in* (by which *grasshopper* is ordinarily written as *chapul-in*) to which I would testily cite the example of Atonal, ruler of the town of Coixtlahuaca circa 1458 whose name is similarly bereft of said suffix. Why Chapal should be so named is ambiguous. Either he was a native of Chapultepec (*Grasshopper Hill*) situated on the western bank of the lake in which the Mexica built their city, or he was a balding boggle-eyed gentleman given to dispensing inscrutable wisdom to David Carradine types. Which seems less likely.

IXTA (Face Dad) - Brave (or perhaps somewhat foolhardy) Jaguar Knight who dared to take on the mighty gob-punching power of Ian 'let's have a fight' Chesterton. Whether by accident or design, his name represents an unambiguous composite of *ix-tli* (meaning *face*,

95

surface or *eyes*) and *ta-tli* (*father*), despite losing the absolutive *-tli* suffix (see also Chapal). Although *Looks Like a Father* might be an equally valid interpretation, *Face Dad* seems somehow fitting in the context of both a television programme broadcast in 1964 and a sharp-dressed cat who might be considered swingin' Tenochtitlan's very own precursor to Michael Caine.

TLOTOXL (Hawk something or other) - Clearly a high-ranking priest of the Tezcatlipoca cult, and a man at the peak of his profession who surely deserved a show of his own. His name might almost be an anagram of Xolotl (meaning *dog*, *twin* or *monster* - take your pick), but is otherwise rendered largely impenetrable by kak-handed application of Nahuatl grammar. The stem *tlo-* derives from *tlotli* (*hawk*) but the rest is anyone's guess. Possibly his parents were idiots whose general ineptitude inspired their clumsily-monikered offspring to do better, as indeed he did. Whatever one might think of Tlotoxl, he clearly knew his theological onions, and it seems unfair to brand him as superstitious given that, unlike Autloc, he was at least able to tell the difference between a living god and a 1960s schoolteacher.

TONILA (Warmth of the Sun) - Young priest and possibly an initiate of the Quetzalcoatl cult. His name renders a perfect translation of *tonal-li* (*solar heat*, *summer*, *day*, or even *soul*) providing it's pronounced in whatever accent the Mexica regarded as equivalent to Cornish or perhaps Birminghamese. Given that there is no other etymological accounting for his name, it therefore seems likely that young Tonila was of rustic ancestry and may even have arrived in Tenochtitlan half expecting the streets to be paved with gold.

YETAXA (Good Father Poo) - Deceased clergyman prone to transgender reincarnation as a lady. Blood from a stone is easier than extricating meaning from the title of said gentleman, and even the somewhat unlikely offering here is reliant upon a dubious (although not unheard of) muted *c* pronunciation of *yec-tli* (meaning something *good* or *clean*) combinated with *ta-tli* (*father*) and *xayotl* (*dregs* or *excrement*) as the word would sound coming from the lips of Elvis Presley. Aside from the wisdom of reincarnating oneself as someone who is singularly unable to name even one of the thirteen heavens and seems shaky on even the most basic theological truisms, you would think the first thing Yetaxa might have done upon finding himself reborn would have been to choose a better name *(perhaps he excelled at changing the baby's nappies - Brax).* Further to which, we are once again compelled to wonder how Autloc (witness to this supposed reincarnation) came to be High Priest of Knowledge when clearly he would have been better suited to the role of High Priest Of Just Saying The First Thing That Comes Into Your Head.

GOING BACK TO THE BEGINNING
by Angela Giblin
Original material for The Best of Shooty Dog Thing

Five years ago the BBC resurrect *Doctor Who* and I'm intrigued. I already think Christopher Eccleston is brilliant and *Strictly Come Dancing* doesn't start for another couple of weeks so what else am I going to do on a Saturday night? It starts well and it just gets better and better, I love every episode (no really) and have to get a recordable DVD player for those weeks where some selfish tart decides to get married and forces me to attend. The most special day in your life? Don't you realise the Doctor got shot by a Dalek last week woman! So when we got to the end of the most recent series I'm left with nothing. There are only so many times you can watch a series and I hit critical mass pretty early. No more Doctor. Five specials over the next eighteen months is not going to satisfy. So I hit the back catalogue.

My grandparents had kept the free *Doctor Who* DVDs a national newspaper had been giving away for me and so I own one episode from each Doctor. It seems sensible to start from the beginning but I haven't heard anything particularly complimentary about Hartnell and he looks grumpy on the cover so I start with Patrick Troughton and *The Faceless Ones*. The set up is good, splitting our team of four up at an airport and having Polly witness a murder - just my cup of tea. There are a couple of officious but well meaning airport staff and a quick glance of an alien in a shipping crate. Where's the next episode? What happens next? What good does THAT do me? I can't watch it like this. I need to know what happens next. The one episode wonders go on to the shelf to stop them tempting and vexing me in equal measure. Now what?

Thankfully, new friends with extensive DVD collections are at hand and let me borrow a couple of stories. Starting with *Enlightenment* I get a little back story from my teacher in these matters before it starts about Black Guardians, conflicted ginger aliens and - Oh look, it's Linda Barron. I'm sold. Big costumes, beautiful dresses, Edwardian ships, pirates AND ancient Greece! I don't remember anything I saw as a child being this flashy. Yes, the special effects are cheap - even for the eighties, but you ignore that and enjoy. The sign of a good story.

Next is *The Five Doctors*. Possibly a bit of a cheat to watch this one so early in my education but it was a really good shortcut to get to know more than one Doctor/companion dynamic and loads of fun. There's everything I remember from the requisite quarry to the goateed Master and again there is mystery, conspiracy and explosions (and who doesn't like them?) There are even Cybermen. I enjoy the journeys they all take to the tower and the introduction (to me anyway) of the half dozen companions, whether real or imagined. I like the obstacles they encounter, especially the ballet/ninja/body stocking killer dart man thing and I love the bickering. It is interesting to see the way the different Doctors interact and I start choosing favourites and planning what to see next.

Now I've started there is no stopping me. I've joined a postal DVD service and have ordered every story to be sent to me over the coming months. *The Invasion* landed on my doormat this morning and it is already in the machine waiting. Listening to everyone discuss what might happen next after *The Waters of Mars* at 'Dimensions' and having absolutely no idea what they were talking about excited me. I don't know how the Ice Warriors would fit in to this or how the destruction of this means that so-and-so can never do whatever. I have no idea who half the people and races of aliens mentioned may or may not tie in to the coming story arc and that means I have a lot to learn and I can't wait.

'AND CUT IT... NOW!'
by Jon Arnold
Originally printed in Shooty Dog Thing #5 - Spring 2008

Right now *Doctor Who* is as popular as it's ever been - we've had an episode that was the second most watched hour of telly not only for the week but for the *whole damn year*. It took nearly 20 years but we old school fans can finally revel in *Doctor Who* being more popular than *Coronation Street*. In *Doctor Who* terms we're in a golden age right now, up there with sixties Dalekmania and the early to mid 70s Pertwee/Baker shows. Anything with the taxi cab logo seems to fly off the shelves. But the old series merchandise... not so much. In fact, Big Finish reported something of a sales slump. So why, generally, isn't the old series being investigated by more of the countryful of new fans Russell T. Davies has delivered?

It's an unfortunate truth but, to anyone but we fans and the odd nostalgic old timer, most of the old series can seem unwatchable, not just because a lot of them are in black and white. The last classic series repeats on BBC2 were cancelled as the ratings were poor. That's almost certainly not a comment on the quality of the show, particularly in the context of the time at which it was made and the pressures of production, it's a comment on the style. A modern audience hasn't got the patience to sit through one story for seven weeks, even one episode at a time. Part of that's to do with television drama during much of the show's original run being produced essentially as a theatrical performance with the camera pointed at it (in *Who* terms it's even the case as late as *The Happiness Patrol*, but that was something of an anachronism even at the time). Part of it is obviously to do with technological progress with TV equipment - superior effects work makes them less accepting of the creaky effects we grew up with, and editing is now an infinitely easier process than the tape splicing technique forced upon 60s film editors, meaning old shows look jumpy and seem to hang together poorly. And, as Russell T. Davies has observed, this latest generation has grown up with television as their main media input, they're capable of absorbing far more information from one scene than sixties or seventies audiences were. Twenty-five minutes in and the Hartnell crew had generally just finished exploring and were having a cliffhanging encounter with the villain of the story, the modern version of *Who* has already told half the story by that point. In modern terms even the early run of a show such as *Star Trek: The Next Generation* looked creaky and slow by the time the last episode of that show was broadcast. Simply put, today's television audience, particularly the generation born after the original run of the series finished, are accustomed to their shows moving far faster than that series ever did, even in its later years. Is it possible to interest the modern viewer in the classic series? And if so how?

Cut them down.

Fair cop, I'm being deliberately simplistic in approach here but to me it's the most obvious and easiest solution. It's the sort of process publishers have used to try and hook readers on Victorian novels (such as Dickens) bloated by the need to meet a monthly wordcount. We're no longer in the situation where fans who want to watch the old shows don't have access to a (musical copyright and Pamela Nash allowing) copy of each episode as originally broadcast so why not attempt to attract a modern audience by cutting what they see as narrative fat? It's hardly as radical as it sounds either, back in the mid 70s and early 80s the BBC used to use such cut down versions as summer schedule filler, even releasing a cutdown *The Brain of Morbius* years ahead of the episodic version on VHS.

I'm not suggesting for one second that the old stories should become unavailable in their former episodic glories; I'm still as hooked on their cheap nostalgic thrills as any fan. Those fans who appealed for that unedited release of *The Brain of Morbius* fought a war for us youngsters you know, and have their re-released VHS tapes to prove it. Nor am I advocating the simple hack 'em together approach of BBC Video from the eighties either, that kind of clumsy hatchet job does neither the show nor the viewer any favours. A skilled editor would be needed, ruthless but sensitive to the basic needs of narrative sense - *City of Death*, for instance, wouldn't be improved by hacking out most of the running around Paris scenes.

As a rough guide I'd think of halving the length of stories (enough to tauten the pacing but not so much that the gist of the story is lost) and format them as per a new series episodes - one 42-45 minute instalment with the odd story extending to an hour. It's not such a sacrilegious idea. These previous omnibus editions cut a hell of a lot of narrative fat from the stories without harming them - it's time to admit to yourself that *Genesis of the Daleks* would really benefit from losing a few capture/escape routines, Muto confrontations and, yes, sadly, the giant clams *(As someone who first encountered the story as a 60 minute audio cassette, I agree - Brax)*. There may be the odd plot hole but the audience weaned on modern *Who* is used to those, and any of us who care enough can use imagination as a plot Polyfilla - that's an age old pastime anyway, particularly amongst *Who* fans. I'm advocating alternative versions you could run on BBC3 or collect together in a special DVD boxed set.

I freely admit that all this is an absolute pipe dream since I doubt 2Entertain has the budget or time to remove the narrative fat or performing such detailed edits or that any such repeats would be worthwhile funding. And of course it wouldn't work for all stories, particularly the Cartmel era which, if anything, often provided narratives which were too compressed by the running time *(Ghost Light* being the obvious example here), neither does it get round the age-old problem of getting new viewers to look at the ingenuity stretching BBC budget and technology to the limits. But to produce a new take on old episodes, to open up what many current viewers see as overlong and dull is surely worthwhile. If you still need convincing I'll leave you with one final thought - it'd be possible to revisit the Saward era without some of those interminable Doctor/companion bitching scenes and maybe, just maybe you can convince yourself that these people actually like each other.

WE'VE GOT LOVE FOR YOU IF YOU WERE WHO IN THE EIGHTIES!
by Erik Pollitt
Original material for The Best of Shooty Dog Thing

Colin Baker was 'My Doctor'. As a 5 year old, I loved watching the sheer lunacy of Tom Baker, falling out with the programme slightly when Peter Davison took over, but it was Colin's Doctor that stamped the *'Doctor Who* Fan' label on my heart. He also sewed it in my school uniform, which I am slightly less happy with.

A friend that I haven't seen since primary school recently

contacted me on Facebook. He'd seen an episode of the new series and had decided to get in touch to see if I still walked around with a tyre pressure gauge in my pocket. I told him that I'd given that up when I was 8. What I didn't tell him was that I'd given it up because the sixth Doctor didn't carry a sonic screwdriver. He didn't need such gadgets, being the Doctor was enough to get him out of any situation.

The sixth Doctor wasn't your best friend or a kindly uncle, he was an alien. He cared more for the butterfly than the storm. If you walked his path, you could quite easily be left behind. He was dangerous, arrogant and exciting. He was the Doctor, whether you liked it or not. And I did.

Looking back at this period in *Who* history, it's very easy to point out the flaws and the cracks. If I'm honest, that's probably because there are many. The uneasy relationship between Doctor and companion seems to mirror that of producer and script editor. It was a turbulent time in front as well as behind the camera. Some bad decisions were made. And I'm not just talking about the coat.

Colin, rather unfairly gets the blame heaped squarely on his shoulders, which is ironic, because he is the only 'right' thing about this period. He played the sixth Doctor, not only with conviction, but to perfection. He had a power in his performance that no other actor bar Tom Baker has been able to match.

Of course, the great shame is that his era was cut so short. The general public only knew half the story. They won't have seen the sixth Doctor's epic comic strip adventures, surely the best *DWM* ever produced. They won't have read his 'missing adventures' in Blackpool and on the planet Magnus. They won't have heard the sheer lunacy of *Slipback* or seen him tread the boards in *The Ultimate Adventure...* And of course, they will not have had the pleasure of hearing the sixth Doctor's audio adventures.

Colin's performance in the audio adventures is second to none. The other Doctors do an excellent job, don't get me wrong, but they don't do it with as much gusto as Colin. You can tell he loves the scripts, loves the role, and gives it his all when performing them. Being partnered up with the perfect companions, such as Evelyn Smythe or Charley Pollard, allows us to see sides of this Doctor that we've never been privy to before. He's caring, compassionate and loyal to his friends. And this is exactly how he is to his listeners.

Thanks to these fascinating alternate takes on the man, he's become multi faceted, intriguing and unpredictable. Perhaps that mix and match costume of his fits the patchwork sixth Doctor better than we ever realised.

Over the years, I've met most of the actors to play the part of the Doctor, shared a brief conversation or a joke with most of them. I've even told one off for pushing in front of me at the bar... Unfortunately, Colin is the one I haven't met. I find this a great pity as he is the one that I feel I could sit down with and have a real conversation with, perhaps over a pint. I don't feel that I could do that with any other 'Doctor'. Why? Well, I'm not sure.

Perhaps it's because of the interviews I have heard with the man, where he just sounds like one of us. He isn't an überfan of the show, but you can tell that he loves it. He sounds so down to earth in interviews that I feel like I know him. Yes, he was my hero when I was 10 years old, but now he's become the friend who sat down and watched the show with me. No airs and graces, no 'I am the Doctor'. He's a humble man who is proud of his association with this crazy show of ours.

I for one am glad of his association, and look forward to the opportunity of buying him a pint to say thanks for being my childhood hero. For teaching me that there are so many shades of grey to be found between black and white. The first round's on me. Of course, he may be driving. In which case I'd be happy to check his tyres, I'm sure I have a pressure gauge around here somewhere...

Heartfelt thanks to Colin Baker and long live the sixth Doctor.

My Doctor.

Whether you like it or not.

THE SHOOTY REVIEW
compiled by Paul Castle

One of the core elements of *Shooty Dog Thing* is the '*Doctor Who* Monthly' review feature, which was born out of the observation that fanzines tend to drown in a sea of reviews of stories that everyone else was looking at. Why should you want to read about the new books, DVDs and telly episodes here when *Doctor Who Magazine*, other fanzines and about a million websites and blogs are doing the same? My solution was to contain all the reviews in one feature, select titles that were printed the forthcoming months *from previous years* and take an example from six different media. The result proved remarkably successful, with a wide range of reviews that were unique to *Shooty*: issue ten, for example, covered *TV Comic*'s *Action in Exile!* from 1969, BBV's K9 audio drama *The Choice* from 1999, BBC Books' *Vampire Science* from 1997, Big Finish's *The Maltese Penguin* from 2002, the Target novelisation of *Slipback* from 1986, and *The Dominators* telly story from 1968.

Rather than choose the best of these for this book, I've commissioned the usual suspects to choose their favourite sixth Doctor story, tying in with one of Hirst Books' other new titles: *Look Who's Talking* by Colin Baker.

So, here's a selection of sixth Doctor stories from each media it's worth dusting off or hunting down. We start with the ever popular *Timelash* from the telly, before moving onto the novelisations, the hiatus, comic strips, stageplays, spin-off videos, novels, audio plays and short stories before considering Baker's post telly renaissance.

'TIMELASH'
TV STORY BY GLEN McCOY
reviewed by Paul Castle
Original material for The Best of Shooty Dog Thing

To say that *Timelash* has something of a bad reputation amongst fans would be something of an understatement. It would be all too easy for me to toe the party line and repeat all the lame shit stirring, but I'm getting too old to wallow in self pity. This story was shown practically 25 years ago now, and if it's guilty of murder then this story has served its time. Get over it.

So, forgetting all the bad, with the sets made from tinsel and Paul Darrow's Richard the Third acting, what's good about it?

Surprisingly enough, it's both entertaining and enjoyable. Winding down after work on a cold and rainy winter's morn, snuggled under a duvet and cradling a mug of tea, I was far too comfortable to let any of the traditional animosity join me. Rather than sigh at the Doctor and Peri bickering in the initial console room scene, I noticed that the performance lacked all the rougher edges that were present in *Attack of the Cybermen* from the other end of Season 22, the last of theirs I'd watched. Whilst the Doctor and Peri's relationship retains its antagonistic temperament, there's an underlying warmth that shows a deep affection. This brings to mind the image of them as an old married couple, something which you'd never have imagined possible just a few stories earlier.

The story follows the usual pattern of the era, introducing the planet Karfel and the situation there before the Doctor and Peri arrive. All is not well, a rebellion against the tyrannical rule of the Borad is on the edge of defeat, with those found guilty cast into the Timelash: an open-ended time tunnel that represents the pinnacle of the Borad's temporal engineering. All progress on the Timelash has ground to a halt though, and serves as nothing more than a crude method of exile or execution (they had no way of telling until the TARDIS got caught up in it).

After bearing witness to one hapless victim of the Timelash passing ghostlike through the TARDIS, the Doctor sets course for the origin point of the spectre. Finding himself on Karfel, both he and Peri are treated like VIPs. It seems that the Doctor had been to the planet before, and was remembered as a hero.

But it's not long before Peri's separated from the Doctor at the behest of Paul Darrow's wonderfully slimy Maylin Tekker, and held as a hostage so the Doctor would have no option but aid Tekker recover a device that was lost in the Timelash.

I'm not going to summarise the whole story. It's basically about a hideously mutated scientist who's hidden away from all but Tekker's eyes, ruling via a proxy on a screen, Big Brother style. He wants to emerge from his self-imposed exile, but is afraid of his people's reactions to him. Half-human, half-reptilian Morlock, he'll be the only survivor if their enemies, the neighbouring Bandrils attack with a Neutron missile. So he's purposely instigated a war, and whilst waiting for the bomb to drop has engineered a repeat of the same accident that mutated him: this time with Peri as the victim. Once all the humans have died, he and his newly mutated bride can start a new race of little Borads.

Now, I'm no fan of eighties *Doctor Who*, and should I choose can pick fault in practically every story. There's nothing, absolutely nothing wrong with *Timelash* that isn't also a factor in the vast majority of mid eighties *Doctor Who* stories. Yes, it looks cheap and dated, yes, it's distinctly over lit, and yes the story's not wonderful. But can you name any of its peers that doesn't suffer from these faults? To single out *Timelash* strikes me as unfair, especially given it's actually better than the likes of *The Mark of the Rani*, *The Two Doctors*, the whole of *The Trial of a Time Lord* and, well, all the other sixth Doctor telly stories. Yes, the story is simple and the villain's plan is pathetic, but a simple story means that it does at least make sense (unlike the complicated mess of the other titles named), and the villain's pathetic plan is defeated by the Doctor pointing out how idiotic it is: the Borad is not defeated in a battle, but by showing that happiness cannot be seized through force, and that you cannot be loved unless you first love yourself. The Borad's driven mad by the force of the Doctor's argument (and a glance at his hideous face in a previously covered mirror), and stumbles sobbing into his own trap: the Timelash. As a story, it works.

My challenge to you is, next time you watch a *Doctor Who* story that's criticised more than it's praised, watch with an open mind. You can never enjoy anything in life if you've got nothing inside you but negativity. Okay, so the Timelash is made from tinsel, some of the actors are straight out of drama school, and Paul Darrow's hamming it up something chronic, but there's also a couple of cute girls (alas, Christine Kavanagh's killed within five minutes, but at least Tracy Louise Ward survives to the end), Darrow's Richard the Third is highly entertaining, and Colin Baker's performance as the Doctor is as brilliant as ever. There's alot to enjoy here, if you give it a chance.

'THE TWO DOCTORS'
NOVELISATION BY ROBERT HOLMES
reviewed by James Gent
Originally printed in Shooty Dog Thing #8 - Winter 2008

The Two Doctors was the only time Bob Holmes novelised one of his own stories. For me, *The Two Doctors* is a great choice for a story to be told in the master's own words. Why? Bob Holmes' stories are notable for being considerably more risqué and daring in tone than many of his peers, with most of them having a jet-black streak of darker-than-dark humour and edgy satirical barbs. In Holmes' hands, *Who* often felt like a sci-fi combo of Pythonesque surrealist satire and Dennis Potter griminess.

The Two Doctors sees Holmes really going to town with these elements for his last hurrah, an essentially moralistic story that somehow manages to skirt the border of good taste with a surreal, gleefully grotesque 'larger than life' quality, which somehow makes it more acceptable than the determinedly dour and pessimistic tone that defines the Saward era. So what better story to be re-told by the master to allow his unique style to flow freely?

The novel doesn't deviate from the televised script drastically, but the story feels better told for the change of medium. As the equivalent of an old school six-parter it seems to take forever for all of the characters to converge. It's much the same in the novel, with the Doctor, Peri and Jamie arriving at the villa exactly halfway through the book, but broken down into twelve bite-size chapters, the journey becomes more enjoyable than arriving at the destination.

One good reason for this is that the characterisation is spot-on and well observed. We see a lot of situations from certain character's perspectives and are privy to their internal thoughts... When we see things from Jamie's point of view, for example, he relates things through his historical frame of reference - when he recalls the Time Lords sending the Doctor on the mission to J7, 'the Doctor had bowed deferentially so they had obviously been chieftains', and (as in the TV script) he likens Shockeye to a 'scullion'. During Oscar's first encounter with the Doctor, Jamie and Peri, en route to the villa, believing them to be from Interpol, the Doctor is the 'senior officer', although this rapidly devolves to 'senior madman' and 'chief lunatic'! Oscar is one of those characters who jumps from the page, fully formed, being the latest in a long line of classic Holmes supporting characters (a la Garron, Jago, Vorg) whose egocentric bluster betrays a deep-set cowardice, and who shares more than a few characteristics with our vain Time Lord hero. Indeed, it could be argued that Oscar and Anita are an analogue for the Doctor and Peri, much like Vorg and Shirna were in *Carnival of Monsters* - a camp old thing prone to hyperbole and self-promotion and patiently humoured by a compassionate, decorative companion. Either way, Oscar supplies some of the ripest comic gems in *The Two Doctors*, from his longing for the security of his much-loved teddy bear, to the sublime 'My dear, departed father was an air raid warden in Shepton Mallet throughout the war. He slept in a steel helmet for five years', a wonderfully droll slice of minutiae worthy of one of Victoria Wood's creations!

Shockeye, too, comes into his own as a fully-fledged grotesque here; his single-minded obsession with eating meat is hilariously all-encompassing. To Shockeye, Peri's impressive form is 'fine-boned but the flanks and buttocks of the little creature were well-packed with firm flesh.' Holmes even treats us to a couple of grisly Androgum nursery rhymes (Sample quote: 'Smash the head and chomp the flesh, And sup the blood and crunch the bones') which are worth the cover price alone!

The only slightly off-key note, character-wise, is that of the second Doctor. From the moment he steps out of the TARDIS and into the space station, everyone's favourite cosmic hobo is in a constant shit-fit, laying into Dastari with a positive thesaurus of wordy insults, and even Jamie is subject to a couple of snappy retorts several leagues more irascible than the jocular back-handed compliments that denoted their rapport, calling him a 'simpering...hyperborean ninny' and berating him for his 'appalling mongrel dialect'. The generally rather didactic and pompous tone the Doctor assumes in these scenes feels more akin to the third Doctor in one of his particularly bumptious moments! Indeed, sometimes one has the feeling that Holmes had the third Doctor in mind when writing these early scenes - wasn't it the third Doctor who was prone to being sent on missions by the Time Lords, and would make reference to his relations with the High Council? That particular can of worms could bring us to consider the whole Season 6b issue but as the novel airily sidesteps issues of continuity placement, so shall we. Suffice to say, the reference to Victoria isn't included in the novel, so your guess is as good as mine. Perhaps this is one of those Targets that seems to inhabit a 'bizarro' canon, the one where three Time Lords in a perfumed garden quiz a 'semi-retired' first Doctor about the events of a differently remembered *Massacre of St. Bartholomew's Eve*, and Jo Grant's first adventure took place on the planet Uxarieus.

One thing that really comes through strongly in this novelisation is that this story does at least have something to say. Many *Who* stories - the ones that aren't basically re-tellings of classic tropes of folklore or genre fiction - have 'something to say', usually something that can be summed up as a bullet-point. I'm at a loss to find the purpose behind the narrative in most Colin-era stories, the prophetic *Vengeance on Varos* aside. *The Mark of The Rani?* Some potentially interesting stuff about the crucially significant changes wrought by the Industrial Revolution becomes background colour to petty Time Lord one-upmanship. *Timelash?* Search me. *Attack of the Cybermen?* Don't even go there.

By contrast, *The Two Doctors'* message can't be missed, taking advantage of the colourfully descriptive, readable style Holmes employs here. In this cannibalistic caper, Holmes is basically writing a good old-fashioned, grim and lurid moral warning about consuming passions - figuratively (Dastari) and literally (Shockeye). In this story, the underlying message is that by being in thrall to lust for greed, one is succumbing to one's most base desires, and they will consume and destroy one. This is illustrated in various ways by the overarching desires and ambitions of Dastari (one of a longline of the series' misguided would-be alchemists trying to play God - there's an article there!) and those uppity Sontarans, and the avarice of the Androgums, and in time-honoured fashion these flaws pave the way to their undoings. It's not the most sophisticated of morals, and I suppose the execution is a bit iffy in places, but I've always found the absolutism of this story's moral to be strangely compelling, even if it strikes me as slightly conservative. Basically, the character of Chessene seems to be a warning against getting ideas above one's station and to know one's place - but in this case it turns out that the Doctor's regard for the Androgums as sub-human is fully justified. There's an interesting internal monologue from the Doctor where he ruminates on the respective virtues of the animal kingdom - '...there was not one of those dumb creatures that knew aught of envy or pride, prejudice or resentment. They were not driven by the thirst for power or a hunger for dominance' - and those of 'the intelligent species, driven by the unquenchable fires of ambition, who made the bad mistakes?'. Ultimately, the Doctor concludes his rumination by coming down on the side of intelligence and the pioneering spirit that enables one to find order in swirling patterns and map the stars. Thus, one can only conclude that he opposes Dastari and the Sontarans as their aims are solipsistic rather than altruistic.

This story's take on appetites and greed is appropriately full-blooded and meaty, the Doctor's description of a gumblejack 'cleaned and skinned and pan-fried in their own juices' strikes the reader as sensuous and evocative until one notes its uncomfortable closeness to accounts elsewhere in the book of the corpse of a space station duty watcher, his remains 'chemically filleted' by a poison gas, and the Doctor's florid monologue on the 'smell of death... fruit-soft flesh peeling from white bones'. Subtle, it ain't, but Holmes' garishly sensual analogies certainly have a primal punch.

In case you're wondering why I haven't yet mentioned the Sontarans, it's because Holmes doesn't much either. It's clear from both the TV serial and the book that they're obviously the one ingredient in the story that Holmes is the least interested in, and we don't get the mandatory mention of their 'probic vent' and 'bifurcated hands' until over halfway through the book! Nevertheless, like the recent Sontaran two-parter Holmes realises that there is much mileage to be had in juxtaposing the Sontarans' single-minded obsession with valour, victory and honour and their complete lack of self-awareness or humour (as the Doctor says in one of his most memorable ripostes here, 'A face like yours isn't made for laughing'!).

The Two Doctors stands out a mile from the more run-of-the-mill mid 1980s Target adaptations and benefits hugely from being penned by its original writer. On this evidence, Holmes' prose is just as detailed, evocative and mature as his skill for characterisation and dialogue in his scripts. Its obsession with viscera isn't to all tastes - too juicy for some palates perhaps? If you can stomach it, get stuck in!

THE 'EIGHTEEN MONTH HIATUS'!
reviewed by Arfie Mansfield
Original material for The Best of Shooty Dog Thing

There's a game popular among *Doctor Who* fans that involves telling people which episode was on in the week you were born. It's not much of a game, but it's something we can all relate to better than which long-forgotten pop toss was at number one (this year, amongst other milestones, marks the point at which children born when *Doctorin' the Tardis* topped the charts can now stand for Parliament). But does it say anything about us? Is someone born in 1969 likely to be slow-moving but vaguely interesting? Are those who were born in the early '80s good-looking and vapid? Do the toddlers of today spend all their time apologising for war crimes?

If so, what does it mean that I was born when the series was off the air for a protracted period? Certainly, the first time I ever heard of *Doctor Who* its future was uncertain and stayed that way for well over a decade (a period called 'my childhood', roughly equivalent to the period between the Cold War and the War on Terror - can it be a coincidence that the series has never been made during peacetime? Well, yes, most likely) but that's hardly conclusive, though it demonstrates that the 'taking *Doctor Who* off the air' pilot proved a greater, longer-running success than most.

Even so, now that I finally get to see a series or two of *Doctor Who* as it's broadcast, we have to get used to the idea that this kind of thing is going to keep happening, if Moffat runs with Davies' notion that to keep things fresh you need a fallow year every now and then, with a spot of ground-cover to prevent surface runoff and eutrophication. Given that last time this happened we ended up with Christopher Eccleston's brief but marvellous tenure, there's compelling evidence that it should work. Given that the time before, however, we ended up with *The Trial of a Time Lord*, there's compelling evidence against. Perhaps a year just isn't long enough; even six years into the Great Hiatus the first attempt was half-baked and set recovery back by quite some time.

In fact, we have some idea of what the 1985/6 season might well have been like - the missing stories are well-documented and mostly

111

novelised, and while they don't set the world alight they look a damned sight more interesting than the eventual Season 23. That's not strictly fair, though, as we're comparing a finished work - with all the compromises production inevitably forces on a story, through budget, practicality and the rather inconsiderate death of the one writer who should have survived - to an idealised concept of what might possibly have been achieved had the constraints the previous 22 years had been produced under miraculously taken a holiday. *The Masters of Luxor* (1964) would probably have been a bit crap, *Lungbarrow* (1989) would have been heart-breakingly poorly realised on-screen, and any of Christopher Priest's scripts would have been pruned back to a fraction of their potential - the best stories are always too broad and too deep.

On that basis, the breather after *Revelation of the Daleks* could well have done the sixth Doctor a favour; it's widely acknowledged that the character was a bit crap, but there's always been an underlying sense that he and - to a greater extent - Colin Baker himself were short-changed. If Big Finish's output has proved one thing, it's that this is undoubtedly true and while we might not have lost a great Doctor outright, we certainly mislaid him for far too long. But even at the time, he was getting up to a lot more than the small screen would allow him to - if there were one era of *Doctor Who* comics that stood out the most, this was it; a particularly well-polished stretch of the golden age. It's a shame he himself was so rarely allowed to shine on-screen, but in the long run it hardly matters.

In many ways, it was more than just the hiatus that returned in force throughout the nineties; through appearance on screen, stage, radio and comics, the sixth Doctor established a precedent that while *Doctor Who* came from television it needn't be constrained by it and, by the time McCoy finally had his swansong, the seventh Doctor was not only the longest-serving but the first whose primary medium wasn't the box. And what of the eighth, who had little over an hour on screen but bore the torch for almost a decade in print and through headphones? It's certainly true that the first hiatus not only set a precedent, but broke the momentum of the old series, and yet it's also true that it established that it didn't *need* to be on the air to survive.

If *Doctor Who* has taught us anything, it's that one man's dinosaur-riddled calamity is another man's Golden Age; so while much of fandom looks back on the post-*Survival* days as 'the Wilderness Years', to some of us it was just part of glorious tradition that's as relevant today as ever but stretches all the way back to when the Doctor took Peri to -

'THE GIFT' DWM COMIC STRIP
BY JAMIE DELANO & JOHN RIDGWAY
reviewed by James Hadwen
Original material for The Best of Shooty Dog Thing

I've never been a fan of *The World Shapers*. It's a confused mess of conflicting plot lines that doesn't really know where it's going or what it wants to do. So in my mind, in that corner of the universe that only I get to control, *The World Shapers* was never published and, instead, the title of 'Last regular sixth Doctor comic strip' goes to *The Gift*, a glorious celebration of a story that should have been the swan song for that most colourful of Doctors... even when he was in black and white.

The Gift doesn't have many pretentions. It starts simply, parties its way through volcanoes and trips to the moon and ends with Peri flapping her way in and out of trouble whilst the Doctor plays pied piper to manic robots and Frobisher does what only a shape shifting penguin could do. In short, it's a triumph of the sixth Doctor's reign and, had it been on television, would have been an audiovisual extravaganza. Replace the word birthday with Christmas at the start of the first part and Russell T. Davies would have done it as a superb family event to end the year on something of a literal high note. So where to begin breaking this down? Why is this such a wonderful story? And how much would I have to pay Big Finish or Mr Moffat to give it life outside of the comic page?

On the small screen, a large amount of the Doctor's time with Peri was spent arguing. TARDIS scenes weren't used to particularly develop the plot or give us a deeper understanding of the characters, they were used as padding full of bitchiness and left us wondering why they ever travelled together. Look at the start of *The Gift* and it's a completely different picture, one I much prefer. The Doctor, Peri and

Frobisher are friends, they're relaxed, the dialogue isn't bitch it's banter. Peri's not complaining about the constant danger she's in, Frobisher's moaning that there isn't enough danger! This is a TARDIS crew who I'd actually willingly spend time with myself and I'm more than happy to read about.

Strictly speaking the plot isn't massively intricate or startling. It is, however, traditional and fun. The characters are larger than life (even the midget Lord Duke of Zazz) and the science funky. What other story could have volcano powered rockets, self replicating robots and the Doctor in an American space suit? The feud between Strut and Zazz (sorry but there's something immensely satisfying about writing about characters with those names) seems realistic without lots of detail. The party atmosphere in episode one feels like a manic party with the Doctor and Peri dancing on the tables before Peri eventually breaks into song (can't you just see the track listings on the CD soundtrack) and the end of part three would, decades later, be echoed by Big Finish when Colin Baker threatens to burst into song in *Doctor Who and the Pirates*.

John Ridgway's artwork isn't the best likeness of Colin Baker and Peri on the planet but at this stage in the comic strip's run this isn't too much of a problem. The comics had 'their' sixth Doctor and Peri (with Peri's hairstyle being the main nod to the television version) but where this story stands out in my mind is the look of everything else. The robots are basic in design yet somehow believable. The characters are all dressed in fairly traditional Earth style 20s outfits (I'm sure that the start of a television version of this story would have attracted much comment about Peri's swimming costume... and the Doctor's more casual look) and there's a token alien. Most impressive though is the change in style for the moon's surface though, it's suitably bleak and dust swept in contrast to the clean lines of the party and the functional rocket area.

The story's resolution is clearly signposted in part three but that doesn't stop the final part being a triumphant race through *The Pied Piper of Hamelin*. Only the comic strip could deliver an army of robots dancing to the clifftops to the Doctor's tune (yet strangely it was Sylvester who ended up playing the Piper on stage) with some waltzing underwater past a bemused looking octopus. This is *Doctor Who* as it desperately wanted to be on telly. Bold, brassy and extravagant with an explosive ending it's always stuck in my mind for one reason. Frobisher completely steals the show with his attitude to life (there's something very Frobisher about supervising work whilst lounging in a deck chair) and his shape shifting finale sums him up the story perfectly.

The Gift takes my breath away whenever I read it. I've tried to put my finger on why I love it so much but, even after reading everything I've put down above, it doesn't quite seem to do it justice. I just find it so much better than I can really express in words and maybe that's its secret. This is a story about atmosphere and music, science and jazz. Get yourself a Sazerac, put the music on and then you'll really understand why this story is so wonderful.

'THE ULTIMATE ADVENTURE'
STAGEPLAY BY TERRANCE DICKS
reviewed by Terry Francis
Original material for The Best of Shooty Dog Thing

From a personal point of view, *Doctor Who: The Ultimate Adventure* is a very special production. It was more than just a chance to see Jon Pertwee playing the Doctor at the Bristol Hippodrome, and that - in itself - is a memory to treasure for those who were lucky enough to see it. You see, before 1989 I hadn't really seen much in the way of theatre - I vaguely recall being sent to the Salisbury Playhouse with a coach load of people to see a version of *Cinderella*, and there was this maths-education play called *Countdown* which the school took us to see at Poole Arts Centre. To be honest, the idea of going to the theatre when I was a child just didn't really appeal to me. But then, one day, *Doctor Who Magazine* mentioned this stage play based on our favourite Time Lord - and, so, at the tender age of 15, I coerced Dad into taking the Francis family to see my first ever play. On that night I saw those people on the stage having a great time, I wasn't 'fan enough' then to be horrified by incorrectly-shaped Daleks or to be dismayed by the pantomimesque nature of the production. Yes, dear reader, *The Ultimate Adventure* made me want to become an actor. Fair enough, I have since seen better examples of work on the stage and I only tread the boards in the world of amateur dramatics - but for this show to create in myself a love of all things theatrical can be no bad thing.

Of course, having seen Pertwee in the role I thought it could never get better. Until I found at that Colin Baker was to take over the role for the second leg of the tour. Unfortunately, I regret that I never got to see 'old sixey' perform the role on stage. I had managed to acquire a ropey VHS bootleg of his version, but the quality was so awful I only skipped through it to watch certain scenes (mainly the three songs - more of which later). I still have that VHS and it remains unwatchable and unlistenable!

There have been several *Doctor Who* stage plays since *The Ultimate Adventure*, and very good they all were too. But, in my heart of hearts, all I really wanted to see was Terrance Dicks' 1989 masterpiece revived on stage. Big Finish have done the next best thing and given us a permanent record of the play via the audio medium. And I, for one, am grateful - especially as it finally gives me a taster as to how Colin Baker tackled the production.

For anyone expecting a complicated, angst-driven, hard hitting drama this really is not a tale for you. It has been mentioned in the past that *The Ultimate Adventure* is the closest we will ever get to 'Doctor Who - The Pantomime'. Some consider this to be derogatory to the show. Having appeared in several pantomimes, I can only consider the comment to be taken as a compliment. A decent pantomime is very difficult to pull off, but can be very rewarding and incredibly entertaining when done well. And that's the point: so what if *The Ultimate Adventure* is a pantomime? If, at the end of the day, it has entertained you and left you with a big grin on your face then its job is done.

The basic plot consists of the Daleks teaming up with the Cybermen and some mercenaries in a bid to start World War III on Earth. The Doctor is vital to the plan and must be kept alive at all costs - which does, admittedly, remove some tension by knowing that he cannot be threatened with death. You can tell by listening to the CD (or the legal download from bigfinish.com) that the play relied on spectacle. The laser tunnel effects and the flying bat creatures don't really work on audio - but the constant jumping from location to location (almost a stage version of the sixties telly story *The Chase* in

116

that respect) is achieved easier here than it ever was in a provincial theatre.

The cast do their best trying to convey a visual adventure into an audio production. In the main it does work, though it occasionally falls into the trap of having the characters describing things in an almost narration like manner. And poor old Zog, whose comic pratfalls and mannerisms were great on stage, merely comes across as this characterless thing that makes strange noises every few moments. Colin Baker certainly tries his best to maintain a balance between a stage performance and an audio performance. One can sense that he wants to retain as much of the original as he can without resorting to shouting so that he could be heard 'in the Gods', but you can tell that he doesn't want to tone it down too much as the whole point of the CD is to resemble the original as closely as possible. As such it creates a version of the sixth Doctor that in both different in style to the television interpretation and the usual Big Finish interpretation. It is a clever balancing act that Colin achieves splendidly. David Banks on the other hand, whilst good, shows how a stage performance does not really go that well on audio as - to my ear - it is obvious that he is playing to the back of the upper circle. That may be good in the correct medium (and it was, I was there - remember), but the contrived nature in which David says his lines does not work when coming out of your headphones and straight into your ears.

What does work, however, are the songs. With the exception of the duet ('Sky High'), the songs fit in rather comfortably on the audio. Both 'Strange Attractor' and 'Business is Business' are sung in cabaret venues, so they really do not jar as much now as they did back in 1989 when the presence of songs in *Doctor Who* set many a fan into apoplexy. It helps that all three of Steve Edis' compositions are pretty darn catchy! Though I must admit it is very sporting of the Cybermen to wait until Crystal's song finished before they massacred the clientele of the Number 10 on Clarendon Road. In fact, it must be mentioned that the Cybermen in this tale really are a waste of time. It is obvious now that they could quite easily be removed from the story with no ill effects - the one time the audio highlights that an element of the show was incorporated purely to put bums on seats.

The only major flaw with the audio is thorough no fault of Big Finish. The end of the play relies on the presence of a large teapot. In

117

a visual medium this is a good payoff as the prop is prominent on stage for the entire scene. On audio, alas, the solution to the Doctor's problem just appears made-up and contrived as it is as if the teapot has appeared from nowhere! Come to think of, an extra - brand new song - featuring the Doctor here would have been fantastic! Ending with do-rah-me-fah-soh-lah-tea!!!!

But why quibble over such minor matters? *The Ultimate Adventure* is simple leave-your-brain-at-the-door escapism. There is nothing wrong with that when it is done well and as a record of something that cannot be repeated unless it goes on tour again. Oh, and the CD extras on this release are the most interesting, informative and worthwhile Big Finish have ever produced - certainly when Terrance Dicks and Colin Baker's enthusiasm for the project comes across so clearly.

'THE STRANGER'
SPIN-OFF VIDEOS FROM BILL BAGGS
reviewed by Paul Castle
Original material for The Best of Shooty Dog Thing

Spin offs from *Doctor Who* tend to fall into three camps. The most successful are those like *Torchwood*, *The Sarah Jane Adventures*, and *Bernice Summerfield*, which liberate a much loved characters from under the Doctor's shadow and gives them centre stage. Another way is to take a situation or monster from the series and give them a story without the constraints of the main series. Such stories often have a Doctor substitute, but occasionally tales such as BBV's *Old Soldiers*, *I Scream*, or Lawrence Miles' *Faction Paradox* series transcend that and tell a damned good story that would never have been possible with the Doctor present. The third is to take the Doctor and put him into a story, changing his name or simply not using it. BBV's *Audio Adventures in Time and Space* series started off telling stories starring Sylvester McCoy and Sophie Aldred, with Ace simply calling her mentor 'Professor' as she so often did onscreen. This was followed by Nick Briggs' Doctor from the fan series of audiotapes - the *AudioVisuals* - losing his memory and being christened 'Fred' after one of the other character's childhood goldfish which suffered a similar problem. Regaining his memory at the end, Fred decided to keep his new moniker, wanting to make a break with his past.

Preceding these, however, was Colin Baker's *The Stranger*. Made by Bill Baggs for the BBC Film Club, the first few stories (*Summoned by Shadows* by Christian Darkin, *More than a Messiah* by Nigel Fairs, and *In Memory Alone* by Nicholas Briggs) featured a pair of characters who could quite conceivably be the sixth doctor and Peri (although Nicola Bryant dropped her American accent, just to muddy the waters a little, and is credited only as 'Miss Brown'). Things get interesting when, at the end of *In Memory Alone*, everyone in the story is 'returned to their proper time and place' and Colin Baker's character arrives, sans Miss Brown, amidst the bins behind a nightclub in *The Terror Game* with no idea of who he is.

This move by writer Nicholas Briggs (who also wrote the final two in the series) took *The Stranger* beyond '*Doctor Who* by another name' territory, as the 'proper time and place' the Stranger is returned to his place as leader of an extradimensional terrorist cell. The Preceptors are a long-defeated people, 'wiped out in their billions' by 'the Protectorate', who strike out against their ancient enemy by randomly assassinating people from the material universe. Taken in by the manager of the nightclub (played by Louise Jameson) he doesn't remember much at first, but the owner of the club is the next hit and he knows that this is precisely where he should be.

Also on the scene are his old colleagues, David Troughton's Egan and John Wadmore's Saul, who're distinctly rattled by their cell leader's disappearance. When Saul runs into Solomon - for that is the Stranger's name - whilst casing out the nightclub, Egan is far from comforted at seeing his friend and leader.

It turns out that Solomon was lifted from the data stream enroute to the current mission, and underwent a new form of mental conditioning called 'the Estrangement Program' which removes all prejudice from the subject's mind and leaves him able to see both sides of the story, freed from historical enmity.

So, Solomon is returned to his Preceptor cell by the closing events of *In Memory Alone*, separated from his Protectorate observer Miss Brown before he's ready. Faced with his past, reunited with Egan and Saul, he's starting to remember who he is.

Breach of the Peace sees Egan and Saul stuck on Earth, desparately trying to find Solomon before their cover as detectives from the Met is compromised. Solomon's in hiding, sharing a house with the editor of a local independent newspaper, helping her with the writing and editorial duties. When Rose has a run in with Egan and Saul, she's so infuriated by their callous bullying she complains to their superior at the station. That, linked with other threads of the story, leads Egan and Saul straight to Solomon.

Threatening Rose's life, Solomon is forced to lead Egan and Saul into a local breach in the dimensional web (something Solomon can only see due to his post-estrangement lack of hatred).

The final story is *Eye of the Beholder*. Secret government experiments with the mind of a telekinetic girl has opened a breach into the dimensional web, through which the girl, Meta, and Egan make mental contact. Ripped from the web, Egan finds himself at a remote farmhouse, and is promptly shot by the soldier in charge of security at the 'Project Metaphysic'.

Falling from the web in Egan's wake, Solomon and Saul land in the nearby countryside. They encounter the project director driving back to the farmhouse. Using his badge, Saul gets them both a lift.

Whilst Solomon and Saul piece together what's going on at the farmhouse, a convalescent Egan falls in love with Meta, who he finds compelling. Usually dismissive of Saul's 'fraternisation with the natives', Egan undergoes an 'estrangement program' of his own, learning that there is value in life beyond the web.

However, the experiments with Meta's mind has damaged local spacetime, and discharges from the web (flashes seemingly caused by lightning, though Solomon recognises them for what they are) are getting worse. Before too long, a couple of soldiers (from a team summoned to the project as backup on Egan's mysterious arrival) are struck down and reanimated by web energy. They're now antibodies, and their task is to repair the breach by sterilising the area, killing everyone in it.

The only way to stop them, Solomon discovers, is to close the breach created by Meta's mind. And the only way to do that is to kill Meta, but first he has to get past Egan...

The Stranger, by virtue of stripping away the 'is it?/isn't it?' *Doctor Who* element and creating its own mythology, has surpassed most other spinoffs and joined the ranks of *Torchwood, The Sarah Jane Adventures, Faction Paradox* and *Bernice Summerfield* as one of my essential recommendations from *Doctor Who*'s leftfield. Whilst not a totally original concept (the Preceptor/Protectorate concept owes much to comics like Grant Morrison's *The Invisibles*, just as *The Matrix* trilogy did years later) it's original enough to feel like a breath of fresh air against BBV's throwaway stories featuring faux Doctors, Zygons, Autons, Cyberons, Sontarans and Krynoids that followed.

'THE AGE OF CHAOS' COMIC BY COLIN BAKER
reviewed by James Hadwen
Original material for The Best of Shooty Dog Thing

I have had the pleasure of meeting Colin Baker on a number of occasions at various *Doctor Who* events and have always found him the most consistently charming person. No matter what the occasion, no matter how busy or quiet it's been, he's always given the fans his full attention. I found this quite strange because, for the longest time, I was under the impression that we weren't supposed to like him. He was the one 'responsible' for the 18 month hiatus after all, he had the vulgar costume and the loud voice. He wasn't supposed to be a good Doctor. Alright, so I was young and naïve on the fan circuit when I started going to events and I've since learned a lot about a lot of people. The thing I've learned most of all though is that Colin Baker, more than pretty much any other actor, really is the Doctor.

William suggested, Jon apparently drafted but got rejected, Tom pleaded with the fans for money but never made it... but Colin Baker did what others couldn't do. He wrote for *Doctor Who*. Okay, so we're not talking television (oh now there's a thought, Colin penning a new series episode) but he did write a comic strip. Not just a short 8 page thing either, he wrote a full blown graphic novel type affair (with a little tidying up by Barrie Mitchell). The truly amazing thing though is that he did it in the mid 90s, not quite a decade after his slightly less than satisfying exit from the TV series. At a time when the novels were angst ridden and dark, *The Age of Chaos* is an unexpected shaft of light with more than a splashing of humour. It even goes so far as to include Frobisher (though the artwork, more of which later, for the penguin isn't the best in the world). If Colin wasn't passionate about *Doctor Who* then this wouldn't have been written and, despite its largely forgotten nature, *Doctor Who* fiction would be worse off.

So, what's the story? Peri's long since left the Doctor under less than ideal circumstances. With Frobisher in tow, the Doctor returns to Krontep a few generations down the line to see how things worked out, thus meaning we spend the majory of the story in the company of Peri's grandchildren. However, Krontep is a world steeped in civil war and the Doctor and Frobisher find themselves at the heart of a power struggle with Peri's granddaughter, Actis, the contender for the crown. But are there other forces at work on the planet...?

It would have been so easy to give us a simple recreation of his television era. Running up and down corridors, needless bickering and ever so slightly uncharacteristic actions? Not a bit of it! This is *Doctor Who* unleashed... lava, monsters, cute lizards and adventure galore. The sixth Doctor leaps off the page (well, admittedly that's hardly surprising but it's still so very good to read) and, although not the deepest in the world, other characters such as Yrcanos wannabe Carf are still pleasant enough company for the 90 pages of this true epic. Yes, it's a little predictable in places (but hey, it's *Doctor Who* so it's allowed to be) and the exact nature of the shadowy figure observing the Doctor and his cohort on their quest turns out to be exactly who you think it is, but this is a *Doctor Who* story that's full of zest. One of the crying shames of fandom is that the comics are often seen as the unwanted family member. In 1996, two years after *Age of Chaos* came out, the seventh Doctor would take continuity off on a different course, one that was darker and bitterer in the novel *Bad Therapy*. Fans seem to give the *Bad Therapy* version of events - where the Peri / Yrcanos union bore no fruit - as the real one and often completely ignore the happy ending that Colin gave to his era. As much as I like the novel, deep down I really do believe that *The Age of Chaos* gives the true ending to the story and would strongly suggest hunting down a copy of the comic to open your mind to the original version.

The artwork is probably the weakest part of the release. Shared between two artists, my mind always jars when you go from John Burns to Barrie Mitchell about a third of the way through, it's a shame that the graphics let this graphic novel down. However, it's got such a wide variety of locales that you don't really stay in one place long enough to let it worry you too much. Frobisher just doesn't really look like Frobisher, the sixth Doctor doesn't massively resemble Colin (I can only wonder what this would have looked like had John Ridgway provided the art as he did for the original run of sixth Doctor comic strips) but with the Doctor's character leaping so vividly off the page it doesn't massively matter.

A few years ago now, Colin was at a convention and rather than the usual photos, video sleeves or target novels, I took along my only slightly battered copy of *Age of Chaos* for him to sign. As I put it in front of him he looked up and, only slightly mischievously, asked me 'You do know who wrote this don't you?' At the time I wasn't confident enough to answer, instead I just smiled. So I want to change that and I want to now openly answer his question. Yes Colin, I know who wrote it. It was written by someone passionate about the series, willing to get into continuity and continue story lines that had only been suggested in passing a decade before. Even if there hadn't been a name on the front, we would have known. Thank you.

'TIME OF YOUR LIFE'
NOVEL BY STEVE LYONS
reviewed by Wesley Osam
Original material for The Best of Shooty Dog Thing

Sometimes you can guess what you'll get from a *Doctor Who* book by the name on the cover. Kate Orman is always good. Trevor Baxendale... not so much. Steve Lyons is all over the place. His books range from competent but dull (*The Murder Game*) to brilliant (*The Crooked World*).

I couldn't recall *Time of Your Life* and had no idea what to expect. Unfortunately this isn't one of Lyons's better attempts. There are some interesting threads among the competent-but-dull bits... but I want to end this review on an up note, so problems first.

My previous reviews may have mentioned the 'house style' the *Doctor Who* novels inherited from the Target novelizations. Like the

Target books, the original novels skipped between short 'scenes' imitating the scene changes of a television drama, rarely staying with a single narrative point of view for even a single chapter. *Time of Your Life* might have been written to demonstrate why this isn't always a good idea.

Time of Your Life juggles at least a dozen major characters who receive only the briefest of introductions before the book bounces to someone else. A few attention-deficit-disordered pages later they're back, but by then it's hard to remember who they were or what they were up to. Short, intercut scenes work on television - we're watching actors; we have an easy visual handle for each character - but it's hard to keep a novel's characters straight when we meet so many so briefly in so few pages. By the end of *Time of Your Life* I was still vague on who Giselle and Hammond were; at times I may have assumed they were the same person. Other characters seemed to vanish in the chaos. I have no idea what happened to half the science fiction geek club, or to Miriam Walker's assistant.

That's the style... and then there's the content. The main thing you'll notice about *Time of Your Life* is how much it reminds you of *Vengeance on Varos*. Exaggeratedly violent television spectacles - gladiatorial game shows, children's programmes about blood-soaked psychopathic bunny robots - keep a city of couch potatoes slack-jawed and passive. By the time *Time of Your Life* was published this style of media satire had been worn to bits by writers who'd seen the multiplication of cable channels and the desperate flood of garbage content needed to fill the expanded air time.

You'd expect *Time of Your Life* to seem more relevant in the era of reality television, with people so desperate for a moment on screen they'll drink a blender of rats. (Really. It happened on *Fear Factor*. A viewer got very sick and sued.) Instead, it seems *less* outrageous. The constant blare of insane television has been with us a while, now. It's background noise, and *Time of Your Life* doesn't say much that hasn't already been said many times.

Its one stab at individuality is in satirizing *Doctor Who* itself. Sci-fi geeks lock themselves in the head office to protest the cancellation of their favorite show. A thinly veiled Mary Whitehouse harangues anyone who'll listen about TV violence. I've never liked self-parody - good satire casts its gaze out onto the world, not into a mirror - and

Time of Your Life is a particularly weak attempt. Yet it's with Miriam Walker, the Whitehouse stand-in, that Lyons' TV-satire achieves its one triumph. After a predictable ritual humiliation, Lyons gives Walker a moment of humanity. She's allowed to argue her position honestly, without arrogance or histrionics. Suddenly she's *human*. It's no coincidence that, of the supporting cast, Walker grows the most by the end of the book.

Which is a good transition into what *Time of Your Life* does well. Most of the supporting cast blend together, but a few characters stand out. Fortunately, one of them is the Doctor.

Time of Your Life was not technically the first *Missing Adventure* to star Colin Baker's Doctor, but it was the first not written by Christopher Bulis, and therefore the first that was likely to attempt something more than a nostalgic recreation of the television series. The Target novelizations of *The Trial of a Time Lord* closed a plot hole by suggesting a gap between Peri's time in the TARDIS and Mel's. *Time of Your Life* confirmed that the sixth Doctor era contained unexplored territory - enough room to take the Doctor in any number of directions and give him the development he never got during Colin Baker's brief time on screen.

Time of Your Life signaled the new freedom with a new companion. For the first time, the books retroactively inserted a new companion into a previous Doctor's era. *Time of Your Life* takes the opportunity to give the reader a sleight of hand gut punch. At the beginning of the book, Angela slips off with the Doctor. The Doctor is rude to her, as he was rude to Peri after his regeneration - but for the first time we understand *why*. It's a defense mechanism. During the eighties life in the TARDIS crew got awfully precarious. The fifth Doctor's era featured the first death of a TARDIS crew member since the 1960s. After the sixth Doctor's regeneration turned him temporarily psychotic, even the TARDIS no longer seemed a safe haven. The Doctor needs people around, but no one who travels with him will ever be entirely safe. He doesn't want his friends hurt... so he pushes them away.

So when the Doctor leaps into danger he leaves Angela in what looks like a safe place. Splitting the TARDIS crew is a common move, part of the core structure of a stereotypical *Doctor Who* story: the Doctor gets the A plot, the companion gets the B plot, and they meet back up for the big climax. Most readers at this point probably thought they knew how *Time of Your Life* would play out. They were wrong. Angela immediately encounters the A plot and, not being the Doctor, is destroyed by it.

The lesson is that the Doctor can't protect people by pushing them away. (Character development for a previous Doctor - how often do we get that?) In the end he's ready to accept Grant Markham as a new travelling companion. Grant has a background suiting a time traveller, having moved from a technologically primitive planet to a more advanced one. Unfortunately, he doesn't come off well - he's one of the many characters who fail to stand out, and never seems to get the introduction he needs. Grant would appear in only one more book - *Killing Ground*, fortunately one of Lyons' better efforts.

Time of Your Life begins a transition away from the violence of the TV stories overseen by Eric Saward (who seemed more interested in space mercenaries than in the Doctor). The book's slog through the Network's extreme televised violence is like a purging. In the end the Doctor finds himself smashing a robot with the TARDIS hatstand and decides he's had enough. Future books and audios would take the sixth Doctor in a new direction. If nothing else, *Time of Your Life* by example helped give them permission to do so.

'THE HOLY TERROR'
AUDIOPLAY BY ROBERT SHEARMAN
reviewed by James Powell
Original material for The Best of Shooty Dog Thing

I have to confess, I'm more than a little apprehensive at the thought of trying to review *The Holy Terror*. After all, many far cleverer and more eloquent people than me have already written at great length about how clever it is, how funny it is, and how scary it is. And if you've heard the play yourself, then frankly you already know that it's clever and funny and scary as well. You'll know that the script is sublime, and the cast is amazing - Colin Baker gives one of his very best performances, and Sam Kelly is breathtaking. You don't need me to tell you all that for the umpteenth time.

So instead, I'm going to talk about how *unexpected The Holy Terror* was. Today, nine years after its release, I own over two hundred *Doctor Who*-related Big Finish audio plays and, while Big Finish's output still very much has the ability to excite and delight me, it's fair to say that I'm *used* to it now.

I can find it very easy, therefore, to forget that at the time of its release, *The Holy Terror* was only Big Finish's fourteenth *Doctor Who* play. The range was still exceedingly new - I could name every play so far released, and indeed, had listened to most of them several times over. And I was excited about each and every upcoming release - except for *The Holy Terror*. I wasn't in the least bit fussed about that at all.

Part of the problem was its placement in the schedules, sandwiched between *Shadow of the Scourge* - which was written by my favourite *New Adventures* author, and starred both the fabulous Lisa Bowerman as my favourite companion, and myself as a screaming, terrified cross-stitcher - and *The Mutant Phase*, which featured Nyssa's first meeting with the Daleks, at a time when a new Dalek story was still rare enough to be excited about.

Another contributing factor was that I'd never heard of the author. The writers of the first thirteen plays were all familiar to me, mostly through their work for the *New Adventures* or for BBC books, but as far as I knew at the time, Robert Shearman was a complete unknown. Of course, now that I'm far more familiar with Rob and his work, I realise quite how foolish I was - Rob may have been new to the *Doctor Who* scene in 2000, but his skill and reputation as a writer in wider circles was already firmly established.

Then there was the fact that much had been hyped about the companion for the play: Frobisher. I had vague memories of Frobisher from reading friends' copies of *DWM*, and I was certainly tickled by the concept of the Doctor travelling with a talking penguin, but I wasn't familiar enough with the character to really be enthused by the idea.

However, I think that the biggest barrier to my caring about the play was the trailer. Have you heard it? It's really very, very dull - the Doctor talking about belief systems, and Frobisher talking about pants, with a couple of clichéd 'I shall be eviler than thou' lines chucked in.

So, combine the underwhelming trailer with my ambivalence for the author and the fact that I'd poured so much energy and enthusiasm into awaiting the hideously delayed *Shadow of the Scourge* (which I thought was amazing then and still think is amazing now) and I'm sure you can imagine how unconcerned I was to hear *The Holy Terror*. And I'm sure you can imagine how delightedly surprised I was when I heard the play.

It was a cold November Friday in Lancaster when *The Holy Terror* fell onto my doormat. I had very little to do that afternoon - my Fridays were lecture- and seminar-free - so I'd resolved to spend my time baking a rather complicated gingerbread recipe that would require most of the afternoon to ferment. So I got my walkman, and decided to give episode one a listen – and couldn't turn it off. I was utterly, utterly hooked. I had a strict rule at the time that I never listened to more than one episode of a Big Finish play in a day - back then, Big Finish was the sole provider of new dramatised *Doctor Who* and, while I'd never have the mental fortitude to make a tape last a whole month, I nevertheless felt that it had to be *rationed* somewhat.

And yet, as episode one finished and the tape wound to a halt, I found myself opening up the Walkman, turning the tape over, and pressing play. Worse, when episode two finished, the first tape was swapped for the second. I couldn't stop! From the perfect opening scene, the play had me in its clutches, and wouldn't let me go. I was actually late onto campus for my evening's role-playing, because I could do nothing but listen to the play. (Which, considering the fact I was listening on a Walkman was a little silly, but there we go.)

The play completely defied my expectations. It wasn't bland and it wasn't dull - in fact, it was about as bland and dull as John Barrowman is shy and reclusive. Lines that in the trailer had seemed flat and trite came alive with humour or menace. The cardboard villains of the piece were cardboard villains quite deliberately and wittily so - and yet, simultaneously, properly villainous. Peter Guinness properly drips venom as Childeric, while Roberta Taylor is a study of world-weary bile as Berengaria. They don't play their characters for laughs, with tongue in cheek, or with knowing winks to the microphone; they give it everything they've got.

(Legend has it that Roberta Taylor was thoroughly bamboozled by the script, and hadn't the first idea what was going on. I defy anyone to detect even a note of that in her performance.)

And as for the real villain of the piece, the Child - it was the first time I'd been properly scared by *Doctor Who* since my childhood. He is *terrifying* - all but omnipotent, and utterly without moral compunction of any kind. What combination could be scarier than that? And the achievement of the character is only magnified when you realise, in that fantastic cliff-hanger, just who has been playing him.

Frobisher, meanwhile - the alleged reason why many people declined to listen to the play - made a very entertaining companion. As I say, I'd known fairly little about him, but that mattered not a jot, as all the salient details were covered in the play in a way that generally felt naturalistic, not expositional. Robert Jezek gave a hugely entertaining performance, capturing Frobisher's quirks and foibles without ever making him irritating. The basic structure and story of the play could have survived entirely intact with any of the sixth Doctor's other companions in the supporting role, but a lot of the comedy in the play derives from the very specific way in which Frobisher approaches the situation, and I feel that a lot of that would have been lost with a more conventional companion in his place.

The Holy Terror triumphs because, like all the best drama, it takes its audience through a wide array of heady emotional responses, from hilarity to terror to poignancy. It makes a virtue out of cliché, while simultaneously turning all our expectations on their heads. It makes a virtue of very deliberately having ciphers for characters, and *then* rounds the ciphers out and makes us feel for them!

Of Big Finish's first fifteen plays, *The Holy Terror* was by far its finest story and by far its poorest seller. I understand it's caught up with its fellows somewhat since then, largely through very positive word of mouth. But there are still a great many people who've never given it a try. If you're one of those people then perhaps, like I did back in November 2000, you've just been underwhelmed and left ambivalent by what's on the surface. Don't be. Give this story a try, and discover what so many of us already have - that it's a real masterpiece.

'TEACH YOURSELF BALLROOM DANCING'
SHORT STORY BY ROBERT SHEARMAN
reviewed by Jon Arnold
Original material for The Best of Shooty Dog Thing

'The world's not gonna end just because the Doctor dances.'

The Muses is perhaps the most bizarre linking concept the Big Finish range came up with - you have to admire Steve Lyons for coming up with a story dealing with 'epic poetry and rhetoric', or Ian Potter for a story of 'love poetry and mimicry'. Dancing's a slightly different matter - while it's not a common topic for *Doctor Who*, it's one that's tended to produce memorable moments, such as Moffat's subtle new series metaphors, or the Doctor learning to dance on the imminently doomed world of Antimasque in Paul Ebbs' *The Book of the Still*. To a short but distinguished list you can add one of the finest tales from Big Finish's *Short Trips* collections, Rob Shearman's *Teach Yourself Ballroom Dancing*.

From a 2009 perspective Shearman looks one of those too obvious choices, by the time of publication he'd already written four plays (five if you include the pseudonymous *Punchline* for BBV) with another on the way. Three of those plays consistently hover around the top ten of any Big Finish poll. Oh, and he's now a World Fantasy Award winning author (and nominee for several more awards) for his 2007 debut short story collection *Tiny Deaths*, with his second collection, the fantastically titled *Love Songs for the Shy and Cynical*, just published (and every bit as good).

Teach Yourself Ballroom Dancing dates from the time when prose works from Shearman were a novelty, when he was still more comfortable in collaborative media, writing lines for others to say rather than exposing his own voice unmediated to his audience. That's something that doesn't show through in the story itself though, it's a very confident piece (helped no doubt by the larger than life presence of the most outwardly confident Doctor). There are already clear elements in place that recur in much of his other work, much of it probably shaped by his background in theatrical writing. Firstly, there's the economy of the writing. For instance, the story's sharply focussed on the two main 'actors' almost to the exclusion of the rest of the world - only a few other characters get any lines, two only as they're essential to main character Becky's life. Despite that tight focus on the characters, the world Becky inhabits is also well drawn, elegantly suggested in a few brush strokes, in the same manner Robert Holmes used to. She's vividly realised through little details of her life, the smoking, the restaurants she visits and her relationships with unseen characters. There's also an Auton invasion suggested in the background simply with an anonymous soldier and the twitch of a dummy's hand.

Like Shearman's mainstream short stories, the story's written as essentially a series of fairly absurd events happening to someone presented to us as very normal. It's a trait also very visible in his first *Doctor Who* short story (*The Death of Me* from *A Universe of Terrors*). It's not necessarily something you could regard as remarkable in a *Doctor Who* story - assuming the companion as the usual viewpoint character, almost every story can be regarded as absurd or at least extraordinary events happening to a relatively ordinary person. More importantly, it doesn't make the mistake a lot of *Who* short stories do and try to cram a whole adventure into just fifteen pages but exploits the short story medium. The other main forms of telling *Doctor Who* stories - TV, novel, comic strip and audio play - are fairly ill suited for character study or lengthy introspection given the action quotient generally required of the series, but writers such as Shearman, Paul Magrs and Joe Lidster were quick to exploit the potential of the short story that allowed us to see aspects of the series through different, unfamiliar, ordinary eyes. It's taking the opportunity to restore a certain sense of wonder to the series. The sense of wonder the Doctor can provide to humans is a key theme here, along with the less explored theme of the sense of wonder humans often provide to the Doctor.

It's interesting to note that, given a choice, Rob always seems to opt for a sixth Doctor story. Whilst his most acclaimed audio (and his oddest and most fascinating one) may have been for Big Finish's then flagship eighth Doctor range, he only wrote for one past Doctor. It may originally have been that the sixth Doctor audios were almost the early flagship stories, rehabilitating the damage done by his televised stories. Or it could possibly be that Colin's Doctor is well suited to the clever use of language in Rob's work. And then again it may be that Rob could empathise with a curly haired chap with a way with words.

It's no bad thing though, while I'd love to see his take on any of the first five Doctors, he delivers a beautiful take on Colin's Doctor. If it weren't anathema to use it of a series with so many fine authors I'd be tempted to call it definitive. Rob's sixth Doctor retains his wit, eloquence, and outward air of superiority whilst always being far more mellow and likeable than he ever appeared to be on screen - he always seems to be writing for the toned down (and more interesting) version heard in the audios (although it's worth remembering the sixth Doctor here is seen through the lens of a sympathetic character's perspective). And while the Auton invasion in the background played for laughs, the Doctor's attitude towards it demonstrates the lack of human perspective that Colin talked about in his early interviews, the type of character who'd mourn a unique and beautiful flower being trodden into the ground by an invading army as much as the humans falling before them. It also suggests that the bluster he often employs does have some substance, an Auton invasion being something that doesn't command his full attention. When the character's as well written as this it makes something of a mockery of Terrance Dicks' oft stated maxim of the Doctor always being the same character - you honestly couldn't imagine any other Doctor working so well in this story.

On the face of it though, this story is far more suited to the seventh Doctor - after all, it involves an attempt to manipulate timelines, pretty much the storyline that was a *New Adventures* stock in trade. So maybe better suited to being set in Season 24? Not quite if you look deeper. For starters, the dancing sequences wouldn't be anywhere near as amusing with the shorter and relatively svelte seventh Doctor, there's already a comedic edge derived from the choice of Doctor you wouldn't get from any of the others. The story also requires a certain warmth and bonhomie that wouldn't really convince with any other Doctor. Also, the Doctor's motivation is close to altruistic, it's almost a favour for a friend. There's no higher purpose at stake, no obvious big universal event. Instead you can see this almost as the Doctor having a clumsy trial run for his seventh incarnation - practice making perfect is one of the story's themes, and the sixth Doctor shows how remarkably unsuited he is to try and manipulate the timelines, how his more emotional nature gets in the way of him seeing what he really needs to do. He blunders down an obvious path in trying to improve Becky's life in some small way - the problem, as he realises, is that it's too obvious, it's the wrong path and the nudge he made in a small attempt to change someone's life won't actually change anything. He's looking at his feet instead of feeling the rhythm. He needs more ruthlessness and focus. Compare it to probably the finest *Doctor Who* short story, Steven Moffat's *Continuity Errors*, and you can see how that ruthlessness and focus has allowed him to perfect subtle and unsubtle manipulation. The difference is here it's a somewhat clumsy and endearing change, made for unselfish purposes, the seventh Doctor's changes are perhaps as altruistic, but often lack consideration of the people caught up in them (for the ultimate illustration of this, read Andrew Cartmel's War trilogy sequentially). The seventh Doctor has nipped off and learned how to dance, but he doesn't feel the rhythm. Of course, it's also a well meaning start down the road to becoming the puppet master of McCoy's incarnation, taking morally correct actions for dubious reasons. If placed in context, with foreknowledge of what was to come, you can see similar questions being asked as were considered in the last quarter of *The Waters of Mars*, albeit slightly more compactly and abstractly.

It's not unflawed - the question of just why the Doctor is helping Becky is never answered beyond vague handwaves, and despite my love of the subgenre of story, there's always the question of why a powerful character who's usually concerned with huge universal matters is intervening in an ordinary life when there's no greater benefit to the cosmos, trying in a painfully clumsy manner to help someone insignificant in universal terms realise her dreams. It's almost the equivalent of foiling a Vardan invasion by blowing up the surrounding solar system. If it were badly executed, such concerns would float to the forefront of the reader's mind very quickly. The thing is, in an understated way, *Teach Yourself Ballroom Dancing* demonstrates exactly why Rob Shearman is one of the best pure writers to work on *Doctor Who* in any medium - it's worth reading this for the prose as much as the story. In fifteen pages, it provides wit, pathos, wonder, questions for the reader to ponder and a subtly fresh take on the main character. And it'll also provide the reader with a sense of wonder - wondering why it took four years for Rob Shearman to adapt himself to prose when he was clearly always suited to it.

IT'S ALL ABOUT UNFINISHED BUSINESS

by Jon Arnold

Original material for The Best of Shooty Dog Thing

It's fairly obvious what the unfinished business with the two main recipients of the fan DIY era of the 90s and early 2000s was. The seventh Doctor's era on TV simply faded away without a satisfactory conclusion, the only onscreen acknowledgement that it might be the last of the original run being Andrew Cartmel's hastily cobbled together speech for overdubbing at the end of *Survival*. There was still plenty of mileage left in the concepts Cartmel and his scripting compadres had come up with to underlie their vision of the show. And the eighth Doctor barely had his potential scratched by an hour of screen time before he was cut short. In both cases there was plenty for writers to get their teeth into, plenty in the toybox for writers to play with.

And then there's the case of the sixth Doctor. Prior to Colin Baker's appointment every Doctor we'd seen had a fair chance to explore the character, even if their departure wasn't as willing as it first seemed. Each of them had at least twenty stories to explore the facets of their version of the Time Lord, a generous amount of screen time to show their abilities. Arguably the only one who might've left untapped potential in their Doctor was Baker's predecessor, Davison. It all seemed so promising at the time of Baker taking over too, with Colin talking enthusiastically of beating the senior Baker's record of seven years. And oh yes, behind the scenes there were grand and glorious plans in place for how things would go.

History of course records that things were not to turn out as brightly as planned. The sixth Doctor's era got off on the wrong foot (for the increasingly vocal fans at least) from the start, following Davison's finale. That last Davison story, *The Caves of Androzani* is a story that lodges itself firmly at the top of all time favourite polls. And it's followed by *The Twin Dilemma*. Which, to say the least, doesn't get close to the top of *any* all time favourite polls. The following twenty second season then got hammered for being overly violent and gaudy, leading to the infamous 18 month hiatus, the staggeringly overambitious 14 week *Trial* saga and then the BBC equivalent of Colin Baker being chucked into the boot of a car with a dip in the river in concrete boots to follow. Eight stories, his tenure officially spread over three and a half years, and out.

This, of course, makes it bloody difficult to create and sustain an engaging character. According to Baker himself, the plan was to start his Doctor off as an unlikeable arrogant character and gradually soften him. Looking at the show at the point where he took over the sixth Doctor's initial character is a fairly logical evolution of the character. Davison, particularly in his last season, had portrayed something of an innocent becoming disillusioned with an often violent world - the death of Adric, *Warriors of the Deep*'s last line that 'there should've been another way', his longest serving companion leaving due to the constant violence of the Doctor's lifestyle sickening her and wearing her down in *Resurrection of the Daleks*, or even the grubby, petty drug wars of *Androzani*. The Doctor becoming less tolerant makes sense as a reaction to the events he's recently seen, becoming overwhelmed by disillusion and realising he can't avoid getting his hands dirty. Or you could see it as a natural reaction to the shock of a sort of Time Lord middle age, the Doctor being nearly halfway through his allotted regenerations. As esteemed fellow *Shooty* contributor James Gent once said over a pint, as you get older you can appreciate the Doctor being a bit more of a bastard at this point. Baker even had a head start with the public of the time in establishing this bastardhood, his portrayal of Paul Merroney, a prototype Thatcherite, in *The Brothers* being the role he was mainly remembered for at the time. My mum actually remarked upon Baker's casting that she didn't like him, entirely due to that series.

The great trouble is that, despite the soundness of the idea, it's not very well accomplished to start off with. It's impossible to imagine any of the Doctors making a decent fist of the role as presented in *The Twin Dilemma*. Even Hartnell didn't come across as quite such a callous companion assaulting git in the abandoned pilot version of *An Unearthly Child*, and that was sensibly revised after a quiet word from the BBC hierarchy. Trouble was that by 1984 there was no-one to point out to John Nathan-Turner or Eric Saward that having the Doctor attempt to strangle his companion was a bloody awful idea. Sydney Newman gave a shit because *Doctor Who* was partially his brainchild, through the 1970s the 'Seventh Floor' at the BBC cared because it was a successful show. As Saward was never shy of pointing out later, script notes were rarely forthcoming from the likes of Jonathan Powell, so the production team simply got on with things.

And the other problem with *The Twin Dilemma*, the one that subsequent events would prove to be probably the worst creative mistake in the show's history, was the decision to transmit it as the last show of the season. Bizarre as it may seem to anyone growing up watching modern TV, including the current version of *Doctor Who*, the 1980s show seemed to lack any concept of a season finale, an oversight that looks even stranger given JNT's famed desire for maximum possible publicity. Instead of being an all-stops-out story to send viewers off with happy memories and thinking they should watch again, those final episodes often turned into the cheap story which had to be made to balance out better looking productions. And they usually ended up being at best unmemorable (*The King's Demons*, although granted that was by accident rather than design) and at worst a car crash of a story (well, plane crash in *Time-Flight*'s case). Here it meant that the new Doctor would be doing the equivalent of opening in a village hall rather than on a West End stage. More importantly it meant that, as the one sustained example of Colin Baker's performance as the Doctor, writers for the next season would be taking their cues from that story.

Bugger.

The big trouble here is that *The Twin Dilemma* falls into the tradition (established since the third Doctor's debut *Spearhead from Space*) of the new Doctor being a touch unstable. Which is fine for the previous three Doctors as those introductory stories were all placed at the start of a season, rather than seemingly tacked on to their predecessor's last season as an afterthought. Their personalities had also stabilised for the second half of the story. And, rather crucially, each post-Hartnell Doctor's debut had been written by an experienced *Doctor Who* writer, each of whom served as script editor at some point. Anthony Steven hadn't written for the show before, didn't have any scripts or performances to go on and seemed to derive all his ideas about sci-fi from the 1950s and earlier - is it any wonder he struggled to come to terms with the show? If the idea of placing the new Doctor's debut at the end of a season had a shot of working it should probably have been written by the incumbent script editor, a man who'd helped devise the new Doctor's character and would have a good idea as to how to establish the identity they wanted. Saward may well have rewritten drastically, but in a story where he's essentially just rescuing what he can from a wreck, establishing the character may well have been beyond his ability. After all, his other work doesn't demonstrate a particular flair for characterisation.

What we're left with as a template for the writers of Season 22 is someone in severe need of mood stabilising drugs, operatically switching from murderous to penitent, to aloof, to arrogant and a million wild mood swings in between. On top of that the Doctor-companion relationship is rather fragile (Peri's smile at the end is at best uncertain), although it's probably the most realistic reaction by any companion to a new Doctor. If someone you've just started travelling with (well, that's how it's intended, despite the myriad audios and books set just before *Androzani*) suddenly changes into someone else looking and acting completely differently it's certainly going to shake you and your relationship with them up, and Peri's cautious acceptance of the new Doctor is more convincing than, say, Ben and Polly's acceptance in *The Power of the Daleks*, Tegan, Nyssa and Adric taking regeneration in their stride in *Castrovalva* or certainly Mel in *Time and the Rani*. The trouble is the companion is the human viewpoint, as close as the audience has to an identification figure and if she didn't know what to make of the Doctor, the audience probably didn't either. God knows what the next season's writers must have made of it, because at the end of *The Twin Dilemma* you really have no idea of the Doctor's character (bar maybe a certain arrogance bordering on callousness and a fondness for portentous quotations), nor of how he relates to his companion. That's not necessarily a bad thing if deliberate - it can keep an audience on their toes - but when it looks like the result of clumsiness and misjudgement it's massively unhelpful.

So through Season 22 writers seem to have latched onto the only evidence they've seen. And what we get is generally arrogant, mercurial and unsympathetic. The Doctor blunders into situations without understanding what was going on, misjudging them and often becoming callous and careless (the best examples being his misjudgements in *Attack of the Cybermen*, the quips after the acid bath deaths in *Vengeance on Varos* and his asphyxiation of Shockeye in *The Two Doctors*). It may be more realistic than the often cartoon like violence of ITV's slick American imports such as *The A-Team* or *Knight Rider*, but it was drastically out of place on a Saturday evening. Dramatically interesting as shades of moral greyness are, it's not what the early Saturday night is looking for. Particularly not when compounded by themes such as relatively graphic violence, video nasties, sadism or cannibalism. This wouldn't be a problem in, for example, *Blake's 7*, a show intended for adults and broadcast in such a slot. In those adult timeslots you can get away with morally questionable heroes in a dark world, in the early evening slot of the Davison years you might just get away with it, but in a Saturday teatime slot with the audience recovering from the horrors of Roland Rat it simply isn't going to work. This isn't, of course, entirely due to this version of the Doctor, it's more Eric Saward's fascination with conflict, violence and body horror that eventually led Grade and Powell to give the show a rest. But the problem lies in there being no contrast between the character and methods of the hero and the villains he faced. The sixth Doctor and his world was far too much of a shock to the system of an eighties audience, who found their white hatted good guy vs black hatted bad guy thrills with those glossy American imports.

Those 18 months clearly saw some lessons being taken to heart by the production team. The first part of *The Trial of a Time Lord* brought us a Doctor who'd slightly mellowed, and whose relationship with his companion was on a smoother footing, with far less bickering in evidence, more in line with a conventional Doctor-companion relationship. Until *Mindwarp*, which threw the Doctor's and Peri's relationship back into flux. While it's interesting to play on the relationship still being uncertain in one story it's really not beneficial to the sixth Doctor or the series overall. The unreliable nature of *Mindwarp*'s narration doesn't help either, what we're seeing may be the Valeyard twisting evidence to cast aspersions on the Doctor's character, but at this point the series needed to show the audience that the Doctor's still the hero they're used to seeing. Instead we're left in doubt as to whether he's a bastard again or not; even the script editor, writer and lead have been reported as not knowing precisely what was going on. Unpredictability should have been off the menu. Mel's arrival for the last six episodes brings out a gentler, more paternal Doctor, although this may just be Pip and Jane Baker's interpretation of the character being more palatable than that of the harder edged version from Saward, Martin and to a lesser extent Holmes. Or it may be that this Doctor was better suited to a less arsey companion.

And then Michael Grade intervened again.

Whether motivated by personal rancour or not, Grade told John Nathan-Turner to fire Colin Baker, later remarking in a 2003 *Daily Telegraph* interview that it was due to him finding Colin's portrayal of the Doctor 'utterly unlikeable, absolutely god-awful in fact'. While that's a matter of opinion, you can see how the violence and inconsistency in the writing of the character contributed to that impression. With a man in a wig bearing no real physical resemblance to him getting a bump on the head in a pre-credits sequence, the sixth Doctor was disposed of. Any ideas about a long term character arc were summarily cut off and all anyone would be left with would be memories of a loud violent man in an even louder coat.

Four years later *Doctor Who* was essentially dead, the BBC not making the mistake of announcing it loudly this time. Instead they tried to euthanise it at the end of the programme's 26th year, tried to let it slip away quietly. This time there was no media outcry, because there was no announcement, and therefore no story to centre outrage around, just vague rumours and statements on possible futures. The BBC didn't want *Doctor Who*, but the fans did. And if none was forthcoming then they'd make their own.

Peter Darvill-Evans and his predecessor at Virgin Publishing, Nigel Robinson, had been floating the idea of original *Doctor Who* novels for years before they became a reality in 1991. When they finally drew up the contracts with the BBC there was such little interest in *Doctor Who* that they were essentially allowed to name their own terms. Initially the range would be the only one that Darvill-Evans found stimulating, the ongoing adventures of the seventh Doctor after he left our screens. And it would include an open submission policy, leaving the door open for the fans to get their hands on the ongoing series for the first time (*Full Circle* notwithstanding). After three books from established *Who* authors came the first book from a fan (albeit one who'd already had some success writing in other media). It'd be an exaggeration to say there was a lot riding on it, but after it was published *Doctor Who* fiction was changed forever.

Paul Cornell's first book was a revelation in both name and nature. I can remember my mum buying it before the official release date at The Chepstow Bookshop's pre-Christmas evening opening. I was supposed to be revising for mock A-levels. But every time I tried to draw my concentration back to the work the book taunted me, demanding that I read the next chapter. Result: Relatively crap mock results and a blown fanboy mind. *Timewyrm: Revelation* was the first book that showed you *Doctor Who* could be so much more than just stories you could've seen on the telly. It was the first book to show you *Doctor Who* could work equally well in the literary medium, unbeholden to its televised origins. It went places (the inside of the Doctor's head for starters) that the TV show could never have dreamed of, played out scenarios that budget, imagination and format would've ruled out - evil child astronauts, sentient churches, the heads of dead Nazis carrying on living, dancing with Death on the moon, the Doctor and Ace being pursued by the hordes the Doctor has killed (or at least feels guilty about having had a role in their death)... It was a wild, imaginative tour de force that blazed a trail for new authors to do what they wanted with *Doctor Who*.

The thing is, it's very much a product of the times - familiarity with the tropes it brought to *Doctor Who* means those who came to it afterwards can't hope to experience the shock of the new that those of us at the time felt. And perhaps, to an extent, the old school *New Adventures* fans do remember the book behind sheen of cosy nostalgia. More relevantly here though, the attitude displayed towards the sixth Doctor is very much of the time. *Revelation* has the first five Doctors appear as aspects of the Doctor's mind, culminating in the fifth Doctor as the manifestation of the Doctor's conscience. The sixth Doctor doesn't appear, partly due to the story *Revelation* was based on being designed for Davison and therefore having no room for the sixth. But it helps establish obliquely what would become the background mythology of the *New Adventures*. The sixth Doctor is almost a pariah, a madman in the seventh Doctor's mental attic. As that mythology unfolded over sixty books we learnt (in Cornell's second novel *Love and War*) that the sixth Doctor was the sacrifice the seventh Doctor made to become Time's Champion, locked safely away where he wouldn't trouble the seventh Doctor's mind. It's almost as if the more prominent *New Adventures* authors bought into

Cornell's vision so strongly that, consciously or unconsciously, they disowned the murky ethics and violence of the second Baker era, preferring the gentler, more conciliatory approach of the Davison incarnation mixed with the manipulative approach glimpsed in McCoy's last couple of seasons. McCoy's portrayal, understandably, would be the one benefitting from the creative renaissance brought about by the *New Adventures*. In fan circles it became okay to like the seventh Doctor, almost fashionable (trolls on the newsgroup rec.arts.doctorwho notwithstanding). The reputation of the sixth Doctor, however, continued to languish.

Colin's Doctor wasn't immediately rehabilitated by the advent of the *Missing Adventures* in 1994. Launched in response to the success of the *New Adventures* and an oft asked question from fans, the *Missing Adventures* scratched the fan itch to see stories featuring previous Doctors. The first book to feature the sixth Doctor was Christopher Bulis' *State of Change*, a fairly workmanlike story of an old SF cliché, the alternate world where Rome never fell. It's brave to do that in *Doctor Who* since you're always going to be compared to *The Iron Legion*, the much loved comic strip that ran in the first few issues of *Doctor Who Weekly*. Instead of looking forwards and seeing what he can do with the character in prose though Bulis instead fixes his authorial gaze backwards, seeking to simply tell a story that could easily have been told on television with a bigger budget (oh, and with the eighties fanboy fantasy of a dripping wet and naked Peri - in Bulis's hands it's not anywhere near as erotic as that fanboy wet dream sounds). In the course of the story he deliberately (and seemingly randomly) uses Colin Baker era icons, going out of his way to reintroduce Peri's transformation into a bird as seen in *Vengeance on Varos* and making the Rani the mastermind (mistressmind?) behind the whole alternate Rome scenario, to the point where she's crowbarred into the story. That retro outlook extends to the characterisation - Peri and the Doctor's relationship is precisely as we'd seen it on screen, they're even bickering in the opening scene. And while the Doctor might appear more likeable it's only in relation to a Peri who has all her character faults exaggerated - snippy, self absorbed and with seemingly permanent PMT, all wrapped within a strange British idea of how Americans speak and act. It's what I imagine Americans mean when they call someone preppy. While capturing the spirit of the Doctor's era was part of the range's remit, to capture it so slavishly when there's an incarnation so suited to prose (with his verbosity and the opportunity to undercut the brash exterior) has to count as a missed opportunity.

The 1995 sixth Doctor novels are where the rehabilitation of the character gets underway. His next appearance was the first appearance of one of the eventual key figures in the sixth Doctor's renaissance, Steve Lyons. Lyons had made his *Doctor Who* debut with *Conundrum*, which had made innovative use of the Land of Fiction from *The Mind Robber*. *Time of Your Life* is important as it's the first book to really make the sixth Doctor work as a literary character. Whilst he's very much the abrasive figure seen on screen, he's less antagonistic for an audience as Lyons uses the strengths of the novel to get inside his head and render his concerns, hopes and fears understandable. It's set in the interregnum between the end of the Trial and Mel actually joining, and shows a worried Doctor trying to avoid the fate of becoming the Valeyard, amply demonstrated in his cautious attitude towards the two companion figures introduced here. He's almost doing his best not to get involved with companions after what happened (or nearly happened) with Peri. The shadow of the Valeyard was an important consideration in the sixth Doctor's development in the *Missing Adventures*, providing a context for his actions here and his fear of his future making him far more sympathetic. The Doctor still resorts to violence (battering a robot to death with the TARDIS hatstand) in a world as violent as anything seen in his time on screen, but the absence of the bickering with Peri, or Mel's relentless enthusiasm, is refreshing and a hint of things to come. It's far from Lyons' best executed novel, perhaps being too self-consciously grim and strongly paralleling elements from *The Twin Dilemma* and *Vengeance on Varos*, but the subtle redrawing of the sixth Doctor's character here means it's more important to his rehabilitation than it might at first appear. Lyons would build on this further with his other sixth Doctor adventure, *Killing Ground*, in which he forces the main character to consider the consequences of his regular interference in the affairs of others and the necessity of it. He also provides a reason for the Doctor to become mellower, moderating the often violent nature of this incarnation.

That somewhat mellower and easier to stomach Doctor is on show in the book which came out six months after *Time of Your Life*. But where it's possible to underestimate *Time of Your Life*'s influence on how the sixth Doctor would be portrayed, it's impossible to miss that of *Millennial Rites*. Which is probably how the much missed Craig Hinton would like it. Again, it's set after the events of *Trial*, but this time the Doctor's accompanied by Mel, a companion written almost as a generic afterthought on screen, and so dependent on Bonnie Langford's performance, that it was almost impossible to imagine her working in prose. But again, despite this being a fast moving epic book of big ideas (such as a mashing of realities and creatures from the previous universe and the next), the author takes the opportunity to flesh out the characters without slowing down the adventure. I'd say Mel's character is utterly revitalised, but as she wasn't really vital on screen let's just say she's vitalised. Instead of being a screaming fitness freak, merely there to get into jeopardy for the Doctor to rescue, she becomes proactive, with her background capabilities (such as her high IQ, strict moral standards and computer programming) becoming more than mere details. This helps drive the story, Mel playing a major role rather than admiring the Doctor's brilliance then telling him to get fit. All this is done without undermining what was established in the series, she's recognisable as the character portrayed on screen and you get the impression she'd still be annoying if you spent too long in her company, but it's the opportunity to get into her head that strengthens her here. So strong is the rehabilitation that this is the template for future appearances such as *Business Unusual*, and especially for the writers in the Big Finish range, more on which later. Mel becomes more a character that the reader can sympathise with, and is therefore more palatable as a viewpoint character. And as the viewpoint character is more sympathetic, so their view of the main character becomes more acceptable to the reader, again helping to remove an alienating edge from this Doctor. This is even more effective when considered in tandem with the same month's *New Adventure*, *Head Games*, from that man Steve Lyons. It uses Mel to contrast the seventh Doctor with who he was and what he's become. *Head Games* sees a crowded TARDIS with all the seventh Doctor's companions making an appearance, and examines the changes wrought upon him by Andrew Cartmel and his team of scriptwriters, and subsequently the *New Adventures* novelists. Mel, a relic of a more innocent onscreen era becomes disgusted by this Doctor's actions, thereby subtly repositioning the sixth Doctor as more palatable than the manipulative seventh. And although the fictional version of the sixth that manifests itself here for a showdown with his future self is ostensibly insane, it's understandable how he's become the equivalent of a bad sector on the computer that is the Doctor's brain. Again, the comparison of methods provides arguments the seventh Doctor can't really answer without looking a complete bastard compared to his ostensibly more violent predecessor.

Back to *Millennial Rites* though. What we get here is a story which is dark in theme but utterly lacks the nastiness and violence seen in the majority of sixth Doctor stories to this point. If you like, it's a dark story told with a light touch and an understanding that to be truly successful a *Doctor Who* story needs to balance any darkness with thrills and entertainment. And this is crucial to the novel's success in rehabilitating this Doctor. We have a story that manages to distil the essence of what a sixth Doctor-Mel era would probably have been like from what we saw on screen but manages the gripping story that partnership was denied. Essentially, unlike much of what we see on screen, the Doctor is at the centre of the story and in the sort of *Doctor Who* fantasy world that exists outside the Saward era, less violent and more enjoyable for the audience to visit (unless you're a masochist). For the first time he's placed in the same sort of moral environment as inhabited by the other Doctors. It has the effect of making him more mellow, as what's there for him to rage against doesn't seem so mundane. It's a rage against the myriad evils of the *Doctor Who* universe we're used to, and makes him the kind of hero his predecessors were. Although stories which fitted the tone of Season 22 were still possible (Dave Stone's *Burning Heart* being a good example, throwing the Doctor into a thinly disguised replica of Judge Dredd's Mega City One where he really doesn't seem out of place) it's this repositioning that makes later books which place the sixth Doctor in lighter, more conventional stories (such as *Business Unusual*, *Grave Matter* and *Players*) viable.

To this point it should be clear that the sixth Doctor is a character who's better served by his print appearances, something that's reinforced when his comic strip era (especially the epic *Voyager* saga) is taken into account. Part of this is that the character's better suited to a medium relying on words rather than images - he's verbose, and his outwardly loud, often violent nature is hard to like without some degree of insight as to his motivations. That degree of insight was something near impossible to achieve through his performance on screen given the unsubtle nature of every aspect of production through his two seasons. Until 1999 Colin Baker had only had one chance to contribute to correcting the mistakes made during his tenure with the graphic novel *The Age of Chaos*. As the cover art suggests, it's a lighter story with the Doctor's personality reined in a little, certainly with less Doctor related violence present. And interviews with him throughout the nineties suggested someone who knew that significant creative errors had been made during his era. As he told Ben Cook in *DWM* #325, he always had the feeling that he never got a chance to finish what he started.

And then Big Finish came along, and gave Baker that chance.

Big Finish began to produce *Doctor Who* audios in the summer of 1999, after impressing the BBC with their early *Bernice Summerfield* range. They launched with *The Sirens of Time*, which is designed to showcase the three Doctors willing to appear at the time. And although the production is by no means Big Finish's strongest, it does succeed in that aim. It's a portent of things to come in the nascent range that the strongest performance we see is from Baker, as he covers some scripting weaknesses by injecting plenty of energy and brio. It's not always easy to judge on first appearances, particularly when each Doctor's share is around an episode and a third, but the sixth Doctor we get here isn't quite what we had on screen. He still attempts to irritate the other characters who appear in his story and quite egotistically insists on being in charge when all three Doctors finally meet - the Pertwee of this three Doctors tale. But the story's not dragged down by the violence that marred his era, and neither does the Doctor resort to violence as easily as he tended to on screen. It's a more thoughtful, measured performance, toned down from the television. Mind you, it might well have helped that we couldn't see that insanely conceived coat.

Whispers of Terror, the sixth Doctor's first solo audio outing, confirms that initial impression. He's accompanied by Peri, but the relationship as portrayed here is less abrasive than on screen, with less bickering in evidence (although it's not entirely absent with several moments of unpleasantness between the two). The slightly different take was an approach producer Gary Russell was obviously keen on from his comments in Big Finish's *Inside Story* (it's also evident in the sixth Doctor stories he penned). What we get is an evolution of the relationship rather than a sudden change, still recognisably the characters from Seasons 22 and 23 but with thought given to amending the on-screen flaws. This is still recognisably the Doctor of Season 22, but again it's a more cerebral take on the role. This Doctor still charges headlong into situations, and can lack self awareness (rather fabulously at one point shouting that he 'doesn't shout'), but he doesn't tend to offer brute force as a solution. *Whispers of Terror* demonstrates that the audio interpretation of the sixth Doctor can be contrasted against the violence in his stories, rather than becoming part of the bloody fabric of it. He'd barely qualified as a flawed hero for much of his televisual life, now thanks to a more skilful performance from Baker and scripting sympathetic to his aims, he's more the heroic Doctor figure we're used to.

However, Peri as companion still presents a problem. To be convincing, there would always need to be a certain edge to the Doctor-companion relationship, the insults flying between the pair not coming across as friendly banter but genuine antipathy. Bluntly, she's better suited to stories with the more laid back fifth Doctor as her aggressive nature (for a companion) provides more of a contrast (a la Tegan), and they don't openly rub each other up the wrong way. Pairing her with Davison's Doctor rather than Baker's was one of Big Finish's more inspired decisions, even if it robs *The Caves of Androzani* of some of its dramatic power if you think about it too hard. Probably the best thing Big Finish did for the incarnation from this point forward was to provide him with companions who could challenge him but weren't as obviously antagonistic. This means that the sixth Doctor is no longer as defined by his relationship with Peri as he was on television. Mel would return for an outing in *The One Doctor*, their lighter relationship allowing this Doctor to venture into outright comic territory that simply couldn't have worked with Peri. Comic strip companion Frobisher, the shape shifting penguin with a tendency to talk like Philip Marlowe, had a couple of successful outings, his often blithe disregard for the Doctor's exasperation working better than Peri seemingly taking each remark to heart. Far in the future of the range he'd be paired with the eighth Doctor's companion Charley, an ongoing story arc regarding him being unaware of her future companion status providing a an fascinating tension. And there'd even be the occasional solo outing. By far the most successful companion for this Doctor though would be introduced in his second solo outing, the time paradox historical story *The Marian Conspiracy*.

The sixth Doctor is a Doctor who likes to show off and impose himself, yet is also prone to childish outbursts when frustrated. He's therefore much more suited to a mature, experienced companion who can realistically and convincingly challenge him intellectually (something it's impossible for Peri to do given her youth and personality). Due to the practicalities of television production, this wouldn't be possible on screen, such a role being likely to take a toll on an older actor, or audiences generally being less inclined to accept an older character as their viewpoint. With audio being less strenuous to produce (for actors at least), the first of those barriers is removed, and with the audios being mainly aimed at fans, you've less need for a universal viewpoint character given they're likely to be more invested in the story anyway. This makes a character such as Evelyn Smythe possible, the type of companion the sixth Doctor needs and who's helped redefine him in audio as much as any other element. There's an easier understanding between the two, a mutual respect for the experience and intellect of the other. Most importantly it doesn't feel like there's an antagonistic basis to their relationship, you can understand why they continue to travel with each other. And with this sort of Doctor-companion relationship, the one denied him for all but six episodes on screen, the sixth Doctor fits better into the Doctor as hero format.

It's noticeable that prior to Paul McGann agreeing to reprise his role as the eighth Doctor, the Doctor who garnered most praise for the audios was Baker. Davison had played the role for three seasons, had twenty stories in the role. He'd had a fair crack of the whip in establishing his Doctor. McCoy had three years, plus a long and eventful literary afterlife in the *New Adventures*. The potential we saw onscreen had been tapped and explored. But the sixth Doctor had neither the onscreen time the fifth Doctor had, nor the book range of the seventh, being confined to sharing the *Missing Adventure*/Past

Doctor spotlight with others instead. In a real sense, his Big Finish stories were the main phase of what the book range started in rehabilitating that Doctor, returning this prodigal son of a Doctor to the fold. With the eighth Doctor also being the centre of a book range, there's a good argument to be made that Big Finish's treatment of the sixth Doctor is the most interesting thing they've done with their licence.

Recently, Big Finish has come full circle with producing the *Missing Stories* range, which for the sixth Doctor means the stories lost to the hiatus. It's a measure of the success of the range in rehabilitating his Doctor that Baker is willing to return to the more loud and aggressive portrayal of his Doctor and his fractious relationship with Peri, something he surely wouldn't have been willing to do when the range began. Colin's business may not be finished yet, but through the hard work of novelists and scriptwriters his Doctor's finally had the chance backroom incompetence and politics denied him.

DO THE M.O.N.S.T.E.R.M.A.S.H.!
by Paul Castle
Originally printed in Shooty Dog Thing #6 - Summer 2008

One of the best things about the monsters in *Doctor Who* is that they're usually rather inventively created, but in just the two dimensions. They're just there to (1) provide a tangible threat, and (2) look monstrous enough to maintain the kids' interest. How, you may ask, is being two-dimensional one of the best things? Surely we want three-dimensional monsters, right? Well, the way I see it, if the production team had fleshed-out their latex and paper-maché horrors properly, what on Earth would there be left for fans to write about them? So, for the next few pages I'm going to be adding my own third dimension to monsters and aliens, asking how the remains of the very animal Mandrels turn into narcotic fungi after death, if the Ogrons are really aping humans, whether the virus in *The Invisible Enemy* is really a virus, why the Sontarans look so different story-to-story given they're all clones, and might the Dals have mutated into the Thals' perfection if they'd not taken to living in the Dalek machine, and more questions of that ilk.

Mandrel heredity

Nightmare of Eden, a classic Tom Baker and Lalla Ward story from 1979, revolves around a drug smuggling plot. Vraxoin is a fungal compound that's a little like marijuana taken to the extreme, where passivity and an inflated sense of humour eventually lead to violent behaviour and death. What's novel about Vraxoin, however, is that its source is the monstrous Mandrels. When Mandrels die, they leave behind a pile of fungal spores, which is Vrax. Vrax is highly addictive and eventually causes death in humanoid life forms.

The question this raises is, how does an animal produce a fungus, and why is the conversion of dead body to pile of fungal spores so rapid? Well, I think that the Mandrels we see here are merely a stage in the life-cycle of the fungus, much in the way that a caterpillar is a stage in the life-cycle of a digger wasp. You might remember from your David Attenborough that digger wasps paralyse a caterpillar and lay their eggs in the still living body, which provides a fresh source of protein for the infant wasps to breakfast on before they emerge into the world. Now, my theory is that when a body becomes addicted to Vraxoin, what it's being compelled to do is ingest enough of the spores to start a colony within the body. These spores, with ingestion and multiplication, soon inhabit every cell within the host. Now, the original infected creature usually dies from this massive cellular hijack, but being dead and buried is no good to the germ-line of the Vraxoin fungus and the body actually stays alive but with the original occupant no longer in the driving seat. Instead you have the Vrax in control, though as it's not a conscious force the 'dead' addict returns as a zombie like creature with no other desire but to rampage. The extended phenotype of the Vrax within the body of the addict is making a nuisance of its host, and when destroyed (as it will have to be: there's no way to contain the beasts), the fungus within each and every cell goes into the sporing. On a chemical signal, the fungus instantly consumes all the animal cellular matter and expires as it spores, and the result is an explosion of dead fungi parent cells and the germ-line spores, which is awfully addictive to animals and the life cycle continues. This life cycle isn't confined to humanoid animals though; its effects are active on all animals from the smallest mites through to whales. Vrax is a decomposer that's gone a bit more 'proactive'.

So, this leaves options open, should BBC Wales (a) want to bring them back, and (b) read *Shooty Dog Thing* and want to buy my idea for a small fee (debate among yourselves which is more unlikely!) then either the Mandrels are not the actual monsters but essentially peaceful creatures made rabid from the effects of the Vraxoin, or that the mutated cellular structure makes the host more and more like the Mandrels in appearance after they 'die'. Just depends on the effects budget and/or level of horror you wish to inflict on the audience. Humans becoming slavering Mandrels and then exploding into dust after a good rampage is far more pre-watershed friendly than slavering humans going on a rampage and exploding into dust.

Ogrons: aliens apeing humans?

I love the Ogrons, they're the *Doctor Who* equivalent of the stereotypical 1930s Chicago gangster's henchman: not much of a brain or personality, but with a physique that more than makes up for any shortfalls. When faced with the prospect of returning the Daleks to our screens after an absence of seven years, but with only the budget for three casings (and one of those a distinctive gold, limiting the onscreen presence to just two soldier Daleks at a time) they needed some humanoid figures to swell the ranks, and so invented the Ogrons. It strikes me very much in the line of Terrance Dicks' sense of humour to make the appearance of these Ogrons a comment on the almost universal humanoid bodyform (two arms, two legs, and one head, standing up straight) in science fiction. It's an incredible feat of anthropocentric conceit for us to state that the natural shape of intelligent (or near-intelligent in the case of the Ogrons) alien life is to 'ape' us. And so, they made them look like humanised apes. But that's a behind-the-scenes explanation: how do we explain our ungainly shapes, which are notoriously prone to bad backs and require toilet paper to clean up after themselves, becoming the pinnacle of evolution on a universal scale? Well, I can think of three options: panspermia, the ancients, or the morphogenic field. Either that or God decided to sod Creation and ran with the first thing he could think of at 4.55pm on the sixth day so he could take the seventh off.

Panspermia is the name given to the theory that life may be seeded on planets by microbes that live within comets, making planetfall in meteorites and getting on with the business of populating a planet by replication and mutation. It's not really an origin theory, or an alternative to the all-but-universally-accepted Darwinian selection, as the question of where the comet microbes came from in the first place needs explaining (and there's no sensible alternative to Darwin's 'dangerous idea') but what this means for science fiction is that all life in the universe might possibly spring from the same source. However, we know from molecular evidence on our own planet that all lifeforms are direct cousins of one another, be they elephants or honeybees, badgers or flukeworms, plumbers or lawyers, mixotrixes or dandelions, so there's no credibility in the idea that all humanoid life is humanoid due to coming from the same single-celled ancestor. Next!

The Ancients. Once upon a time there was a popular notion amongst the more hippy-inclined members of society that all human progress is down to visitations from outer space, beings from more advanced civilisations or planes of existence who liked nothing better than to periodically visit us to drop a few hints and vanish off again. This space-aged version of the idea comes from Von Daniken's *Chariots of the Gods*, but is more or less a sci-fied up concept of the Djinn from Islamic myth, who according to my Muslim friend at work, are responsible for all the ancient monuments like the Pyramids and Stonehenge, etc. This, frankly, is an insult to the very human people who actually did build these things, especially those who died in the process. But, personal opinion aside, the ancients are a huge part of human prehistory in the *Doctor Who* mythos and a strong contender for the manipulation of evolution to form humanoid creatures across the galaxies. There's loads of them: the Osirians, the Daemons, and the Jagaroth are all contenders. Oh, and not to mention the Time Lords...

The morphogenic field. Hmm, bit of an odd one, this. I first encountered it in one of the early *New Adventures*, possibly 1992's *Lucifer Rising*, where the idea was put forth that rather than today's accepted science of embryology, where all living beings are grown from the recipe encoded in a zygote's DNA using materials passed down from the mother (who's eating for two), somehow an organism's shape is informed by its aura. Now, the first successful intelligent species in the universe somehow encoded their aura into the space-time vortex and all intelligent creatures that evolve are moulded in their form. It's pretty much an idea inspired by Plato, who postulated higher planes of existence and that all mortal creatures are shadows of their Platonic ideals: here you could say that the ideal form of intelligent life is one head, two arms and two legs, standing upright and all the humanoid aliens we see are shadows of this, of the first civilisation. This is kinda cool and hoopy, so a good contender for a telefantasy explanation.

'Nucleus' of the 'virus'?

In *The Invisible Enemy*, the 1977 fourth Doctor and Leela story that introduced K9, the title refers to the Nucleus of the virus, a teeny, tiny shrimp-like creature which somehow infects the Doctor through a sort of radiowave-teleport transmission thing (it's a bit vague, like half the stuff in *Who*, but doesn't matter) with the intention of using him (amongst other 'infected' humanoids) to hijack a moonbase on Titan and use it to incubate millions of the virus's next generation which'll swarm across space. All very exciting, but one does wonder in what ways this equates to being a virus? It's more like a parasitic infection, a microscopic queen that nestles in an unfortunate brain and extends her phenotypic influence; in short using her host's arms and legs to further her, and not their, objectives.

What I think we have here is a classic case of mis-description, something which happens in *Doctor Who* all the time. Calling a parasite a virus is the biological equivalent of mixing up solar systems, galaxies and universes (see *The Daleks' Masterplan* for some shocking examples of cosmological ignorance), or the geological equivalent of confusing the Jurassic with the Pleistocene (see my review of *Time-Flight* last issue) and failing to pick a geological era in the Mesozoic where you might conceivably have met dinosaur-men, instead choosing the Silurian period (where the most you'd expect to find are spiders and scorpions) or the later (still incorrect) correction of the Eocene (where mammals had long filled all the niches vacated by dinosaurs, but early hominids were still several tens of millions of years off). In short, the science in *Doctor Who* is pretty much as dodgy as that last rather elongated sentence. And it's not just the older episodes where you'll find clunkers: just a couple of months ago we visited the *Planet of the Ood*, where the question was asked how a species could evolve that's totally subservient to other species. Fair enough, but in explaining that they gave us an even bigger problem: how can a species evolve where they have to carry their forebrains around in their hands? It's conceivable that a mutation might arise where a nasally-carried forebrain might be expelled, but surely any mutant infant with such an exposed brain wouldn't survive long enough to reproduce, and even if it did, precisely what advantage would there be in having to carry your brain everywhere? No, the science in *Doctor Who* hasn't gotten any better and the Nucleus of the Virus should have been called the Queen of the Parasites.

Sontaran diversity

One of the key points about Sontarans is that they're a cloned species, if indeed a non-breeding people can be considered a species at all: the definition of 'species' is they only breed with each other to produce fertile young, and the Sontarans don't breed with anyone and are sterile.

Anyway, the main thing about them is that they're identical to each other. Which is fine in theory, but far from the truth in practice. Even by their second story, *The Sontaran Experiment*, differences were starting to creep in, as due to the failing health of the actor Kevin Lindsay, his costume from *The Time Warrior* had to be loosened, and he wore gloves that were five-fingered rather than three. Their next appearance, in *The Invasion of Time*, saw even more marked differences. The masks had been remoulded to make more use of the actors' faces, replacing the huge slit for a mouth with makeup around their mouths. By 1985's *The Two Doctors*, the difference from the original was startling. No longer short and stocky, they were now played by actors who could have been equally uncomfortable (on account of being filmed in Spain in the middle of summer) as Ice Warriors or Cybermen, and their heads were quite visibly bobbing on top rather than tapering up from the shoulders. Thankfully, more thought was put into their 2008 return, but again they're markedly different from previous appearances and despite never being better, this brings us to the main question. For a cloned species (or whatever), why aren't they exactly the same from one story to another? Of course, the boring answer is that different productions have different designers and make-up artists and producers, but how can this be explained within the mythos?

Well, two authors have paved the way for me. Firstly, David McIntee suggested in his 1995 novel *Lords of the Storm* that Sontarans have different castes. It's been over 12 years since I read that book now, so can't recall the full extent of DM's work on building up the Sontaran society, but I clearly recall his description of a technician class, where they have five fingers for greater dexterity. As the book is a direct prequel to *Shakedown* (which had a radically different Sontaran design for an independent spin-off video) but featured the more familiar type on its cover, you can be sure there's further caste variability. The other author is Lance Parkin, whose explanation for a different design of Ice Warriors in 1997's *The Dying Days* (as a nod to how they might have looked if Philip Segal's eighth Doctor series had gone ahead) was down to there being different family groups/nation states of Martians in that era, something which was worked into the resolution of the plot.

I would suggest that the reason why we have different-looking Sontarans in different stories is due to a combination of Lance and David's theories. Having an identical genetic heritage for everyone is a weakness that the Rutans could exploit, for if a virus was engineered to attack Sontaran cells and there was no variance, then the whole species would be vulnerable. But if you have dozens (or hundreds) of gene-streams (you can't have a gene-pool if there's no sexual recombination: there's no pool in which the genes can mingle over the generations) then you've got enough genetic diversity to withstand such a targeted assault.

So, whenever we see a different face or body-shape amongst Sontar-kind (as you could now justifiably call them) then it's simply down to their having different ancestral genes. To support this theory, can you imagine that in such a militaristic people, they'd come to a consensus over whose genes should be immortalised back when the cloning process was initiated? No, more likely the best warriors from each tribe or nation or family would have been chosen, and it's those who we see today.

But this doesn't answer every question. Sontaran soldiers are not known for their intelligence: you usually find that it's the officer classes who have the brains, and the 'grunts' are literally that. But if the officers and the squaddies come from the same gene-stream,

154

shouldn't they be identical in every aspect? Well, if you consider your own body, you'll find that all your cells (except red blood cells) have your complete genome held within, but not all your cells are the same. Your liver cells are different from your brain cells and your brain cells are different from your bone cells, but this doesn't mean that liver cells have only the genes inside that code for your liver. No, your liver cells contain the very same information that's in every other cell; it's just that certain functions were turned on during your embryonic development. Now, think of how we can apply this to individual Sontarans. Supposing that at a crucial moment in the clone vats, you added a special instruction that acted upon the foetus's nervous system. The Sontaran would be augmented from grunt to officer. Both officer and squaddie would have identical DNA, but only one of them would have had the development required for leadership. And if you think that's far-fetched, bees do it all the time: their royal jelly is the only thing that makes a queen a queen; she would have been a sterile drone without it.

Thal full circle

According to Thal history, before the *Genesis of the Daleks* reboot changed everything, there were two peoples living on the planet Skaro. There were probably a lot more than just the two, but history's not an exact science, so presumably the Aals, Bals, Cals, Eals, etc etc, were also happy inhabitants of the world. Who these long dead races were and what they were like has been long lost, but history records that the Thals were a race of warriors and the Dals were scientists and architects. For reasons unknown there was a terrible nuclear war, and Skaro was all but destroyed. When we met them, in those early episodes back in '63, what remained of the Dals were pitiful to behold. Their bodies were shrunken, their skin shrivelled, and could only survive within the metal shells they'd created to protect themselves from the harsh environment. They were confined to their city, as their casings could only run on metal through which they drew all their power. They were barely hanging on to life, and dearly wished to shed their casings and live on the surface once more.

These Daleks, as they were now known, were horrified to learn of the existence of their old enemies, the Thals. This wasn't solely due to any lingering enmity, but also because they could only imagine the extent of the mutations which the Thals must have undergone without the protection of the Dalek machine. The Daleks warned the Doctor's granddaughter Susan, when she was sent to claim more of the anti-radiation drugs for her travelling companions, that the Thals must be hideously mutated.

They weren't, of course, the Thals had turned out to be like Adolf Hitler's wet-dream: tall, muscled, and blond, with dazzling blue eyes and an interesting taste in strategically-cut leather trousers. Far from hideous, they were the epitome of *fit*.

There are several questions this raises; did the Thals pass through the mutation stage that the Dals were presently enjoying? And why did the Thals pass beyond the ugly troll stage when the Daleks required a machine in which to survive? Of course, there's no way we'll know this, unless of course we ever visit this period in a new story. That's pretty unlikely given the way in which the 'Davros genesis' permeates the *Who* mythos, so we'll just have to assume only sixties-philes and *Faction Paradox* fans (of which I am both) will care: humour me for a few lines.

After the Neutron War, the Dals and the Thals would have responded to their new and unforgiving environment in quite different ways. The Thals were warriors, and therefore trained to survive in harsh environments. They lived off anything that could sustain them, and certain rare sheltered areas of the planet over which they wandered were found capable of supporting agriculture. With these more sheltered areas and a better diet, sexual selection would gradually increase the preponderance of better-looking examples of Thalkind, and whilst lifetimes were probably still limited to just three or four decades due to cancer and other post-apocalyptic maladies, they were on an upward spiral and went to the very other extreme of beauty. Whereas the Daleks are scientists, and sought refuge in technology. Only trouble is, whilst the Thals were constantly adapting to their environment, the Dals built an environment around themselves and became dependent on that. This halted any further mutations, but also halted any recovery. So, whilst the Thals struggled through their troll-stage of the mutation, the Dals tried to shield themselves from it and got stuck.

It wasn't just the bodies that were affected by the new Skaro; the psyches of the two races underwent considerable upheaval as well.

The Thals turned from warriors to farmers out of necessity (beating their swords into ploughshares?), but that doesn't fully explain their pacifism. These guys are so totally against conflict of any kind at the time they first encountered the Daleks, that it took considerable effort on Ian Chesterton's part to get them to even so much as defend themselves and their way of life from the Daleks' twisted xenophobia. It wasn't so much that they didn't want to fight; they had no concept of it until Ian struck a nerve deep enough in Alydon's heart. By contrast, the Dals turned from scientists and lovers of beauty into vile creatures twisted by jealousy of the Thals' unjust inheritance of the planet: their ugliness wasn't merely skin-deep.

To conclude with a question, would the Daleks still have become one of the universe's most feared menaces if the Thals had never encountered them on their nomadic wanderings? Would the Daleks just have found a way to shed their casings and gone full circle like their cousins before them?

Eocenes and the fossil record

As has been noted before, *Doctor Who and the Silurians* is a bit of an odd name for a story, given that it features neither a character called 'Doctor Who' or creatures that call themselves 'Silurians'. Their name, of course, was taken from the geological layer their hibernation facility was buried in, but on the logic of calling the unknown by the first thing that springs to mind surely any monsters that terrorise the English landscape should be called 'horribles' as in 'ooh, by gum, 'orrible it was!'. But I'll leave off on that now; it's not as if they made the same mistake again. Well, not until the Silurians' aquatic cousins came along and were called 'Sea Devils' after the ravings of their first surviving human witness...

Of course, their name was corrected to Eocene by the Doctor, but as I've already mentioned (not that I have issues, right) that period was well after the reign of the 'terrible lizards' (more of our dodgy nomenclature: dinosaurs are to lizards as us apes are to monkeys!), and tens of millions of years before the Silurians could conceivably shape the lineage of mankind.

But anyway, the main point I want to tackle with this section is why there's no trace of the Earth Reptiles in the fossil record. Relics of the dinosaurs are so widespread that analogies of all modern

157

mammals have been found (except for a dinosaur that burrows like a mole) so why wouldn't evidence of a global community of walking talking *Homo Sauropsids* survive?

The thing to remember here is that civilised species might actively reduce their fossilisation potential; if they were a people who cremated their dead (as would be wise in a world with massive scavengers on the prowl) then any 'present day' people would leave behind no buried bones. And if the species evolved in a forest environment (as has always been depicted in artwork inspired by their stories) then you have to note that the forest floor is not a 'healthy' place for bones to reside. If you look at our closest cousins, the Chimpanzees and Bonobos, you'll find that trails of ancestral bones from their current species back to when those two lineages diverge and then further back to when our and their progenitors had our parting of the ways are distinctly lacking. That doesn't mean those creatures didn't live, just that they didn't have the consideration to curl up and die anywhere they'd leave any remains to fossilise. There's more than enough evidence from our symbiotic mitochondrial family trees to be able to draw up a family tree of all modern species on this planet though, so we'll make no bones about a few missing links.

But, wouldn't a globe-spanning civilisation of cities and agriculture leave some sort of evidence behind for the Bernice Summerfields, Indiana Joneses, and Tony Robinsons of this world to uncover? Well, just consider how long our own species has been practicing agriculture and building permanent settlements. I haven't got any dates here to refer to, but it's several tens of thousands of years. The most we have from a mere handful of thousand years ago are a few pyramids and ziggurats, some stone faces in the Pacific Islands, and a few standing stones dotted around northern Europe. These are all items that have only survived due to not having had enough time to erode yet. Nothing else of the civilisations of five or more thousand years ago exists (Atlantis has sunk without trace, for example), and even the huge relics they left will be gone in a smallest fraction of the time that has passed since the time of the Earth Reptiles. Five thousand years might seem like a long time, but you can fit twenty such periods into one hundred thousand years, and one hundred of those spans into a million. And there's been sixty-five of those since the demise of the dinosaurs. That's something like 13 *thousand* times the age of the

Pyramids and Stonehenge since the time when there were reptile monuments. And whole mountain ranges have risen and eroded away in that time.

So, with no descendents to use molecular heritage techniques on, no fossils to reconstruct and date, and all exposed construction long since turned to dust, it's little wonder we didn't know about them until they started waking up and getting irritated about all the over-evolved shrews (as we would have looked way back then - apes were a long time off) that filled the niches vacated by the dinosaurs.

Ooh, there is one place where we might find traces of intelligent life in our prehistory: if a highly advanced species used agriculture, then maybe pollen traces in ice cores could hold tell-tale clues of genetic manipulation (trademarks, serial numbers or company logos perhaps?). Trouble is I'm not sure how far back ice cores can go. There were no icecaps in the Jurassic, but not sure if there were during the Cretaceous. Maybe pollen trapped in amber is the only avenue of research?

Refusian invisibility

There's a rather barmy reason for the Refusians being invisible. The 1966 story *The Ark* tells the story of a seven hundred year voyage of a giant space ark, travelling from the doomed planet Earth (which the Doctor, Steven and Dodo arrive just in time to see plunge into the sun) towards the only other Earth-like planet in the heavens. The Earth people found the planet using high-powered telescopes and deduced that there was no intelligent life on the planet. Meaning (if I need to spell it out) that the reason there were no intelligent inhabitants seen on their space-telescopes is because they were invisible. Damn fine telescopes they must be!! The only way we can detect planets from other stars today depends on analysis of light waves being bent by gravity. But still, this is the future so you can get away with this sort of thing by calling on Clarke's Law: 'any sufficiently advanced technology is indistinguishable from magic'. Though I think *Doctor Who* writers often veer more towards Cole's Law and chop up any science into shreds, mix it with salad cream and slop a dollop into the script now and then. So we just have to accept that the people from the 57th Segment of Time could simply point a telescope into the sky and spy on their neighbours: though shame their instruments weren't quite good enough to make out the strange footprints left in the sand...

This brings us to the Refusians, the invisible inhabitants of Refusis. There's really no question about the benefits of invisibility: if you're able to conceal yourself from predators and prey then it's easy enough to get a meal whilst avoiding being gobbled up yourself and you can simply concentrate on finding a mate. Hmm, though finding a mate would be rather tricky unless you used senses other than vision, like smell or taste (which is the same thing really), sound waves or some form of sonar. But then, if you can find your way around without needing to see anything, chances are that you're not the only species on the planet that doesn't need vision otherwise you'd have quickly gobbled up all opposition and died out: your advantage is therefore likely to be shared by your relatively close cousins (just as all mammals, with only a few exceptions, have the same faculties). Hey ho, that's the trouble with evolutionary arms races: they usually cancel each other out in the longer term.

But how can they be invisible? What's the mechanics involved? Surely anything solid enough to leave impressions in soft ground wouldn't be able to avoid reflecting a bit of light? It all comes down to the molecular structure of the creature. We know from our day-to-day lives that some things are opaque and some transparent, no matter now solid they are to the touch. Glass, for example, is transparent because the atomic structure is ... oh hell, I don't know enough about the details but some things you can see through due to the way the atoms are arranged. This can be demonstrated by playing with two sheets of Polaroid: hold them together one way and they're transparent, turn them another and they're opaque. It's all very well saying that about unliving matter, as anything that's governed merely by physics and chemistry is relatively simple in structure, but when you add biology to the picture, that's when it gets a bit more improbable. I think I'll evoke Cole's Law though, and just say the Refusians are silicon-based lifeforms and leave it at that. Doesn't answer any questions, indeed it adds even more (like how can you have a silicon-based life form, it's not an element as versatile as our own carbon-based molecules...) so this one's got me beat.

Mondasian inheritance

When we first met the Cybermen back in the 1966 story *The Tenth Planet*, they were survivors of a cosmological disaster. Their planet used to be Earth's twin, but thousands of years ago our shared orbit was disrupted and Mondas was thrown to 'the edge of space'. Already a rather advanced people, though not necessarily more advanced than our own people back when this happened (I postulate a *Battlestar Galactica*-type situation but with two worlds rather than twelve, an Ur-civilisation on each world supporting each other in a couple of worlds full of primitive cultures) the Mondasians turned all their attention to survival. The people from that Ur-culture on Earth simply diminished (as with the Babylonians, Ancient Egyptians, Sumatrans etc, leaving behind legends of ancient wisdom - like with hippy ideals of Atlantis) and the less advanced human peoples thrived in their absence. On Mondas, however, only the advanced people we'll now simply call Mondasians survived the loss of an atmosphere, their technology allowing for airlocked habitats and eventually underground cities: necessity is the mother of invention. And so, the Cybermen developed to survive their space-flung existence, and human civilisations on Earth rose and fell and slowly advanced under their more comfortable environmental conditions.

But that's not what I wanted to talk about; those are just the background details. The main *modus operandi* of the Cybermen for their first few appearances (before they just became like any other humanoid monster as their very point was eroded with each costume update) was simply 'we will survive', repeating the mantra like a tin-plated Gloria Gaynor at times. The main question here is: just *what* is surviving?

Before you just shrug and say 'the Mondasians are,' let me explain. When we think about what it means for a group of organisms to survive, it really comes down to four key points. These could be the likeness (or phenotype), biological heritage (genotype), culture (meme-pool) or simply niche ('comfy place this, I think I'll simply shape myself to fit it better'). Let's tackle each in turn.

Likeness: well, two arms, two legs, one head and one torso but that's as far as it goes. There are no individual features such as the original Mondas-born ladies and gents would have exhibited before the catastrophe. Survivability factor: 2/5 on account of the basic body shape.

Biological heritage: well, there's no actual reproduction anymore, so any talk of heredity or gene-pools is firmly in the past-tense. Survivability factor: 0/5 'nuff said.

Culture: Now, this one's a tad more complex than it might first appear. Culture is something that can change from generation to generation, or something that can last for thousands of years. What determines the survivability of a culture is the demands and needs of the current generation in relation to the culture of the previous generation. Even with natural cultural drift the differences can be staggering, just consider Sam Tyler's experiences in *Life on Mars*: going back a mere 33 years is akin to visiting another planet. Now imagine your whole world is destroyed, and you and your people's very survival is very much dependant on the direct actions of you and everyone around you. What would that do to your culture? Old values like the best school for your child or saving money on your credit card repayments by putting your home at risk would go out the window, and even ideas like sky gods would be deserted just as the skies deserted the Mondasians. Of course, that's not to say religion would vanish, you'd just get new ones linked in with the changing culture: the Order of the Iron Lung as mentioned in Phil Purser-Hallard's *Faction Paradox* novel *Of The City of the Saved...* would arise to champion the cult of the machine. So, survivability factor: 0/5 for the pre-disaster Mondasian culture, but 5/5 for the Cyberman culture.

Niche: Well, again, the old niches would vanish, and all that would be left are opportunities for more Cybermen. Flesh and blood people would find themselves diminishing in number as the resources required for their survival got scarce - how would you grow food, how would you replenish vital gases? The niche would shape the people, so survivability factor for the Cyber niche is 5/5, and 0/5 for every other.

So, does that mean that the people of Mondas had no chance of survival? Is there no way in which that once-great people could carry on? There's one I can think of, but it's a cold desolate survival devoid of all the small beautiful things that life is all about. The Cybermen are immortal, barring accidents and battle damage, and in that very individual sense, their race survives.

Of course, if this is the case there's a certain illogical aspect of their existence: their downright altruistic foreign policy. They appear to retain an evangelistic element from their long-forgotten religions. They have it hard-wired into their brains that they must survive, and that survival is good, and logically all intelligent peoples should want to be like them. But the way in which they go about it puts them in direct danger - in order to save everyone from biological failure and death they must go to war. Before too long, there'd be no Mondas-born Cybermen left as their off-world converts take up a greater and greater proportion of the ranks. The only survivor from Mondas would be the Cyber-Meme itself, rather than any actual life.

But, there is a logical way in which the Mondas-born Cybermen could maintain their survival whilst actively converting alien peoples, though it'd only work once they were successful enough to hold their own kind back. The Cybermen could then have a caste system, where the Mondas-born are the officers and (for want of a better word) their understudies (who'll upgrade to leaders in event of tragedy), leaving the warrior-caste to remain 100% recruits. That way it wouldn't matter how many warriors perish in conflict provided their deaths are spent in active recruitment and/or defence, and that the Cyberleaders and (I thought of a better word!) their back-ups are small in number and kept relatively out of harm's way.

They would need to install the majority of their people in a safe-house, a deep-freeze tomb buried in an asteroid or alternatively a freighter idling in deep space would be ideal, with a Controller in charge to ensure that Mondas-born Cybermen are kept fully upgraded and protected and that strategies for maintaining recruits were optimal. If that were so, then the survival factor for individual Cybermen from Mondas would be 5/5.

Ah, except... after a thousand years or so it'd drop to 4/5, then 3/5, as over this time the purebreds would still diminish through combat and would need replacing from a finite source. I guess they could use cloning techniques to ensure that the officer caste were all genetic Mondasians and the actual Mondas-born Cybermen stayed frozen forever. Hmm, but is that survival, or mere preservation? Ah well, that's their lookout.

Auton plasticity

I can't give you a full definition of what plastic means, as I've not done any research for this article so far and don't intend to start now. Suffice to say, plastic is a material which can be moulded or reshaped into different forms. There are lots of different types, but the Nestene Consciousness has an affinity with them all, and whether they're thermosetting or whatever the Nestenes can use them. The question this begs is: why don't the Autons have full shape-shifting abilities?

The Autons are best known as shop window dummies, which is their most memorable guise from *Spearhead from Space*, but that's really just the tip of the iceberg as regards bodyforms the Nestenes can possess. In *Terror of the Autons* they've been used to animate artificial flowers (which spit fast-setting sealant that covers the victim's mouth and nose), inflatable armchairs (which hold you down and proceed to envelope you), telephone wires (which wrap themselves around your throat), toy dolls (which throttle you), and we'd already met the facsimiles (which take over your life and install you in Madame Tussauds like some kind of bizarre revenge for their wax cousins!). But one thing we've never seen is a versatile shapechanger.

One possibility may be that the plastic we have here on Earth is simply not advanced enough. The Autons we see are able to bend the plastic they are made from to a certain extent, allowing them ability to walk and talk and throttle people, but they require a production line in order to make those bodies.

There is another possibility. We've seen that the Autons can be made in the image of real people, but these advanced facsimiles are few in number. This could well be due to the complexity of both the bodies and the way they have to interact with the world around them, and therefore require a greater proportion of the Nestene's mind to operate. With the basic Autons, the spitting daffodils, troll dolls and so forth all the automatons have to do is follow basic instructions in bodies that don't have to be very convincing and one Nestene can control thousands with ease. However, if the Autons require a mind, then that one Nestene needs to put more of itself into it.

To create a shape-shifter for the first option then, all you'd have to have is more advanced plastics industries (just set the story on New Earth in the year five billion and ninety-nine or something) and you could have dozens of fully convincing morphing Autons running around and replacing anyone (or anything!) they like from just the one Nestene creature (who'll find it easy to animate the various bodies due to their high-tech plastic). But if you want to have a story set on present-day Earth, then you could use the second option with one Nestene for each Auton, or one Auton at any one time, maybe with another Nestene controlling the window dummies or drone units. All the Nestenes would still be remote controllers, and would be installed in a factory on the outskirts of Cardiff or somewhere, but they'd have plenty of protection. Why would you have loads of the creatures when they've only been met individually before? Well, we know from the episode *Rose* that their breeding planets were destroyed in the Time War, maybe they have another go at setting up shop on Earth. Anyway: bored now. Next!

Sensorite sight

In the 1964 story *The Sensorites*, the inhabitants of the Sense-Sphere are the identical Sensorites. So identical that the only way they can tell each other apart is through the sashes and insignia they wear. It's the closest *Doctor Who*'s ever gotten to all-out racism, in an 'all these blasted foreigners look the same' sense, but the story is likely to turn-off non-fan viewers before this ever becomes an issue due to being so ridiculous: there's no way an intelligent species who communicate partially through telepathy would be fooled by a costume change.

So, how can we explain how a short and dumpy Sensorite can fool the First Elder into thinking he's his second-in-command, a position which belongs to someone of a somewhat leaner stature and snootier aspect?

We know from the story that the eyesight of the Sensorite people is not much good, and only really of any use in well-lit areas. It's possible that these eyes weren't even that great in the daylight, allowing them only enough vision to be able to make out people and objects and obstructions in relation to themselves. In this sense then it's excusable for the City Administrator to get away with duping the First Elder (and everyone else) into thinking that he was the Second Elder by wearing the Sash of Office.

But the Sensorites also use telepathy, and the First Elder should have spotted the impostor immediately. The question is, why not? Well, the ersatz Second Elder knows and fully understands his people's abilities and shortcomings and in dealing with the First Elder he could back up his costume change by subtly mentally projecting 'I am the Second Elder' again and again, so when the First Elder regards him there'd be nothing suspicious, and no reason to take a closer look. It's a bit of a tenuous explanation, but it's more than you got in the episode.

Humanity - the worst monsters of the lot?

And so to the final letter in our monster mash. In *The Christmas Invasion*, after witnessing the destruction of the Sycorax's honourably departing ship, the Doctor angrily turns on Harriet Jones (Prime Minister) saying 'I gave them the wrong warning. I should have told them to run, as fast as they can. Run and hide, as the monsters are coming: the human race!'

Is that fair? Are we really that bad? Sadly, I think we are, but perversely I think that's just nature. Not just human nature, but nature full-stop. You don't get cultures of bacteria saying 'hang on guys, we're using up resources pretty quick, don't you think we'd better slow down, think of the future!' or Lemmings saying to each other 'hadn't we better think about family planning? We don't want to do that whole hazardous swarming thing again!' No, the natural way of things is to simply get on with making the most of what's on offer and crashing periodically as resources or lebensraum runs out. The trouble with humans though is that we've got the brains to break the rules of nature, or at least bend them. We only preach sustainability when we're up against the boundaries of our environment, when the effects of our actions are making the world unviable for our immediate future, and everything we do to try and sustain our present lifestyles is having equal and opposite reactions: we're running out of the resources to run our technology, so we turn to biofuels. Biofuels require land to grow on, land which would normally be used for growing the less profitable food. The result is food riots on several continents. There's nothing unnatural about this, we only think natural is good because of health food marketing. But think about it, dying from cancer is natural, wars are natural (and we're not the only species to fight amongst ourselves for resources - no matter what Roald Dahl says in *The BFG*), using up all the resources we have at our disposal and not considering the future is natural.

Conversely, a lot of good things are unnatural: the clothing that keeps us warm or protects us from the harmful rays of the sun is unnatural, contraceptives are unnatural but free us to enjoy sex without fear of unsupportable offspring, and thinking about preserving our environment is unnatural.

I kinda got carried away there with the whole natural/unnatural thing, but the point I want to get onto is more or less related to that: it's quite natural for a species to use up resources and not worry about the future, and that the only reason we're getting concerned about sustainability rather than simply using and abusing our world is because we're capable of foreseeing our own destruction.

But, and this is where the whole 'I should have told them to run, as fast as they can. Run and hide, as the monsters are coming: the human race!' thing comes into it. In the fictional world of *Doctor Who*, the human race finds a way of transcending their resource problems, and make a break for the stars. Once spaceflight becomes self-supporting, the technology improves and travelling between the celestial spheres becomes as routine as crossing the oceans, then there's really no need to worry about conservation and sustainability. You've stripped a world of its minerals or biological wealth? No problem: plenty more stars in the sky! You've wiped out worlds full of life? Who cares: life's abundant in the cosmos! And if you have to fight or 'civilise' aliens for the possession of more territory, then it's for the Empire: for the good of humanity!

We've done all of this before, just look back in the history books or in the extinctions recorded in the fossil record whenever humans colonised new territory. Every time we tread on virgin land we bring with us the promise of death and destruction to the aboriginal environment. Every time we land on inhabited soil where the indigenous populations are weaker or 'less civilised' than us we bring war and our idea of how to live and tell them we're their saviours. The only reason we're not still doing this in our 'enlightened' 21st century is because we're got no more easily crossable frontiers and the world's gotten too small and our actions too visible for us to get away with murder. But in space no-one can hear you scream. Look out universe, run and hide: the monsters are coming!

ALIEN BODIES: THE END WAS NIGH?

by Jon Arnold

Originally printed in Shooty Dog Thing #7 - Autumn 2008

Alien Bodies was the novel that made Lawrence Miles' reputation. At a point where the newly launched Eighth Doctor Adventure range was directionless and appeared to be evaporating any goodwill Virgin's *New* and *Missing Adventures* had engendered it was simultaneously smart, funny and packed with some startling big ideas. But it was probably the worst thing that ever happened to the EDAs.

To explain why we have to go back to 1996 and the BBC seizing control of the *Who* novel range in the wake of the Paul McGann TV movie. In 1990 the BBC had been so disinterested in the *Who* novel range that they allowed Virgin to draw up the terms of their own contract. Six years later, with the Virgin range selling around 20,000 copies of each novel and a new Doctor and potential new television series to launch the range it made sense for them to take the licence back for BBC Books. They were thinking on the right lines of course, it just took them eight more years and a far more successful revival for that anticipated success to happen. Unfortunately things went wrong for the nascent BBC range from the off - well before their June 1997 launch it was fairly clear that, despite good viewing figures in the UK, the pilot movie would not be optioned for a series, robbing the range of the high profile and potential expanded audience that a parent series would provide. Secondly, commissioning the new range was placed in the hands of Nuala Buffini, whose choice of initial titles was fairly eccentric and by her own admission lacked an understanding of the book audience Virgin had built up and maintained over six years. On the face of it *The Eight Doctors* is a fairly sensible choice to launch a brand new range, setting up the lead character and new companion as well as getting newbies up to speed on previous Doctors for the past Doctor books. In practice it's exactly what the range didn't need - Terrance Dicks writing the lead as his standard generic Doctor and new companion Sam Jones barely featuring, leaving little impression or any interesting character points for future authors. It's in stark contrast to the strongly designed and realised companions previously created for the *New Adventures* and later on in Rose Tyler, who comes from a similar background but is far more strongly defined from her opening scenes, due as much to Russell T. Davies' writing as Billie's performance. In the second EDA, *Vampire Science*, Kate Orman and Jon Blum made sterling efforts to set up the new Doctor and Sam as viable lead characters for a literary range, but in practical terms there was no real immediate impact, Sam turning into an author's idea of what a goody two shoes London teenager was. That lack of direction with the lead characters was matched with an overall lack of direction with the initial batch of books all being standalone adventures with each adventure having little impact on the next in terms of character or even in terms of a potential story arc.

Into this creative void came *Alien Bodies*. There hadn't been an impact to match it since *Timewyrm: Revelation* six years earlier. Both came at a time when the ranges had gotten off to what could kindly be called inconsistent starts, almost have more ideas than a relatively short tie-in novel could possibly contain and introduced big ideas which suggested myriad creative directions that the range could take. In one book you get an alternative (and more interesting) version of Sam, a creature made from pure concept, a sci-fi'ed up Brigadoon, an audacious reveal that breathes life into one of the old series' weaker villains, the introduction of the enigmatic Faction Paradox and, an idea so good Russell T. Davies nicked it for the new series, a Time War. Oh, and a Schrödinger's Relic which contains something you'd probably never have expected to see in the series. But while *Revelation* seemed to come out of nowhere, *Alien Bodies* could have slotted seamlessly into the *New Adventures* by giving these ideas a playfully snarky sense of post modern humour. For a book about death it's surprisingly full of life. After the *NAs* had tied up their ongoing background mystery about Gallifrey it gave the new series some fresh background mysteries and mythology to be going on with. Which looked like a really good thing at the time. Like everything that looked too good to be true it was.

Firstly the big ideas that the book depends on for inherent grandeur are best left in the background. Take a look at the way Russell T. Davies has used his Time War in the new series - it's there to create a mythology for the series, provide some dramatic meat for the Doctor's character and a sense of a wider universe. Despite a fan clamour to see the big Time War events mentioned we've seen next to nothing, instead letting the viewer's imagination fill in the gaps. Davies understands that the more you show, the more prosaic these events become since the more you make explicit, the less there is to engage the imagination. Instead a reference here, a mention there, a few background details and it's lent some depth and gravitas to characters and stories under Davies' reign. Gradually we found out more about the EDA's Time War, culminating in *The Ancestor Cell* making a lot of concepts disappointingly explicit. It's hard to disagree that revelations such as the identity of The Enemy, which had book fans talking for years, were a huge disappointment, but then again in an adventure series such as *Who* it's impossible to take what became Miles' preferred option of never revealing their identity. Revelation and disappointment were inevitable, although it's doubtful the identity of The Enemy could have come as a bigger disappointment.

That leads on nicely to the second point - in terms of the *Who* range at that time Lawrence Miles was something of an auteur, not suited to a range dependent on cooperation for success. His *Faction Paradox* novel range shows that he's well suited to being in charge of a fictional universe - there's a clear vision and consistent tone across the novel series, each novel from *The Book of the War* to the recent *Newton's Sleep* is clearly part of the same fictional universe with a consistent portrayal of the Faction and their motives. But when it comes down to co-operating with other novelists in a shared universe series he's not quite so good - he's on record as not liking either *Unnatural History* or *Camera Obscura* because they misuse concepts he's created. You can see his point - while Faction Paradox's agent in *Unnatural History* is evidently an agent of chaos, he's also less amoral and more obviously a black hatted baddie than any of those Faction members appearing in Miles' work. And yes, Sabbath in *Camera Obscura* does revert somewhat to 'generic black hatted *Doctor Who* villain'. But if you're placing characters and concepts in a shared universe it's churlish to complain about other authors getting things so wrong. Yours may be the original vision but in a shared universe series you've given new toys over for everyone to play with. Given Miles' dissatisfaction with interpretations from other authors it's difficult not to conclude that Steve Cole didn't understand Miles' ideas in anything more than a superficial sense, despite leaping on them to provide the backbone to a range which otherwise lacked one. Miles' more anarchic vision for Faction Paradox is clearly working against Cole's simplistic use of them as black hatted bad guys. Faction Paradox, as conceived and realised by Miles, isn't suited to that role. That's not necessarily a problem but it meant there were two different interpretations fighting against each other, resulting in no real direction for the range despite the superficial appearance of an ongoing plot. Faction Paradox as portrayed in the likes of *Unnatural History* and *The Ancestor Cell* wasn't really reconcilable to the versions in Miles' own work or the likes of *The Taking of Planet 5*. And to be fair to Miles, *The Ancestor Cell* version was just a bunch of fairly dull cardboard bad guys with superpowers for the Doctor to beat.

The range had, by that point, put a lot of regular readers off with this confused 'arc' story. It's no wonder that when Justin Richards took over, he decided to cut through the confusion by simply having Faction Paradox excised entirely. This led to a well intentioned zero continuity approach, but this alienated a further percentage of the *Doctor Who* readership whose pleasure lay in the occasional reappearance of the familiar (not the occasional oblique appearance in a new guise), or the joys of a universe with a rich background, alienating another section of the book's fans. Removing the *Alien Bodies* influence had further damaged the range's appeal and, intentionally or not, given dissatisfied readers a convenient jumping off point. The range rallied briefly but meandered to a close with arcs hamstrung by a release schedule change, the range editor now being only a freelance part timer (down from three personnel allocated during the Virgin days), confusing explanations and most of the key books only making sense if you'd been following the range very closely. Faction Paradox themselves would no doubt have appreciated the irony of history repeating itself with one of those vital works of the arc, *The Adventure of Henrietta Street*, being written by Miles. And, as I've briefly outlined, all of this can be traced back to *Alien Bodies*, intentionally or not, becoming the key work of the early EDAs.

Brax's bit:

Alien Bodies was the novel that defined the EDAs, I agree, but I don't think it should have to shoulder the responsibility for their shortcomings, any more than the production crew of *Doctor Who* in the seventies should be blamed for the failures of their eighties counterparts. Lawrence Miles' book is a masterpiece, a novel that rose head and shoulders above its fellows and restored hope in the BBC's eighth Doctor range when *New Adventures* fans like me were reading the continuing adventures of Bernice Summerfield instead.

There will always be peaks and troughs in ongoing franchises, but to blame the existence of such troughs on the peaks themselves ignores the possibility that without the influence of *Alien Bodies* the other books would have been totally directionless, and we'd have missed out on all the superb novels influenced by Miles.

The legacy of *Alien Bodies* in the shape of the future Gallifreyan War that dominated the ongoing novels in 1999 and 2000 gave us something to talk about, and more importantly, something to look forward to. For a time, it gave strength and focus to a range that had lacked both of those qualities during its first couple of years.

But there was a price: the Time War belonged to the future, and that's possibly where it should have stayed. *Alien Bodies*, much as I love the other books it inspired, works best as a one-shot. To bring the future to the present demands closure before long, but such a resolution could never have a chance of satisfying everyone. It's rather like the whole Valeyard situation again, something which the TV series very wisely totally ignored and just got on with telling new stories. In short, my argument is that the problem isn't with *Alien Bodies* or its legacy; it's that the BBC Books - some excellent individual novels notwithstanding - had no direction or drive as a whole. *Alien Bodies* didn't kill the EDAs by being too brilliant, the EDAs withered and died by not being good enough *regardless*. Do we blame a rainy summer on a sunny day in May? No, without that I think all we'd have gotten was a wet summer without the memory of that beautiful day.

TUNE IN, TUNE OUT
by Nick Mellish
Originally printed in Shooty Dog Thing #7 - Autumn 2008

Ever feel like the *Doctor Who* you are watching isn't really *Doctor Who*? That maybe you've slipped into a parallel world of eyepatched Brigadier proportions and that that most wonderfully chameleonic of shows had become something else entirely? That *The Dæmons* is in fact a lost *Famous Five* adventure? That *The Unicorn and the Wasp* really belongs to *Midsummer Murders*?

Let us slip sideways, past Lumic Cybermen and Inferno-crippled Earths, to an England where BBC Adventure is about to launch...

Tin Dog's Telly Choice

For all you TV fans out there, a new variety channel from the BBC is about to launch. Titled 'BBC Adventure', the channel shall continue the corporation's move towards specific channels catering towards fans of specific genres.

Channel Executive Ian K Cimm told us: 'it's the future of broadcasting, and once again the BBC are leading the way. If Sports or Films fans get their own dedicated channels, then why shouldn't fans of other genres? We've seen efforts like the Sci-Fi Channel in the past, so it's not as if it's an alien concept, but the BBC has a far larger name for itself in the world of television, and we aim to push the concept further still.' Teasingly, Ian added: 'if this is successful, then you can fully expect other such channels to appear: one for Soaps fans perhaps, or maybe Quizzes? Again, such channels are already in existence, but no one seems to regard them. Perhaps with the BBC logo, things will change.'

Perhaps. If tonight's opening line-up is anything to go by, then the BBC have definitely nailed the corner of the market they were after by offering a variety of adventurey programmes guaranteed to appeal to the old and young in equal measure.

It remains to be seen if the viewing public shall agree. Ladies and Gentlemen, we may be witnessing the future of television as we know it...

BBC ADVENTURE

18:35 BBC ADVENTURE on CBBC: Look and Read
Galaxy 4. Today, the children discover that looks aren't everything. Can they defeat the wicked Drahvins in time? Also, Wordy reveals the results of his experiments with Magic E.
19:00 Launch
19:05 Blackadder
The Myth Makers. Hilarity ensures when Edmund's latest plan to get him out of fighting the Trojan War unwittingly leads him to getting more involved than ever. Meanwhile, Baldrick's statement that his

sore throat has rendered him not so much a little hoarse as 'a big hoarse' proves inspirational to say the least...

19:35 Firefly Double Bill

Mission To The Unknown / The Reapers' Master Plan. Joss Whedon's *Buffy* follow-up continues when the newly directed Reapers begin their universal conquest by exploiting the greed of the planetary leaders. But, they haven't anticipated on the intervention of a group of smugglers trying to restore outlaw and disorder to the star system. Contains violence.

21:00 Torchwood

The Massacre of St. Bartholomew's Eve. The Rift sends Torchwood Cardiff through time and space. They land in France, on the Eve of the infamous St. Bartholomew's Day massacre, and Jack must do what he can to prevent Gwen interfering with history's true path. Contains nudity.

21:50 Primeval

The Ark. An anomaly leads the team to a Space Ark in the future where animals are preserved for the future. However, another anomaly takes them even further into the future and reminds them how dangerous it can be to intervene with the course of history.

22:35 The Avengers

The Celestial Toymaker. Steed and Peel find themselves at the mercy of a crazy toymaker. The twist here though is that you are not fighting to merely win the game in question, but fighting for your life itself!

23:25 Quantum Leap

The Gunfighters. Sam finds himself thrust into the famous gunfight at the OK Corral with only a shaky knowledge of Cowboy films to aid him historically, and an even shakier knowledge of how to play the piano to help him survive the days before the fight...

00:15 Star Trek

The Savages. On a planet in the future, Kirk and his crew discover that they have been expected. Trapped on a world divided, should Kirk help in the uprising against the Elders, or is Spock right in his assertion that a balance of power between the Elders and the Savages is just like the Class system back on Earth?

01:05 Quatermass

The War Machines. Professor Bernard Quatermass finds himself in a tight spot when the authorities refuse to believe that the new

computer installed in the Post Office Tower is not as innocent as it appears to be. With time running out, can Quatermass stop an alien invasion of London itself?
01:55 Close

MISSING EPISODES?
by Paul Castle
Originally printed in Shooty Dog Thing #7 - Autumn 2008

Back when I was a very young fanboy, I learned something very upsetting about my favourite television series. It may well have been the publication of a list in *DWM* 158 (way back in Feb 1990) when I first heard about the legendary missing episodes of *Doctor Who*. At the time, much of my knowledge of *Who* was fragmentary at best, and the mental map of the series I had in my head had loads of 'here be dragons' markers. I didn't mind, as that just meant I had lots of stories to look forward to. However, what I learned on that fateful winter morning when quickly flicking through my subscription copy before school was that practically *everything* from the first three Doctors was gone for good. Of course, there were still the novelisations, but I was looking forward to buying the videos with my paper round money and experience *Who* first hand.

I became wistful when thinking about the early years, saddened by the fact that I would never get to see them, and it seemed less and less likely that I'd get to read them too as John Fitton Books & Magazines started returning credit notes instead of books I'd ordered when the Targets started going out of print. If the past was a foreign country, certain parts of it were no fly zones.

Then, suddenly, a few audio tapes of these forever lost stories started turning up in WHSmiths from the BBC Radio Collection. It seems that there have always been obsessive fans of the series - even as far back as the sixties - who recorded the episodes for posterity on reel-to-reel set-ups with the microphone held near the speakers (what amazes me about those recordings, incidentally, is the lack of voices in the background saying 'who wants a nice cup of tea?' and 'shh mum, I'm recording!'). These audio releases were only a handful, but it was the first indication that things weren't quite as bad as I'd imagined. I mean, there I was enjoying legendary lost story *The Evil of the Daleks*, something (with even a lack of a novelisation to fall back on) I never imagined I'd experience.

Despite this though, lack of a sustained release schedule meant that these stories were still well and truly missing, a fact which was emphasised by such videos as *The Hartnell Years* and *Daleks: The Early Years*, which gave us the chance to watch orphaned episodes from fragmented stories. The audio tapes were just curios, isolated examples of what was lost forever.

At the turn of the century, things started to change on this front. The end was in sight for the video releases, and I guess they were after something else to sell, but whatever the reason the BBC started to release the missing episodes on CD. This time though, rather than shove out a handful of poor quality examples, they utilised the most talented fanboys at their disposal to clean up the soundtracks, and employed actors who originally starred in the episodes (most notably Peter Purves and Frazer Hines) to provide linking narration so even the quieter moments or scenes of chaotic action were easy to follow. Such was the top notch quality and accessibility of these CDs that they had wider appeal than a few dedicated fanboys, and sold consistently enough that by a couple of years ago every 'lost' story was available for anyone to enjoy. Indeed, such was their success that even complete stories that could be released in full on DVD were given the audiobook treatment.

So, the question I want to ask is, how can we justify our stance that these episodes are 'missing' or 'lost'? Okay, one facet of them is, but of all the things to lose from a television story the visual aspect is the least important. What matters is that these stories can be fully enjoyed through our ability to hear the actors speak their lines and the musicians and sound effect people doing their thing. If it were the other way round, with silent pictures flickering on the screen, things would be very different. Even with subtitles and newly composed music, such stories wouldn't be commercially viable, and remain the remit of the hardcore fanboy. But as things are, the so-called 'missing adventures' of sixties *Doctor Who* lead a full life in the audiobook market.

TENNANT'S HAMLET
by Jon Arnold
Originally printed in Shooty Dog Thing #7 - Autumn 2008

Probably the greatest disservice ever done to Shakespeare is to make him a compulsory part of the school English curriculum - as a result generations of schoolkids have had Shakespeare taught to them as a literary piece rather than a performed work. And plays very rarely work read straightforwardly from the printed page, even with language as rich as that of Shakespeare. Teachers taught them as something to be revered as a classic rather than be promoted as an engaging work on their own terms. As a result most of my generation saw it as something to be endured, works that were around 400 years old not being overly relevant to them. It's probably the main reason that I've not been to a Shakespearean production since I left full time education. Fortunately *Doctor Who*'s always been a culturally broadening experience - not just the explicit policy of the first couple of production teams, but also indirectly, with innumerable other cultural references, or creative personnel going on to other projects. That's why I find myself in Stratford for my first Shakespearean theatrical experience for the better part of two decades.

This production of *Hamlet* was caught up in a theatrical controversy before it even opened. Jonathan Miller bemoaned West End theatres being reluctant to launch any productions without a star name attached, and one of the names he specifically cited was David Tennant's. In this case that's more than a touch unfair, with Tennant having extensive stage experience, including previously playing Shakespearean leads such as Romeo for the RSC, and if his subsequent *Doctor Who* inspired fame can make Shakespeare one of the hottest tickets of the year then what's wrong with that?

Of course the criticism would still sting if this was a grandstanding vanity performance from Tennant, if he played Hamlet as a variation of his Doctor. That's emphatically not the case though, with only the occasional mannerism being reminiscent of his most famous TV role. Instead it's far more subtle, with a visible progression in character throughout the play. Initially, in the aftermath of his father's death and mother's subsequent remarriage, his Hamlet's wired and nervy, radiating nervous energy. Following the first encounter with his father's ghost he pulls off the difficult trick of portraying what he interprets as Hamlet's faked madness without overacting, always conveying to the audience his intention that there's calculated reason behind Hamlet's actions right to the end.

He brings the same vibrant energy to the performance as he does to *Doctor Who*, which energises the production in a way that's vital if you're to keep a modern audience interested for over three hours. The play's other big draw, Patrick Stewart, is less flashy in his twin role as Claudius and the Ghost, but his subtle and solid performance as the play's villain is a fine contrast to Tennant's often manic lead. Both make the actions of their characters at least comprehensible, almost sympathetic even in their darkest deeds. Stewart's Claudius is a hugely interesting interpretation of the character, rather than a flat out evil usurper he's guilty and almost regretful at his misdeed. Of the rest of the cast Oliver Ford Davies' performance as Polonius is the standout, his absent minded and lovable performance making it easy to understand why Ophelia goes mad with grief over his death. It's easy to notice the performances, the inspired minimalist set design - all reflective surfaces, and just enough indication to show where the scene is set - and dramatic use of lighting seems designed to focus every scrap of the audience's attention on the cast.

For me though, the best element of the production was the willingness to play up the comic elements in the play, to highlight the inherent tragedy even more. After so many po-faced interpretations it was something of a revelation to see that a Shakespearian tragedy could actually be funny, ranging from verbal sparring to knob gags. The play within the play is all out bawdiness - I'll never think of a Slinky spring in the same way again - but there's verbal wit aplenty in the remainder of the play to balance that.

As I've mentioned, I'm not overly familiar with recent Shakespearean productions but this one drags Shakespeare into the 21st century. The language aside this is a fast moving piece that seeks to draw the audience in with talented big name actors and then hopefully to snare them by showing how gripping Shakespeare can be, particularly when presented in a modern manner. It's a daring take that deserves all the praise it's received and, even without the presence of either science-fiction icon, would be well worth an evening of your time.

DOCTOR WHO AND THE
WAR MACHINES OF THE DALEKS
by Paul Castle
Originally printed in Shooty Dog Thing #8 - Winter 2008

I've got something of a soft spot for wild fan theories, and whilst it's almost always a case of 'I love humans, always spotting patterns that aren't there...' that doesn't diminish their appeal. Like the 'Take Five Theory' I waxed lyrical about in issue 4, I don't know where this little gem originates (if it was you who came up with it, drop me a line and say hi!) but it cropped up in conversation with Finn Clark a couple of months back and I thought I'd run with it and see if it holds together on retelling and not a little bit of personal elaboration.

If you know your *Doctor Who*, then no doubt you've already guessed the gist of the idea from the title, but for good measure I'll start from the beginning and flesh it out from there.

At the start of *The War Machines*, The TARDIS lands in London in the middle of June 1966, and right from the moment the Doctor leaves his ship he's bothered by something. He gets the same sort of heebie-jeebies feeling that he associates with the Daleks, and soon walks right into the middle of an adventure where robotic tank-like War Machines controlled by a computer based in the Post Office Tower are set to take over London, with the whole world to follow! It doesn't take long before WOTAN, the computer at the heart of the story, has identified 'Doctor Who' as a threat and things come to a head. Naturally enough, the Doctor wins to fight another day, and heads off into time and space with two new companions, Ben and Polly, acquired during the adventure.

The next time the TARDIS arrives in contemporary London, for the story *The Faceless Ones*, Ben and Polly discover (once the baddies have been defeated) that the date is 20th July 1966, the very same day that they left. Taking the opportunity to return to their normal lives, they say their goodbyes and rush off leaving the Doctor and Jamie to face their next adventure on their own. This is *The Evil of the Daleks*. Now, the TARDIS has been stolen by an agent of the Daleks in order to lure the Doctor into their trap yadda yadda yadda but this is where the fan theory kicks in. The first Doctor made a big thing about

179

sensing the presence of the Daleks in London in June 1966, only a day or two before the second Doctor runs into them. Once the first Doctor learns of WOTAN and its War Machines the Daleks are totally forgotten, but is *The War Machines* to *The Evil of the Daleks* what *The Long Game* was to *Bad Wolf / The Parting of the Ways* in 2005?

You may remember that these three 2005 episodes with the ninth Doctor were all set on board Satellite 5, a news and entertainment broadcaster. The Daleks had infiltrated the news network and their agent, the Mighty Jagrafess of the Holy Hadrojassicmaxenrodenfoe, was using the media to suppress humanity's outward urge and limit their aspirations to simply wonder what was on the telly. The Doctor removed the Jagrafess, but the Daleks had cemented their position by this point and simply carried on through other agents their long game. When the Doctor turned up on the station in *Bad Wolf*, the Daleks had been established for 100 years and used the resources of the Earth to rebuild their race and their fleet, and were finally ready to face our hero.

It's worth wondering whether we can ascribe a similar backstory to the events of *The War Machines* and *The Evil of the Daleks*. We know from *The Chase* that the Daleks have gotten a tad fed up with the Doctor scuppering their every scheme, and it seems feasible that they would wish to take revenge upon the Doctor by attacking his favourite planet. Though they've learned from experience that it's unwise to risk their own shells, so have started to use decoys. It's telling that the War Machines are not much more than primitive versions of the Daleks, with WOTAN as their Emperor. More solid than that though is the nature of WOTAN's control: Professor Brett (the man responsible for WOTAN) is soon under the central computer's hypnotic influence, and he and his subordinates are reduced to little more than Robomen, able to follow simple orders and carry out basic procedures without any trace of humanity. One has to wonder quite how Brett could have built a machine with a mind control circuit, or indeed one with a voice synthesizer when data readouts were still being printed onto paper rather than displayed on computer monitors. No, there is nothing about WOTAN that fits: it just seems too capable of highly advanced technology when the shell is still very nineteen sixties. What's more, all the malevolent aspects are both hidden and as much a surprise to its creator as everyone else.

It's a prime contender for a non contemporary or alien origin if ever I saw one, and if any more argument needs to be made it knew that 'TARDIS' stood for 'Time And Relative Dimensions In Space', not something that could be expected to be known by any human agency in the pre-UNIT era, or logically worked out from the acronym alone (as seems to be the implication here - but you cannot logically deduct anything from a cold acronym).

That's convinced me, but where I'm really struggling to work out is quite why. Okay, I said about the Daleks wanting to attack the Earth without putting themselves at risk, but how would they know the Doctor would turn up, and why are there two Doctors on the scene?

I suppose the same question can be addressed to their presence in 1966 on a straight viewing of *The Evil of the Daleks*, but with more force. There's more chance of the Doctor landing in a Dalek trap if the tinplate terrors have engineered a red herring, as they will have observed by this point that any threat to the Earth will be joined at some point by the wheezing groaning sound of the TARDIS arriving. There is an argument to make that they used the context of *The Faceless Ones* to know that he'd be there (but that would imply they can follow his travels closely, and if so why can't they see how they are defeated?) but I'll maintain here that the presence of the Doctor in the adventure at Gatwick is outside the Daleks' calculations.

Of course, the spanner in the works of that idea is that the Daleks have a photo of the second Doctor and Jamie to give to their agent Waterfield, and not the first and Dodo. Such a photo is a bit of a problem in the straight viewing of the story anyway, as they would have had no experience of Jamie before *Evil*, and they'd only have expected Polly and Ben to be the second Doctor's companions. But if the Daleks had some intelligence on the Doctor and his companions, then it might not be too much of a stretch to suggest that they chose the date of Ben and Polly's departure and return as a time to set their trap. And John Peel's novelisation of *Evil* does have Waterfield discarding Ben and Polly's photos in favour of just the second Doctor and Jamie. I'm fudging it a bit, that that's the nature of fan theories, especially when thinking on your feet. So, to tie up all the loose ends there, polish and present it a bit more coherently, what we have is:

1. The Daleks have intelligence that Ben and Polly's time traces converge on London, 20th July 1966, and they know from a previous

encounter with them that they travelled with the second Doctor. Ergo, this is when they joined and left the Doctor and the Daleks leave their trap for the Doctor somewhere that Polly works (ironically causing Polly and the Doctor to meet).

2. They infiltrate Professor Brett's organisation, and 'upgrade' WOTAN to their specifications. Also, if you've ever wondered at the speed of manufacture and assembly of the War Machines when watching the episodes, they designed and prepared kit versions of the robots for easy overnight warehouse assembly by a bunch of brain dead zombie wannabes.

3. The Daleks provided details of the second Doctor and his companions to Waterfield, and Waterfield's subcontractor Kennedy kept his eyes peeled for them and any incongruous sightings of a Police Telephone Box (it's far more out of place in *The Faceless Ones* than it was in *The War Machines*, where its disguise, for once, worked perfectly).

4. The second Doctor and Jamie are captured easily by Waterfield's simple secondary trap, whereas the first Doctor is left to deal with the more complicated primary trap of WOTAN and its War Machines easily enough. Knowing that he has to depart safely in order to maintain the timeline, the Daleks leave the first Doctor unmolested, knowing they've as good as caught his future self.

CY - FI: THE SIXTIES
by Paul Castle
Originally printed in Shooty Dog Thing #8 - Winter 2008

As you may recall, I'm currently in the middle of a rather laid back marathon viewing session of all televised *Doctor Who*. Starting last March with SDT#5, I've been vaguely devoting each issue to each of the seasons. We're now up to season four, and short of going off on one about regeneration (what's left to say about it anyway?) the most notable thing about the run of episodes from 10th September 1966 to 1st July 1967 is the introduction of the Cybermen.

I have to confess to have had a bit of a rose-tinted view of the silver giants ever since I was a child, something which until now has remained unshaken by reality. But one thing suddenly struck me as I was watching (and listening to, given it's half audio) *The Moonbase* a few months ago: the Cybermen are a bit pants. Until now I kinda regarded the sixties episodes as being at the height of their excellence, with a sharp drop in quality as the seventies arrived (surely everyone *knows* that *Revenge of the Cybermen* is a load of tosh...) and by the eighties all they do is stand around saying 'Excellent!' and getting killed by a most ridiculous Achilles' heel. Okay, so maybe my rose tinted view of them was starting to fade, but it's only now when the lenses have fallen out that I'm starting to see the early appearances with a bit more of a critical eye. And do you know what changed my mind?

'Only stupid Earth brains like yours would have been fooled.' Smugness is an emotion, surely?

It seems that tinfoil and sellotape aside, those first Cybermen from *The Tenth Planet* were the best we ever encountered on telly. *The Moonbase* ones, once they started saying stuff like that, just sounded like the Cadburys Smash robots from *The One Doctor*.

But I'm not going to swing to the other extreme without giving them a fighting chance. I'm going to take in every story on their own terms and have a little think (just a little one, haven't got time for anything too strenuous) about whether the Cybermen have been given a fair outing.

Oh, and given that this is *Shooty Dog Thing* - and I am me - I'll be covering the comics, audios, cameos (if I can justify it), stageplays, short stories, and anything else that comes along. And just to prevent me veering too far off course, I'm going to try and use the following tools to judge each story:

Cy-Fidelity - Whether the basic premise of the Cybermen is upheld.

Cygh! - Anything that makes you roll your eyes and think 'why, for the love of... why?'

Cylly Cyence - Might as well be magic.

Cy-Hi! - Welcome developments!

Cytation - Any notable mentions of other stories (I won't get too precious about these: I'm not writing a definitive guide here).

Cyan - Anything that might colour my thoughts leading to a biased appraisal.

Cyn-off - My conclusion.

N.B. I'll only give a cursory story guide for the telly episodes, but as the comic strips are not commercially available and a little hard to get hold of I'll do my best to do a fuller breakdown.

The Tenth Planet
by Kit Pedler & Gerry Davis
(BBC1 4x25 minute episodes 8th - 29th October 1966)
The first Doctor, Ben and Polly arrive at the Antarctic Space Tracking Station just in time to witness the first observations of a new planet that's suddenly appeared between Mars and Venus. As all hell starts to break loose when the gravity of the planet affects the ability of the station to bring their astronauts home safely, the Doctor observes that very soon they will receive visitors from this other world...

Cy-Fidelity - They're people like you and me who were so desperate to survive they lost everything worth surviving for. Their genetic heritage was lost to a memetic one: instead of their DNA passing down the generations their ideas of what constitutes survival does.

Cygh! - They both look and sound a bit silly in retrospect, but I cannot with any seriousness criticise them for this. Instead I revel in their originality: I'd love to see BBC Wales try something similar: perhaps as an adaptation of Steve Lyons' *Killing Ground* novel, where in order to fight the Cybermen, some hard liners become the very thing they're fighting.

Cylly Cyence - Ah, well, the whole parallel evolution thing between Earth and Mondas and everything that lives on them: even going so far as simultaneous continental drift. Also the beaming down of energy from Mondas. Exceedingly improbable events that makes the science reader in me <sigh>.

Cy-Hi! - The first welcome development is the creation of an interesting new threat!

Cytation - It's interesting that the Doctor already knows about the Cybermen and the origins of Mondas, yet he'd never heard of the Daleks before meeting them, even though Skaro must have been high in the thoughts of the Time Lords since the Old Time. That's continuity for you :o)

Cyan - Only bias I have is that I think these Cybermen are bloody brilliant!

Cyn-off - Well, it'd be a bit unfortunate if they'd lost their way in their debut story. The first of the Cyberman stories is really the only one to treat the central concept of losing precisely what they were trying to save. The thing that's left - machines who used to be people - is the only thing that passes onto future stories. A subtle difference, maybe, but one that gradually reduces them to mere robots that were barely distinguishable in essence from the Cylons in the original *Battlestar Galactica*.

The Moonbase
by Kit Pedler
(BBC1 4x25 minute episodes 11th February - 4th March 1967)
The second Doctor, Ben, Polly, and Jamie arrive at the weather control station on the moon just in time to take the blame for both sabotage and introducing a mystery space plague. Both are caused by the Cybermen who've infiltrated the base and intend on using the station to disrupt the Earth's weather, thus leaving the planet open to invasion.

Cy-Fidelity - Well, they've seemingly forgotten about converting the population of Earth and just want to kill everyone off: didn't take long to diminish to 'monster of the week' status, did it?

Cygh! - If the Cybermen can come and go as they please though that sodding great big hole in the dome, why bother with poisoned sugar, controlled humans and frontal assaults?

Cylly Cyence - Remember that great big hole in the dome the Cybermen use as access? Well, they seal it with sacks of sugar. They'd not be enough to hold back flood water, let alone keep the base's air from leaking into space. A shameful error for a scientist: is this why Dr. Kit Pedler was writing kids stuff for telly rather than doing his day job?

Cy-Hi! - Much as I like the original design, these new costumes are the bees' knees. Also the first time we see humans being used as remote controlled undercover agents.

Cytation - The events of *The Tenth Planet* are nothing more than a homework assignment for kids: 'There were Cybermen, every child knows that, but they were all destroyed ages ago.'

Cyan - The music that's all but the Cybermen's theme, *Space Adventures*, is so evocative and sing-along (closest thing *Doctor Who*'s gotten to the *Imperial March* from *Star Wars*) that you quite forget that

185

the easiest way to attack a well-defended fortress is through the gift shop at the back, as Bill Bailey would put it.

Cyn-off - Highly enjoyable *Doctor Who* but very very silly. It's pretty unforgivable that one of the co-creators of the Cybermen, the scientific advisor of the team no less, should write a story that's not only scientifically shoddy but also forgets the *modus operandi* of his creation after a mere 14 weeks off screen.

The Tomb of the Cybermen
by Kit Pedler & Gerry Davis
(BBC1 4x25 minute episodes 2nd - 23rd September 1967)
The second Doctor, Jamie and Victoria arrive on the planet Telos just in time to witness the discovery of the legendary final resting place of the Cybermen. It's not long before it turns out that it's just a trap for unsuspecting archaeologists and power seekers to fall into, as the Cybermen are not dead, merely sleeping...

Cy-Fidelity - A vast improvement on last time, as the Cybermen are shown to be intelligent and manipulative. Relatively so, anyway: it's still a bit silly. Nice to see they've remembered that the Cybermen prefer to convert people rather than kill.

Cygh! - Rather than include charging units in the tombs themselves, the Cybermen wake up depleted and far from ready for battle. Given the tombs are a trap for unwitting resurrectors, they should have been prepared for visitors at the very least. I mean, what if it had been a military expedition who found them?

Cylly Cyence - The whole logic system of the tombs control desk all looks very nice, but makes very little sense: to work out a system logically you need information to work on, not just a bunch of unmarked levers and a chart on the wall that the logician Klieg hardly pays any attention to.

Cy-Hi! - The first appearance of the Cybercontroller and the Cybermats! Also great to see the first semi converted human, rather than merely brainwashed ones.

Cyan - I still remember when this story was lost from the archives and had attained near legendary status that the elders of our tribe related with great reverence. It's a powerful influence! Looks gorgeous too. These things outweigh most problems when watching for entertainment alone.

Cyn-off - After *The Tenth Planet*, *The Tomb of the Cybermen* is the most effective Cyberman story. It builds on their mythos, and treats them with some measure of respect. However, they're still very much the monsters of the week to send the kids diving behind the sofa. Maybe what I'm looking for isn't there: maybe there's no sense in seeking rhyme and reason when all this stuff is designed to do is simply be an adventure serial of the week.

The Coming of the Cybermen
art by John Canning, writer unknown
(*TV Comic* 4x2 page colour spreads 30th September - 21st October 1967)

The second Doctor Who, John, and Gillian arrive on the deserved planet Minot where they discover a crashed spaceship. Dr Who investigates, leaving the children hiding amongst the rocks. They witness the return of the Cybermen to the ship, laden down with sheet metals. Dr Who is trapped in the spaceship as it is repaired, and cannot escape before it takes off leaving the children stranded and the Doctor an unwitting stowaway! Given as he's stuck aboard, the Doctor investigates what the evil Cybermen are up to, and finds a flying bomb which is programmed to destroy the Earth. The Doctor finds an escape route (using the two man shuttles the Cybermen use to patrol outside) and then sets the bomb to explode in 20 minutes. However, he's spotted making his escape and the Cybermen open fire! He flees to the shuttle bay, but finds that guarded, and doubles back to the bomb where he's counting upon the Cybermen not looking for him. Luckily, he's right, but when the Cybermen have passed the hatch is jammed: he's trapped inside with only 15 minutes to detonation! The Doctor manages to kick the hatch open and escapes to the shuttle bay, where he kills the sole guard by pulling a tube out of his chest unit. Fleeing the ship with moments to spare, he succeeds in avoiding the Cyberman gunners just long enough for the bomb to detonate, taking the ship with it. The Doctor pilots the craft back to Minot, where John and Gillian are relieved not to have to go all Robinson Crusoe!

Cy-Fidelity - Well, the Cybermen have no interest in converting Earthlings, as they call the Doctor, and would rather destroy the Earth and everyone on it than invade. So these guys are just generic baddies again.

Cygh! - If Minot is a deserted planet, where do they get their supply of nice shiny metal sheeting from? They're definitely seen approaching across the rocky terrain, so not from round the other side of the ship. Must have been a B&Q nearby... Also, it seems pretty implausible that the Doctor could kill one with his bare hands: if the Cybermen are impervious to bullets surely their vital hoses should be pretty sturdy too...

Cy-Hi! - This is the first example of a decent Cyberman battleship: all previous craft haven't shown any indication of weaponry: in *The Tenth Planet* they were simply landing craft, and even in *The Moonbase* a cannon had to be set up on the moon's surface rather than using a ship mounted weapon. They also had to use the Moonbase's own gravitron to deflect an approaching Earth ship into the sun, rather than shooting it down. Here they're combat ready!

Cyan - Odd as it is, given that the first appearance of the Cybermen in the comics happens seven months after the redesign, their appearance is still that of *The Tenth Planet*, and remain so throughout the rest of the *TV Comic* Cybermen stories. This is really welcome as I rather like that original design, and the faults with the costume onscreen do not apply here.

Cyn-off - Frankly, I'm astonished. I've only really got the haziest notion of what these *TV Comic* strips were like from the odd read here and there, and was expecting something utterly without merit. However, this story holds together better than those off the telly: possibly because the Cybermen and their plans rest easier in comics than they do in live action telly. High time these comics got a proper multi volume release like the *DWM* strips.

N.B. As is the norm with magazines, the issue date is the final day the comic was available in the shops. *TV Comic* was published every Monday, so the issue dated September 30th was available to buy from the 25th, just two days after the final episode of *The Tomb of the Cybermen*.

Flower Power!
art by John Canning, writer unknown
(*TV Comic* 5x2 page colour spreads 25th November - 23rd December 1967)

The second Doctor Who, John, and Gillian arrive on a peaceful meadow-like planet where butterflies are abundant. There they meet Professor Gnat, who's an avid butterfly collector. However, the Doctor finds a dead Cybermat in the undergrowth and warns that Cybermen may be nearby. Unheedingly, the Professor dances off with his net in search of rare specimens and runs straight into a Cyber Patrol, who arrest him before starting a search for any other intruders: Doctor Who and the two children are bound to be caught! Looking for something they can use as a weapon, the Doctor remembers the dead Cybermat. Postulating that the flowers killed it and two more of the metal rodents they discover, they grab a bunch of flowers each and allow themselves to be captured, getting close enough to be able to thrust the plants in the faces of the Cybermen. This has an immediate and deadly effect and they gain entry to the Cybermen's city, but they set off an alarm and are moments away from being heavily outnumbered! Luckily they find somewhere to hide, and take the three Cybermen who are hunting them by surprise. They find the Prof's cell easily and dispatch the guard, but the prisoner is too fascinated by a flying spider which has made a web in the cell. With more Cybermen moments away, they face capture as Prof. Gnat refuses to be rescued! Well, not for long, as Gnat sees sense. But bad news: the delay has allowed the Cybermen to develop and issue masks to protect themselves from the pollen. Learning of this, the fleeing earthlings return to the cell where Doctor Who uses the dead Cyberman's ray gun to widen a ventilation shaft that leads to the surface: but the Cybermen are on their way with orders to shoot them down with their ray guns! The shaft is collapsing behind Dr. Who and company as they continue to blast their way up, but this just tricks the Cybermen into thinking the humans have been buried alive, and they remove the masks. Our heroes make it to the surface and make a run for the TARDIS, but they're spotted by the Cybermen who open fire. Needless to say, they make it to the TARDIS unscathed and escape: even Gnat who stopped to catch his flying spider.

Cy-Fidelity - The Cybermen imprison all intruders for life: don't they convert people any more?

Cygh! - Cybermen - who don't need to breathe remember - are killed by an extreme case of hay fever. Give me strength.

Cylly Cyence - When the Doctor's melting a tunnel to the surface, they're able to crawl up without suffering any burns. Also, the Cybermen develop a mask and distribute hundreds of them within minutes of learning of the poisonous flowers.

Cy-Hi! - The Cybermen are doing pretty well for themselves, they've settled down on a planet and built a city. Though presumably not one with window boxes...

Cyn-off - All in all, I suppose it's not bad. Very silly, but credible enough on its own terms.

Cyber-Mole

art by John Canning, writer unknown

(*TV Comic* 4x2 page colour spreads 3rd - 24th February 1968

The Cybermen land in some woodland near London in 1970, and shedding the outer casing of their rocket reveal a corkscrew-shaped Cyber-Mole. The Cybermen destroy the outer casing, leaving no trace, and burrow into the earth in their machine. As predicted, the human authorities write it off as a meteorite strike, until Doctor Who, John, and Gillian arrive. The Doctor finds a scrap of metal, and recognises it as a product of Cyber technology! Doctor Who, John and Gillian spend all night in shifts watching the hole in the hope that the Cybermen might reveal themselves, but the silver giants are elsewhere: raiding the Doomsday Bomb from a high security underground bunker in order to hold the world to ransom. The Doctor reads about it in the paper the following morning and realises what a fool he's been! (Duh) The time travellers make all speed to London where the Doctor offers his services to the MOD. The Cybermen have demanded that all the world's weapons are destroyed within 5 days or they'll detonate the bomb: they've got a legion of Cybermen up in space ready to invade once the planet is defenceless. The Doctor's in the MOD HQ and demonstrates the effectiveness of his ray gun, which impresses the military enough for Doctor Who to lead a squad into the tunnels after the Cybermen, deep deep deep within the bowels of the Earth! Having caught up with the Cyber-Mole, which is now stationary, John asks how they're going to get in. Dr Who simply bangs on the hatch, which causes the Cybermen to investigate what's causing it. The Doctor leads a full-on assault, ray guns blazing, and the Cybermen are destroyed. The captured Cyber-Mole delivers its deadly cargo back to the safety of Earth's scientists!

Cy-Fidelity - Spot on! The Cybermen plan a bloodless invasion where they'll neither be at any risk, or have to destroy any of the planet's resources: it's an all or nothing venture where they stand to gain a whole world at the risk of just three Cybermen.

Cygh! - Having discovered the Cybermen are up to no good, the Doctor just sits around all night watching the pit in the hope the Cybermen might come back rather than actively investigate what they're up to.

Cylly Cyence - If the MOD's map of the position of the underground bunker and the present whereabouts of the Cyber-Mole is to scale, both are well below the Earth's crust, deep in the magma and thousands of miles away. Doesn't stop the Doctor leading the army after them on foot...

Cy-Hi! - The Cybermen appear to have worked out a damned fine plan that's more credible than anything on telly. Also they have decent spacecraft that can land with pin-point accuracy (shame they don't have that in *The Invasion*!) that can deliver a groovy Cyber-Mole, and their weapons can melt metal to nothing. Groovy!

Cytation - The Doctor's ray guns are presumably the same as the one he uses in *Flower Power!* He must have been working on reproducing them as everyone in the team he leads appears to carry one.

Cyan - I quite possibly covered all this in 'Cy-Hi!' :o)

Cyn-off - This is practically a pre-empt of *The Invasion* which was broadcast later in the year. Whilst there's no human baddies here, the Doctor teams up with the military and helps save the Earth from a full scale invasion. The Cybermen are spot on, aside from the somewhat idiotic reaction to someone banging on the Cyber-Mole's hatch that cost them their lives. However, it's shocking to watch the Doctor lead a fully armed assault shouting 'finish them all...'

The Cyber Empire!
art by John Canning, written by Roger Noel Cook
(*TV Comic* 4x2 page colour spreads 30th March - 20th April 1968)
The Cyber-Empire is at its height, so the Cybermen have abducted thousands of human slaves to build a city in the honour of the Cyber Controller. The TARDIS arrives just after a huge gold statue of the Controller is erected in the main plaza, and Doctor Who and his two

grandchildren observe the construction work from hiding. However, they have to duck out of sight when a Cyberman lands his glass-domed hoverchariot and investigates the incongruous addition of the TARDIS in the building yard. The Doctor whacks the Cyberman over the back of his head with an iron girder and steals his transport, painting the glass dome black (save for a slit in the front so they can see where they're going) to disguise their presence on board. They fly around the city observing its defences and fortifications, planning how they'll rescue the slaves and get them to the rocket pads. That done, the Doctor scruffs himself up even more than usual in order to mingle with the slaves and organise a revolt. He gets the slaves to pass the word around that in the morning that the giant Cyber Controller statue will be destroyed, and plants a small bomb. Next morning, he sets off his device and the statue collapses in pieces. In the confusion, the slaves start to storm the ray gun towers. Noting that they don't stand a chance, the Doctor picks up a ray gun from a dead Cyberman (crushed under fragments of the fallen statue) and shoots the Cybermen manning the gun. After that, all hell breaks loose as more ray guns are liberated from blasted Cybermen on the ground and other ray gun towers are captured. In no time the Cybermen are all dead and the slaves board the rocket ships: destination Earth!

Cy-Fidelity - Convert, convert, convert! Why do they never convert?! The whole base concept of the Cybermen is to convert people to give them the strength of ten men and never tire. So why build a city using inferior labour? It's hardly logical. Also, the Controller is very proud: a rather odd attitude for the leader of a race of machine creatures who have eliminated all emotion from their brains.

Cygh! - Doctor Who paints the hoverchariot's dome black so they cannot be seen inside, hoping that a black dome would just look important enough to appear to be high ranking Cybermen travelling in secret. But why would high ranking Cybermen do that anyway? I mean, the leaders wouldn't have to hide from their unquestioning inferiors or care what the human slaves thought. Aside from that, how could the Doctor and the children observe so much of the city as they flew around? Try painting your car windows black aside from a slit in the front next time you go sight-seeing and you'll see what I mean!

Cy-Hi! - The lanterns on the top of the Cybermen's heads are used as lanterns! I know, simple pleasures for simple folk, but they do make the Cybermen look rather scary in the dark.

Cyan - It doesn't seem right that a *Doctor Who* story should end with the Doctor and his companions running around shooting Cybermen with ray guns. It just isn't how *Doctor Who* works!

Cyn-off - A stupid premise, a silly middle, and an uncharacteristic ending. This is awful stuff that hardly does the Cybermen any favours: they're weak in mind and in body throughout the story.

The Wheel in Space
by David Whitaker (from a story by Kit Pedler)
(BBC1 6x25 minute episodes 27th April - 1st June 1968)
The second Doctor and Jamie arrive on a space station just in time to prevent yet another invasion of Earth by the dastardly Cybermen!

Cy-Fidelity - The Cybermen want to invade Earth, which is fair enough as they presumably want to convert everyone and utilise the planet's resources.

Cygh! - The Cybermen, in order to deflect meteorites towards the Wheel, destroy a star. If they have the technology to destroy stars, why bother with a sneak attack on the Wheel? Especially when they're still reliant on radio signals to guide their spaceships.

Cylly Cyence - The Cybermen grow from eggs - er, what? Also that star going nova thing: the energy would take far too long to reach Earth's solar system to affect any meteorite activity near the Wheel, and any beam sent to destroy the star would take too long to reach it.

Cy-Hi! - Well, the Cybermen have a Cyber Co-ordinator, which is a bit like having a less mobile version of the Cyber Controller, which begs the question: why not just have the Cyber Controller? I guess you could argue that the Co-ordinator is a less sophisticated version (given the story is set something like 500 years before *Tomb*) in order to focus on the regular Cybermen more.

Cytation - For the first time, the Doctor is recognised as an enemy of the Cybermen.

Cyan - I cannot see how any nostalgic bias could improve this story in the eyes of any beholder. Okay, the chief medic Gemma is very nice, and Zoe is the cutest companion to join the TARDIS to date: but those two factors are irrelevant to the main subject.

Cyn-off - This story does not make sense. The Cybermen arrive in a spaceship which would have been destroyed under normal circumstances. Their plan is so convoluted, even just a few weeks after listening to the story I'm a bit unclear what was going on: Cybermats were sent to consume a vital resource needed to power a laser that is used to deflect meteors, so the humans would bring a crate of the stuff onto the Wheel (with a Cyberman hidden inside) from a human ship they hijacked so they could take control and launch a sneak attack on Earth using the human's own ships. It's a mess. And why do the Cybermen now have a dribble-hole to match their teardrop holes? Are they salivating at the prospect of invading Earth?

Masquerade
art by Patrick Williams, writer unknown
(*TV Comic Holiday Special* 2 pages black and white June 1968)
John and Gillian are alone in the console room of the TARDIS when a Cybermen suddenly bursts through the interior door, scaring them both. But it's okay, it's just Doctor Who in a Cyberman suit he's been working on in case they ever need one. A short while later, they've landed in a meadow somewhere peaceful, and the two children go exploring whilst the Doctor makes some tea in his space-aged tea maker. It's not long before the kids are captured by Cybermen, and hearing Gillian's scream the Doctor investigates. Learning of the Cybermen, the Doctor rushes back for his Cyberman suit and uses it to rescue the two children. All's going well until they're just outside the Cyber Outpost, when some barbed wire rips the leg of the Cybersuit and reveals the distinctive checked pattern of the Doctor's trousers and they have to run all the way back to the TARDIS.

Cy-Fidelity - The Cybermen take prisoners, but unlike *Flower Power!* there's no indication what's to become of them. Shall we give the Cybermen the benefit of the doubt and imagine they convert their prisoners?

Cygh! - The Cyber Outpost is clearly labelled as such with the words Cyber Outpost above the main entrance. Also, the Cyberman on guard waves the disguised Doctor through saying 'Pass friend' which is not something you could imagine a Cyberman saying at any other time.

Cy-Hi! - The Cybermen are no longer vulnerable to hay fever, as presumably Gillian might have at least have tried to thrust her bunch of flowers (which she'd picked to brighten up the TARDIS) in her captor's face! (Okay, I know, grasping at straws here!)

Cyan - It's a bit mean of the Doctor to dress up as a Cyberman to scare the children at the start.

Cyn-off - This is an extremely brief story, so not really much to commend or object to. All I'd say is that it's harmless summer holiday fun. Like *Flower Power!* though, there's no suggestion that the Cybermen should be prevented from whatever they're up to, it's simply enough to escape from their clutches.

The Time Museum
art by John Canning, writer unknown
(*TV Comic Annual 1969* 4 colour pages October 1968)
Doctor Who, John, and Gillian discover an abandoned museum of spaceships and technology, including a dead Cyberman. However, the Cyberman is merely laying in wait and starts firing at them. The travellers hop aboard a mini rocket craft from 2150 as more Cybermen appear, and zoom around the museum avoiding ray gun blasts. They're shot down before long and hide in some empty Trod suits to avoid capture, before scampering back to the TARDIS.

Cy-Fidelity - Does this respect the original idea of the Cybermen? Take a wild guess...

Cygh! - How long was that Cyberman standing around the deserted museum waiting for 'earthlings' to fall into his trap?

Cylly Cyence - When the dart crashes, the Doctor and the children are thrown to the ground. The Doctor comments that it was lucky they only fell about six feet, but even so at the speed they were flying it's still the equivalent as being thrown through the windscreen of a car at speed, yet they were only a little bumped and dizzy. Maybe they had inertia dampeners as standard in 2150?

Cyan - Well, compared to *The Wheel in Space* this is good.

Cyn-off - It's reasonably exciting for an annual story, but hardly going to win any credibility points for the Cybermen.

The Invasion
by Derrick Sherwin (from an idea by Kit Pedler)
(BBC1 8x25 minute episodes 2nd November - 21st December 1968)
The second Doctor, Jamie, and Zoe arrive on Earth in the near future

just in time to prevent an invasion of Earth which is masterminded by leading industrialist Tobias Vaughn.

Cy-Fidelity - The Cybermen plan to destroy all life on Earth rather than convert people. Same old same old ignorance of their original *modus operandi* yet again.

Cygh! - The Cybermen require a radio beacon to guide their ships down to Earth safely. For a spacefaring race, this is pathetic.

Cy-Hi! - The Cybermen in this are, at least until their 2006 reappearance, the most solid we ever see them. Their costumes really give the impression that they'll clang if you whack them with an iron bar, and protect the actor inside from anything up to and including mortar fire.

Cytation - The Cybermen have encountered the Doctor before on 'Planet 14', though it's unclear where or what Planet 14 is.

Cyan - The Cybermen look tremendous. These are quite possibly my favourite of all the designs

Cyn-off - Well, despite the shortcomings, it's still a very good Cyberman story. All you have to do is switch off your brain first and it's hugely enjoyable.

Eskimo Joe

art by John Canning, written by Roger Noel Cook
(*TV Comic* 4x2 black and white pages 5th -26th April 1969)
Doctor Who arrives on a planet that's got weather conditions similar to the polar regions of Earth. He dons some skis and explores, but soon spots some Cybermen. In his haste to return to the TARDIS he loses his footing and tumbles down the slope, alerting the Cyberman Ski Patrol to his presence. They investigate, but find he's gone over the edge of a crevasse to his certain doom. There is much rejoicing. (They know it's him as they've spotted the TARDIS). The Doctor hasn't died though, he was hiding under the overhang after faking his death. Climbing back up, he meets a man called Joe who's dressed like an Eskimo. Eskimo Joe helps the Doctor across the crevasse with the use of a radio controlled gull, before taking him back to his hide-out where he's planning on launching an attack on the Cybermen using exploding eggs dropped by his squadron of seabirds. The Cybermen have detected radio signals though, and close in on them. Doctor Who and Eskimo Joe retreat out the back way and fly to a nearby

hillside using the gulls, with the Cybermen hot on their tails. There they make a stand, using the egg bombs to slow down the Cybermen. Guards from the Cyber-base investigate the explosions, and are killed by the Doctor and Joe as they fly overhead dropping their bombs. Doctor Who advocates attacking the base, but Joe is almost out of eggs! However, the Doctor has a plan: they drop the last six eggs high up the mountainside and the resulting avalanche pulverises the Cybermen and their base. The Doctor is finally able to continue his skiing holiday, helped by the gulls which make a rather fine ski-lift!

Cy-Fidelity - The supposedly emotionless Cybermen all but jump for joy when they think the Doctor has died. It's kinda sweet really, but hardly respects *The Tenth Planet* ;o)

Cygh! - Astonishingly enough, I've nothing to say in this section!

Cylly Cyence - Eskimo Joe has got a radio controlled gull that's strong enough to carry the Doctor across the crevasse. Even with the Doctor swinging on a rope, the gull's hardly an albatross and would surely be too small to support his weight.

Cy-Hi! - You've gotta love the Cyberman Ski Patrol! :o)

Cyan - <Sigh> I spotted a typo. One of the Cybermen says 'veiw' instead of 'view'. You expect the odd typo in a book containing tens to hundreds of thousands of words, but in a comic with a mere hundred or so it's just careless. Really distracts me!

Cyn-off - 'What stupidity is this? Are they throwing snowballs?' asks a Cyberman shortly before they first encounter Eskimo Joe's egg-bombs. This is rather fun and possibly the perfect Annual story: it's ideal for reading in the early hours of Christmas morning before Mum and Dad wake up! Shame it's published in April though! ;o)

The Champion
art by Patrick Williams, writer unknown
(*TV Comic Holiday Special* 2 pages black and white May 1969)
The TARDIS is caught in a web. The makers of the web use it to ensnare travellers in time. As well as the Doctor a human and a Cyberman have been caught. The people on the planet like their wrestling, so the Doctor's thrown into a ring with their national champion. Knowing that he'll not last long against a strong opponent, the Doctor uses his scientific knowledge and uses his opponent's size and bulk against him. He's declared the new champion, and the

Cyberman answers the challenge to fight him. Again, the Doctor uses his guile and the Cyberman's defeated (headlocked in the ropes). The Doctor is allowed to go free after being such entertainment.

Cy-Fidelity - 'The strength of ten men', huh? The Cyberman wasn't even trying!

Cygh! - It's hardly likely that the Doctor will be set free so easily: surely they'd want to get the most fun out of him as they could?

Cy-Hi! - By implication, the Cybermen can travel in time! Shame it's never utilised...

Cyn-off - Erm, yeah. It's alright for a two page filler. Uninspiring and brief. Foreshadows the next Doctor's love of martial arts.

Test Flight

art by John Canning, writer unknown

(*TV Comic Annual 1970* 4 duotone pages October 1969)

Doctor Who arrives on Earth just in time to be invited on a test launch of a new rocket powered aircraft called The Dart by the officer in charge, Commander Knight. But there are Cybermen aboard the B52, planning on sabotaging the demo and kidnapping the leading specialists in the field. Doctor Who leaps into action as the others stand in stunned silence, and jumps down the launch tube into the Dart. The scientists prevent the Cybermen from stopping the Doctor by punching them on their jaws, but are soon overwhelmed. The Doctor finds himself in a dogfight with Cyberman fightercraft. The main Cybership flies alongside the B52 and the Cybermen are about to herd the scientists onboard when the Doctor notices and shoots the craft down. The Cybermen on the bomber are kicked out in the confusion. The US military are impressed by the test flight, and offer the Doctor a job, but he graciously refuses.

Cy-Fidelity - Presumably the scientists are being kidnapped to be converted and add their genius to the Cybermen war effort. I'll give the story the benefit of the doubt.

Cygh! - The scientist on board the plane are able to best the Cybermen with their fists. Hardly likely!

Cytation - Commander Knight knows Doctor Who from the events of Cyber-Mole.

Cyan - Funnily enough, *Test Flight* foreshadows the direction that *Doctor Who* on telly is heading, with the Doctor flying rocket planes and being offered jobs by the military.

Cyn-off - Pretty good stuff! It's probably the best of all the Annual stories.

Watching all these sixties Cybermen stories, it's incredible that they've got a reputation for being a great *Doctor Who* monster to rival the Daleks. They might grab the imagination of the viewer, but any potential they had to rival the Daleks within the fiction is squandered: it's only really the comic strips who've set them up as some kind of galaxy spanning empire. When *Shooty Dog Thing* returns with issue 11 in September 2010 I'll be looking at the development of the Cybermen through the seventies and the eighties, and my hypothesis is that any reputation the Cybermen have owes more to the public perception than the actual telly episodes.

The main thing I have noticed here is that the Cybermen seem to be far better suited to comic strip adventures than telly episodes. In the comics there is greater scope for impressive looking technology and dozens of Cybs, and whilst their plans of conquest are often as silly as on telly, they're far more excusable in a comic strip. It'd be interesting to see whether this pattern continues into the seventies and eighties. Issue 12 in December 2010 will continue into the nineties and noughties, where the explosion of stories in the so-called 'Wilderness Years' provide a wide range of novels, comics, audios and spin-off videos for us to consider and hopefully enjoy.

THE GOOD, THE BAD, AND THE UGLY!
by Paul Castle
Originally printed in Shooty Dog Thing #9 - Spring 2009

This issue it's the turn of Season 5 to be my muse, and as it's often fondly recalled as 'The Monster Season' I thought I'd take a look at the monsters in *Doctor Who*. Now, I cannot just point at aliens and call them monsters; I have to distinguish between benevolent alien people, malevolent alien people, and animalistic monsters. Or, in other words: the good, the bad, and the ugly. And so I have a good balance across the whole of *Doctor Who*, I've chosen a set from each decade.

Oh, and I can never resist the cute ones...

The Sixties
The Good: the Rill
Large and monstrous looking, the Rill are a benign intelligent species who the first Doctor, Steven and Vicki meet in the story *Galaxy 4*. The singular Rill we meet in the story reminds me of the Elephant Man, gentle and learned but considered a monster by the beautiful but villainous Drahvins. Very little is seen of the Rill onscreen, and even less survives in a visual format, but it appears to be a spacefaring Giant Squid like creature, shut away in a tank of ammonia. A notable and very welcome inversion of the 'aliens are bad' ethos of sixties *Doctor Who*.

The Bad: the Voord
I fell in love with the Voord in 1993. The 30th Anniversary Calendar featured a whole load of old monsters that, whilst not totally reimagined, were painted without being bound by the budget or techniques of the original episodes. The Voord onscreen are men in rubber wetsuits with funny shaped helmets, the Voord as painted by Colin Howard were more like Schwarzenegger's Predator. Way cool! I hadn't seen *The Keys of Marinus* at that time, or read the novelisation, but whenever I watch it now I imagine them as looking like that beneath their suits. It makes their villainous plan to capture the Conscience of Marinus and enslave the world to the will of Yartek, Leader of the Alien Voord more credible, somehow.

And The Ugly: the Slyther
Like the Voord, the Slyther is regarded as being a bit rubbish. It's a monster that the Daleks use to patrol the Bedfordshire mine workings in *The Dalek Invasion of Earth*. It's intended as a hideous land-based cousin of the creatures in the Lake of Mutations (from the Daleks' debut) and provided you don't look too closely and lose yourself in the moment it's genuinely scary. The wailing shriek that heralds its arrival sends a chill down your spine if the story's viewed in the right frame of mind.

Plus The Downright Cute: the Optera
Heh, another of the oft-dismissed-as-rubbish ones, the Optera are the subterranean cousins of the Menoptra in the all-alien world

ambitiously portrayed in *The Web Planet*. They're gruff, not hugely intelligent, and move with a shuffling hop. I find them highly endearing, these serious little creatures who live life on the edge. At the end, when they're hopping around in the sunlight after living underground for generations, I can't help grinning: you just want to hug them!

The Seventies
The Good: the Draconians
Well, you know as well as I do that the Draconians were Jon Pertwee's favourite alien, and for good reason. They were the first *Doctor Who* alien to look like they stepped off the set of a big budget *Star Trek* movie. They're superb creations, combining the skills of the mask sculptors, make-up artists, costumers, writers and actors in a way that's unsurpassed until BBC Wales made the series thirty years later. They've returned time and time again in the *DWM* comics, BBC Books, Reeltime videos, *Bernice Summerfield* audioplays and novels, and deserve an outing in modern *Doctor Who*! They're a fully rounded people and can be goodies or baddies or a bit of both, c'mon Grand Moff, bring 'em back....

The Bad: the Jagaroth
When we meet Scaroth in *City of Death*, he's the last of his people, the Jagaroth. They're 'a vicious, callous, warlike race whom the universe won't miss' who Scaroth is on a mission to save at the cost of life never evolving on planet Earth. A highly advanced people capable of assuming human form and living a full human life (Scaroth is married!), their only weakness seems to be the occasional need to rip off their human face to admire their true visage in the shaving mirror...

And The Ugly: Krynoids
Ooh, the first *Doctor Who* monster to be as big a threat to the planet as *The Thing*. I remember being delightfully terrified whilst reading *The Seeds of Doom* as a kid. Never before has the Doctor come so close to losing the fight for the Earth to a single alien creature. The story is crafted such that we appreciate how near impossibly hard it is to destroy one of the vegetable creatures (the seed pods of which always

travel in pairs, presumably so storytellers can utilise this fact dramatically) at an early stage in its development before showing the second one grow to truly monstrous proportions.

Plus The Downright Cute: Alpha Centauri

Well, there's not much competition for this nomination in the seventies, Alpha Centauri with its huge blinking eye, overwrought / excitable temperament, and high pitched girly voice is the only one I can think of. I've not seen *The Curse of Peladon* or its sequel for way over a decade, so I'm not sure whether to listen to my cringing teenage self or my adulating pre-teen memory on quite how cute the ambassador from Alpha Centauri is... A bit from column A and a bit from column B?

The Eighties
The Good: Terileptils

'Terileptils?' I hear you ask 'Have you *seen The Visitation*? It's the Terileptils who destroy the sonic screwdriver, almost making the fifth Doctor cry...' Well yeah, I know all that. Point I'm making here is that the Terileptils as a people can't be judged by the few escaped convicts we see here. Until we learn anything to the contrary we should assume that they are a people no better and no worse than the human race. You wouldn't write off our people as bad due to the actions of Blackbeard the Pirate, would you?

The Bad: the Destroyer

Yeah, I know, in *Battlefield* this geezer stands there and does nothing. Thing is though, we have to trust Morgaine's fear of his powers. She'd not have brought this demon to our dimension to use as an ultimate weapon if she didn't know of his ability, or have bound him in silver if she was confident of her control over him. This guy's a real badass, and intelligent too: he'd probably be reading Dante if he'd not been summoned sideways and upwards in time to do her bidding. Good job we had good old Brigadier Alistair Gordon Lethbridge-Stewart on our side with a gun loaded with silver bullets, eh?

And The Ugly: Haemovores

Pretty much a cross between zombies and vampires, this lot, with some *Class Of Nuke 'Em High* thrown in for good measure. They get the rampaging from the first, the appetite from the next, and the looks and toxic waste element and looks from the latter - and all at 7.35pm! Gotta love *The Curse of Fenric!*

Plus The Downright Cute: Zyglots

We first meet the Zyglots in the fifth Doctor strip *The Moderator*, but it's the sixth Doctor comic *Polly the Glot* where we fall in love with them. Majestic space-born creatures, the Zyglots are intelligent spacecraft sized jellyfishythings. They're gorgeous, and Dr Ivan Asimoff's dedicated to saving them from being hunted to extinction.

The Nineties
The Good: Ice Warriors

On the telly, the Ice Warriors from Mars are usually the bad guys, with three out of four of their appearances cast as the villains. In the *New Adventures* it's the opposite, with any villainy an aberration dealt with by their own people, and any conflict between the humans and the big green men from Mars consigned to the history books. The Martians found a place as part of the galactic Federation, supplying military resources in much the same way that the Shadow Proclamation have the Judoon. Tensions can run high between humans and Martians though, and a single spark (say, the spilling of a pint) can lead to a fight (UNIT and Martian troops having a pub brawl at Bernice Summerfield's wedding) but that's just soldiers for you, it's still happy endings all round!

The Bad: Chelonians

These guys, first met in Gareth Roberts' novel *The Highest Science*, regard humans as parasites, and much as we'd exterminate any vermin we find on derelict land we intend to utilise, the Chelonians do the same to any humans they discover on planets they colonise.

And The Ugly: N-forms

The N-form is the ultimate killing machine. Created by the Time Lords way back to seek out and destroy vampires, this one remained dormant until it detected a psionic vampire waveform in a council estate in London. All hell breaks loose as the N-form slips through into our dimension in RTD's *Damaged Goods*, intent on eliminating the vampire (in this case an unwitting psychic parasitical link between separated twin boys: one a strong alpha male, the other sickening and close to death) and Time Lords tend to build their weapons BIG: think Unicron's assault on Cybertron in the animated *Transformers: The Movie* on somewhere out of *The Bill* or *Skins*...

Plus The Downright Cute: Ptou

Colin Baker's own *Doctor Who* comic strip *The Age of Chaos* from 1994 saw his Doctor and Frobisher arrive on Krontep, meet the warrior princess Actis (granddaughter of Peri and Ycarnos) and go on a terribly important quest. This was a much slated story, but I remember it a being rather charming. Ptou was the cute lizard pet of Actis (like the one in *Primeval*, though I can't recall if Ptou could fly or not). It was called Ptou because that's the only thing it could vocalise.

The Noughties
The Good: The Forest of Cheem

Jabe was one of the tree-people we met at *The End of the World* when we were just starting to get used to the ninth Doctor. BBC Cymru's *Doctor Who* loves to give us anthropomorphised versions of non sentient life (let's coin a phrase: *Hetero Sapiens*) from walking talking trees and birds in that early episode, right up to walking talking flies in last week's *Planet of the Dead*. I think it's rather charming, like Beatrix Potter for kids of all ages!

The Bad: the Sycorax

I have to admit to not being awfully keen on them on first viewing of *The Christmas Invasion*, but these fellas rock the socks off the other Bads listed! Physically dangerous, they have no regard for other life, and their seriousness allows for some humour from the Doctor.

And The Ugly: the Reapers

Ooh, from *Father's Day*, these are the ultimate monster! No intelligence, they're there to feed, and nothing else! Plus, they look very very cool. I want a plush Reaper to go with Am'bu'ehl, my plush Cthulhu. Dear Mr Moffat, can we have more monstery monsters please!

Plus The Downright Cute: the Adipose

Heh, aren't they just adorable! *Partners in Crime* introduced us to the cutest *Doctor Who* aliens ever! And you get to lose your excess body fat too! If only there was a way to take advantage of their creation *without* dying!

IRIS? IRIS? WHO THE HECK IS IRIS?
by Jon Arnold
Originally printed in Shooty Dog Thing #9 - Spring 2009

So eight million or so people tuned into BBC1 on the Saturday of a Bank Holiday weekend to see yet another of *Doctor Who*'s outlandish scenarios - a London bus in an alien desert. Me? I took it in my stride - quite apart from being a long term *Doctor Who* fan I'd seen all this before, the London bus taken to an even stranger alien environment. As a long term book fan I didn't just have the Doctor to drive the bus, I had the even stranger and just as interesting Iris Wildthyme.

So who exactly is Iris? It'd be spectacularly missing the point to go into mundane biographical detail about her, not to mention migraine inducingly confusing. The easiest thing to say is that she's the Doctor's polar opposite - the yin to his yang. She's a Gallifreyan of indeterminate origin who travels in a mode of transport familiar from twentieth century Britain that's just a touch smaller on the inside, with young human companions. And the adventures that she recalls are often strangely similar to the Doctor's experiences, although obviously as she keeps a record of her adventures in her diaries, they're truer than the Doctor's (our fictional lawyers insist that we insert the word 'allegedly' here).

Like most *Doctor Who* fans I popped my Iris cherry in *The Scarlet Empress* (although we'd had a quick fumble during the BBC's first *Short Trips* collection). Sure, she'd been around the block before, debuting in Paul Magrs' first (unpublished) novel before introducing herself to the wider world in his official debut, *Marked for Life*. But back in 1998 she barged seamlessly into the Doctor's universe without warning, making sure that universe budged over to make room for her. Even though we'd barely met before it *felt* like she'd been around for a long time, a fully fledged character who'd been waiting for the right moment to make her Big Entrance into the *Doctor Who* universe. She drank heavily, chainsmoked, listened to *ABBA*, cocked things up royally and loved every minute of it. She brought a shameless *joie de vivre* back to a range which had been in danger of losing its sense of fun. Hell, at times you hoped the Doctor didn't turn her down because Iris was the literary equivalent of going from black and white to full HD. Thankfully you can't keep a good woman (nor Iris) down, and she returned at regular intervals over the next four years, appearing in every one of Paul Magrs' classic series stories for BBC Books and Big Finish. Paul's tendency to introduce ideas and techniques from modern literature, therefore pushing *Doctor Who* into strange and unfamiliar territory, upset a lot of fans who liked a more traditional type of story. Iris, of course, was inextricably linked with this and, as a result, ended up being less popular with that sector of fandom. Even in the opposite corner, the more radical fans who liked to see *Doctor Who* taking chances, there were accusations that Paul was more in love with his own creation than *Doctor Who*, which is again missing the point. As a mirror of the Doctor, he seems to love the characters equally.

Given that she'd already displayed the tendency to shift fictional universes, moving between media was nothing like as challenging for Iris. It's probably appropriate to suggest that Iris found the perfect actress to play her rather than the other way round. Katy Manning nailed Iris perfectly from the first line, memorably playing the character as something of a force of nature on the outside but with a certain vulnerability within. Her performances in the first and last of the *Excelis* plays merited the series which she eventually got. Like a dragon though, Iris knew better than to appear too often. After two plays and - finally - her very own short story collection she went into semi-retirement for nearly four years, biding her time until the time was right for her to reclaim the spotlight. And now, in 2009, she's judged the time has come for her to once again give her public what it wants in the form of a sumptuous box set of four new plays from Big Finish (with a Christmas special for the festive season!) and a brand new short story anthology from Obverse Books. If you've encountered Iris before you know what to expect, if not, now's the perfect time to give her your adulation.

MISSING PIECES
by Jon Arnold
Originally printed in Shooty Dog Thing #9 - Spring 2009

Let's call them Kennedy moments, the events that 'you always know where you were when it happened'. Fandom being the microcosm of society that it is, it's got plenty of those events in miniature. You probably remember where you were in September 2003 when you found out the series was coming back, when they cast Eccleston in 2004, when the *TV Movie* was announced in 1996, when JNT 'raped our collective childhoods' with *Dimensions in Time* in 1993 and so on. If you're of a certain vintage you'll remember where you were when you heard that one of the holy grails of lost *Doctor Who* episodes, *The Tomb of the Cybermen*, was returned in 1992.

It might seem strange to modern fans that we got excited over a then 25 year old piece of black and white telly that the majority were too young to remember, but in those days you had to take what you could get with *Who* - the *New Adventures* helped but we had no prospect of any new episodes. To most of us, it was a new story, albeit one we knew from the Target novelisation. We'd been told for many years that it was one of the high points of Season 5. That's Season 5, the renowned 'Monster Season' which those fans who were around at the time assured us was one of the peaks of the show.

There was a glow of instant euphoria. Initial viewings of *Tomb*, through those ever useful rose tinted specs, told you that yes, it was as good as we'd been told. And then gradually, ever so gradually our illusions started splintering, then shattering. Yes, there were plenty of moments every bit the equal of what we'd been told - the Doctor/Victoria scene where they talk about family, or the Cybermen waking - but suddenly it began to look a little shoddy. All of a sudden JNT's derided words that 'the memory cheats' didn't look as self serving or daft as *DWB* had painted them. You could see where budget and time had stretched the production staff, the wires that held the Cybercontroller up at a key moment were visible, or that the Cybercontroller that Toberman later flung across the room was clearly an empty suit. And the cliffhanger to part one was obvious. And... well, we'll stop there because I do still have a soft spot for the story. The reputation of *Tomb* and the producers of the time gradually began tarnishing, along with some treasured childhood memories. Justin Richards's first (and arguably best) *Who* novel, *Theatre of War*, seems partially inspired by *Tomb*'s rediscovery, questioning whether such artefacts would be better served by remaining lost. And you know, he had a point. Maybe their absence really has made our hearts grow fonder of them.

But then would any of us rabidly completist fans really turn down a chance to see the glory of *The Evil of the Daleks* or *Fury from the Deep*? To journey to Shang Tu with *Marco Polo*? To explore the eerily deserted Underground of *The Web of Fear*? In the unlikely event that they ever resurface I doubt even I'd turn down the chance; you'd struggle to find a fan of the old series who would. But the trouble for me is that they'd be replacing what, in my mind, are, for example, tense, claustrophobic base under siege tales or commendably overambitious galaxy spanning epics. Like most of the 70s fan generation my mental images of the stories come from novelisations by the likes of Hayles, Pemberton and even Dicks, and even when I listened to the soundtracks, the images in my head were those I'd conjured up from the novelisations. It's a world where the zips aren't visible on the costumes, and the airholes in the Cybermen's faces aren't visible. Where you can't see the wires or a jarring jump to a filmed insert. A world where the budget was limitless rather than about the same as the collection box at Eleanor Rigby's funeral. And there's not much they could achieve on screen to match my mental pictures of Mondas exploding, Ping Cho's tales of the Hashashins, or the Web flooding the London Underground. Yes, there'd undoubtedly be some pleasant surprises along the lines of the Spar modelwork in the most recently returned episode of *The Daleks' Masterplan* but such moments would likely be overwhelmed by the limitations of the studios, budget and the technology available to the production team. I guess with those lost stories Target spoiled me.

But the Target effect wasn't limited to those long lost relics. In the early 90s, for the first time, I actually had some disposable income. And oh yes, the video section of the Newport branch of WHSmith became my source of fanboy crack (particularly around Christmas sale time, students have never had *that* much disposable income), all those Pertwee and Baker Senior episodes I was too young to have seen but had heard and read so much about. Those old stories were as good as new episodes to me, the completist thrill of placing another piece into the jigsaw of the show's past meaning I even derived some unfashionably non-ironic enjoyment from the likes of *Colony in Space* or *The Monster of Peladon*. And, although I didn't have satellite TV at that point, those who did could work their way through the show's history with just about every extant story receiving a repeat transmission. The age of home video and regular repeats, where every fan could finally have the thrill of eventually owning every remaining *Doctor Who* story (until the tape wore through, snapped or became snaggled in the player) meant that many of those older Targets were near obsolete. Why read an often word for word transcription of a story intended for television when you can watch it in the form it was originally intended? Much of the speedwritten cack from the sweat shop era of the Targets doesn't do justice to the source material: the likes of *The Seeds of Doom*, *The Androids of Tara* or *The Sunmakers* for example, even though they smooth out some obvious shortcomings of time, budget or carelessness. Much of Graham Williams' era was far more clever and funnier than came across on the printed page, which obviously appealed more as I moved into adulthood and my tastes grew more sophisticated. Arguably the rise of Williams's reputation and the parallel fall of that of the Pertwee era in the late 80s and early 90s is down to the stories actually becoming generally available to watch rather than remembered or experienced via the novelisations.

But the joyful moments of finding fresh delight in previously dismissed tales were usually outweighed by the moments where stories didn't live up to the terrifying epics I'd constructed in my head. *The Claws of Axos*, in my head a terrifying tale with one of the finest monsters in the show's history, was simply disjointed, often cheap and bedevilled by the type of carelessness that forgot to insert the background for a CSO shot. Malcolm Hulke conveyed more of the confusion and horror of finding dinosaurs in modern day London in his brief prologue to *The Dinosaur Invasion* than the TV story did in six episodes. And *Colony in Space* was just plain dull in comparison to its retitled telling, *The Doomsday Weapon*. Particularly in the case of those Pertwee era novels, the better novelisations had allowed the stories and characters room to breathe, far away from the harsh realities of the production line of series television.

I've pretty much come to terms with all this now by the rather useful expedient of not having an absolute mentality on the subject. If I want to relive just about any fourth Doctor story then the DVD or increasingly archaic video cabinet will be raided. But if I want to revisit the third Doctor taking down another Earth invasion it'll be more than likely that I'll turn to the sterling prose efforts of the likes of Hulke or Hayles or even early Dicks to burnish the stories in my head. To let go entirely of the Target fuelled memories would feel like a betrayal of my childhood self and the books that helped fuel my love affair with the printed word, yet to keep them in place would simply be deluding myself and imposing a false nostalgia along the lines of the 'I ♥ the 70s/80s' shows so prominent at the turn of the century.

But then there are those 60s tales, forever beyond my reach for simple reasons of time and subsequent non-existence. In all probability they'll only ever exist for me as a mix of Terrance Dicks' words and Chris Achilleos' covers, and never have their prose and pointillist filters ripped away. They'll never be betrayed by shoestring realisations, poor acting or an unconvincing costume. On the other hand, we may never get the chance to see something simple but great which might have gone over the heads of impressionable young minds. So instead of forlornly hoping for more episodes to be rediscovered I'll revel in what we have with them, letting the words paint a thousand pictures. Living with the versions I have in my head that can't be ruined by time or a BBC budget.

Missing episodes? I'm happy with the versions I've got, thanks.

DOCTOR WHAT IF?

by Nick Mellish (and Paul Castle aka Brax)
Originally printed in Shooty Dog Thing #9 - Spring 2009

'What if…?' is a game played by most, if not all, fans of *Doctor Who* at some point. And why not: after all, it's a fantastical show that has as its very core a healthy investment in the speculative-cum-explorative and it makes sense that academic (for want of a better term) appraisals of the show take these very values as a root for the direction of said appraisals. Or am I just trying to justify my article?

What I mean is, a fan's 'what if?' is not necessarily a bad thing.

Sometimes, it can take one on a flight of fantasy that has no basis in anything bar a writer's own personal dreams, but here the aim is to try and restrain such flights and go for 'what if's that could, at a push, have conceivably come to pass. So no 'what if we'd all had the Internet back in the Hartnell era'-style arguments, but hopefully three forays into the more possible. We shall see. (For what it's worth, I imagine Dodo would have got a proper grilling.)

What if... the Doctor had not regenerated?

It's the end of *The Tenth Planet*, the 'grotty plonet Mandos' has been destroyed, the Cybermen threat vanquished, and the Doctor doesn't seem to be so well. He staggers his way to the TARDIS, enters, collapses, and... what?

First: nothing. He becomes Patrick Troughton, but not through rejuvenation or regeneration or any such means; he's just replaced without a word said about it. A bit like James Bond in that respect: the actor's gone, but it's supposed to be the same guy. Of course, that's exactly what happens in *Doctor Who*, but we get regeneration to tidy this up. (I almost typed 'we get regeneration to make it all more believable', then realized how silly that was. Ahem.) What would this have done to the show as a whole though? For certain, it would have made for a very different future as the show dipped further and further into its own mythology. Probably no *The Deadly Assassin*, quite possibly no trial at the end of *The War Games*, definitely no Valeyard, *The Caves of Androzani* is a no-no really, and you've got yourself very altered plots for *The Five Doctors* and *Mawdryn Undead* among others.

So often you hear people spout how regeneration was what saved the show and gave it its longevity. Really though, its more longstanding legacy was to give the series a unique plaything to work with in its mythology and plots: any show can replace an actor, no show does it in the same way *Doctor Who* does.

This avenue of 'what if' robs the show of a bit of its indefinable 'something'; that special ingredient that moves it apart from the rest. I'm not saying the whole show rests on this one thing, but it's interesting to look at what even removing a portion of its background does to the show as a whole. It's suddenly very different. It may have been a neat way to swap one Doctor for the other, but by having it happen *via* regeneration in *The Tenth Planet* and not as if by magic as proposed for *The Celestial Toymaker*, the show gets an added bit of wonder.

Brax's Cutaway #1:

So, how does the audience accept this new Doctor without any explanation? Come to that, how do his companions, Ben and Polly? *Doctor Who* is not the same as James Bond, as one is a series of connected television episodes and the other is a series of standalone movies. Casting 007 is more akin to casting Hamlet than Doctor Who, as there's a distinct discontinuity between productions: there needs no explanation. But with a weekly ongoing series there's no way you can pull it off. A Toymaker exchange aside (which'd fit with Ben's suspicion about the Doctor in Troughton's debut *The Power of the Daleks* nicely) the only other solution I can think of is to have the Doctor revealed to be a human aspect of the TARDIS itself.

Say what?! This would introduce a whole new mythology to the series of *Doctor Who*, something equal but rather different to the concept of regeneration. My suggestion is that, rather than the Doctor being a pilot/inventor/stealer of the TARDIS, he's an aspect of the ship itself. The original Gallifreyans (or Jewelians, or whatever they could be called) were a highly technological race whose bodies sickened and died, and instead of their essences being transferred into a Computer Matrix (like what was revealed to happen in Season 14 story *The Deadly Assassin*) they were transferred instead to their increasingly sophisticated time machines (thematically tying in with the debut of the Cyberman in *The Tenth Planet*). As time went by, these machines developed the capacity to grow (or Block Transfer Computate?) themselves organic pilots which could interact with the universe through which they wandered (producing a seemingly independent Doctor/TARDIS symbiant that's in essence no different from what we have on screen), or at an even later time managed to incorporate their physical structure within these biological human-forms, producing a Compassion-like entity as introduced in the *Doctor Who* novels of Lawrence Miles (or even my own post *TVM* Master/TARDIS hybrid from a short story in the *Cloister Bell* fanzine in 1997).

What this would mean, sticking to the 'pilot' aspect rather than the 'human shell', is that on the death of the biological aspect of itself, it could grow a new body that would essentially be the same person as the old one (the person being the TARDIS itself, after all) but with a whole new personality (stemming from a whole new set of glands and stuff, as Terry Pratchett's Death would put it) to express through. The Doctor, rather than being the owner of the TARDIS, *is* the TARDIS. Or rather, the Doctor is the TARDIS's real world interface.

Of course, this could have interesting implications. If, upon visiting a totally alien society, the TARDIS considers the current Doctor and companions to be physically unsuitable, it could put them in stasis and grow itself an alien Doctor through which to explore this new realm. What we know as the Doctor could suddenly be revealed to simply be the 'human space' interface, one of many such interfaces living in conjunction with our human Doctor. This is not to say that a Doctor could be switched on or off at will, but in the moments before materialisation different control rooms with different Doctors could be frozen or unfrozen at choice: allowing the TARDIS to arrive in the time vortex and interact with the inhabitants of that realm without being torn apart by the forces there, or arriving somewhere on a subatomic or superstellar scale.

Back to Nick:
To go back to the original speculation in hand, what if... Ben takes charge. Dashing male lead, one female companion, time machine at his disposal... it would be like having *Action Man* travel through time and space, really; a little bit *Buck Rogers in the 25th Century*, but with a heart (bless Ben and his regret at killing that Cyberman; it's a lovely moment that gives him more character than half the companions ever got).

Again, we're losing some of the show's uniqueness. Already, we're seeing a theme in this speculation. Sometimes, playing with the show just shows that - on the whole - they knew best, or at least, it was their combined ideas that make the show what it is today, in a good way.

Another one put forward, this time by our esteemed editor Mr. Castle (hello, Paul), is, 'what if Ben inherits some sort of TARDIS like essence from the Ship, and steps up into the void left by the death of the Doctor? What if this essence is shared equally between Ben and Polly?'

(Waits for money in padded envelope to be slipped over to me.)

Good question, Paul. (Pockets cash.) *[now you really are stretching reader credibility! - Brax]* This would fall between the two other proposed options, really. We'd lose the have-a-go-hero vibe from the latter and the Bondian casting approach from the former, but in terms of mythology we'd be opening up a whole new, parallel, can of worms.

Okay, so we know that the TARDIS has unusual properties. We've seen in it *Boom Town* with its heart, and with something like *Logopolis* with its ever-changing geography, and in some of the spin-off novels (*Dominion* specifically springs to mind here) we see a deeper connection between TARDIS and Doctor like never before. This, though, suggests something further: that the TARDIS has an inseparable link to the Doctor. In some ways, that's easy to swallow given how the Doctor and his TARDIS go together hand in hand. In other ways, that's a big ask: that the two are one and the same beyond any metaphorical sense. What do we make of it?

Again, it robs the show of its established regeneration-based mythology, but it does so in a way that moves the show into different avenues. What would we have seen? A story in which we see more of the Doctor's people sharing their lives with their ships? One where Ben and Polly relinquish the essence to other humans? One with hordes of human-Time Lord hybrids (DoctorDonna, eat yer heart out!)? One in which Ben and Polly struggle with their humanity against their new alienness? The last one rings true in some ways, but it's taking *Doctor Who* into territory that feels like it belongs to a wholly different show. More than anything, this avenue of exploration feels like it could potentially turn the series into one dealing with far deeper subjects than it was doing at the time. Less base under siege, more existential crisis. With their bodies now containing the Doctor, would that make Ben and Polly little more than Cyberman-like repositories for new creations? It's a strange thought, isn't it? 'What if the Doctor died and in doing so 'killed' his two friends?'

For certain, it doesn't feel... right. Certainly not with what did happen.

Brax's Cutaway #2:

'But it's taking *Doctor Who* into territory that feels like it belongs to a wholly different show.' Now, this raised an eyebrow, not only because we're discussing 'what if' possibilities, but also because you can take a story from each year *Doctor Who*'s on telly and have a completely different show:

1963's *An Unearthly Child* - Audience identification is with two human teachers who've unwittingly stumbled into the lives of aliens hiding out on Earth, and been kidnapped to prevent exposing their disguise.

1964's *The Aztecs* - visitors from the future taken to be representatives of the gods. Attempts by the visitors to use this influence to change the lives of the people for the better goes awry and puts their very survival at stake.

1965's *Galaxy 4* - A parable which demonstrates that not all monsters are ugly, not all babes are lovely, and that it's what lies within that counts.

1966's *The Smugglers* - A simple pirate story of hidden treasure and double crossing.

1967's *The Moonbase* - Evil robot men want to destroy the Earth and plunder its resources.

And so forth. There is no *Doctor Who* format: the idea that changing the format of *Doctor Who* would make it a different show is ignoring the fact that this happens all the time: the series positively *thrives* on such changes.

My suggestion of Ben and Polly inheriting the mantle of the dead Doctor is not really any more radical than the Doctor regenerating into a new body, nor was it to rob them of any of their individuality or possess them in any way. My concept is more comparable with developing in a job role: you start out providing column inches for a newspaper and you end up responsible for the whole publication. The essence of the Doctor that Ben and Polly would inherit wouldn't make them alien, but would instead give them confidence and the resources of the Doctor's (and his predecessor's?) memories and experiences. The stories would be about how to use that new-found knowledge and resourcefulness, but they'd still remain the same people. We're talking empowerment, not possession. *Doctor Who* would become something like *The Avengers*, or even *Sapphire & Steel.* But again: these changes happen with *Doctor Who* all the time...

What if... we really had got an American Doctor Who?

Okay, first things first, by 'really' I am, of course, referring to *Doctor*

Who, the 1996 *TV Movie*, which many showcase as being the show made by Americans for Americans. I'm not sure I agree with this. Oh, sure, it feels like an American production with its pacing, visuals and Britishisms in the script, but still it has the English-slash-British at the front in a way that shows like *Star Trek: The Next Generation* don't quite, and it has more continuity in its little finger than *Attack of the Cybermen* has in one of its Cyberconverted bit parts.

What I mean by American *Doctor Who* is quite simply an American version of the show that stands alone from the British one. What would we get: something like the *TV Movie*, or something other? I'm plumping for perhaps a hybrid of the two. I think script-wise we're aiming for the former with the romance and action (something the Russell T. Davies era often goes for) but without most of the continuity trappings. Why bother having unknown English visual tics such as a Police Box when something American will do equally as well? Why bother having an eccentric English lead: has not *Back to the Future*'s Doc Brown shown us all that eccentricity is not an English exclusivity?

I think we'd see the show started afresh, from scratch, with no trappings, as is the case with every other show remade in America. No reason at all for 'our' show to get preferential treatment as far as I can see.

Brax's Cutaway #3:
What do I imagine a completely American unbound version of *Doctor Who* to be like? Like Nick, I picture a reasonably young and dashing action hero type in the lead role, with a romantic interest (funny, suggest that five years ago and we'd have chorused 'NO...!': just shows how our series can change) and a huge dollop of anti-institutional charisma. I picture each episode set in a totally different location, kicking off in an *ER* type hospital drama where a contagion emergency is just the first step in an alien invasion, with patients showing early signs of a parasitic infection are starting to 'chest burst' giant insect monsters. Just as all hell is breaking loose from the latest admission to the operating room, a completely unknown medic strides in and uses a tubular device to pacify the creature, enveloping it in a light web which fades to a stringy bag like we use to carry onions. He rushes from the theatre with the alien in hand, chucking the creature

into a trolley pushed by his assistant who's reading from a handheld computer telling him where the next creature is emerging and noting how the instances are increasing exponentially. Bursting from the OR behind them, the blood spattered surgeon cries for our hero to stop, asking who he was: 'I'm the Doctor, sorry, must dash!' before he and his gorgeous and totally in charge assistant pulls both him and the trolley into the elevator. Of course, the invasion is averted as they learn more about the creatures and what can prevent infections (water, with the fire dept. hosing down the city and its inhabitants much to the chagrin of the officials and the Doctor's delight). Next week we see the Doctor in a steampunk wild west with *Transformers*-type robot monsters (yes, just like the film *Wild Wild West*) with no explanation of how they got there, the following week they're in Afganistan battling giant centipedes that live in the mountains, the week after they're on Mars the day the first humans make planetfall, trying to prevent a war between the Earth and the Martians. Week after, it's *Frankenstein*, then the War of Independence with zombies, then Bigfoot in the mountains, etc etc etc. Standalone episodes, with the only link being the two leads coming from nowhere to save the day and vanish just as suddenly. After a few weeks we encounter a government agency tracking them, aided by teleporting Dalek-like creatures who claim to be enforcers from the future tracking down rogue elements. As the series progresses, we see the Daleks get deeper into the heart of American security services, and the penultimate episode sees the Doctor fall into an FBI trap. Of course, the end of this episode reveals the true nature of the Daleks, and the Earth is invaded, *Independence Day* style, and only the Doctor can save the day! But he's imprisoned deep under Area 51...

That's how I picture an American *Doctor Who* series: just 12 episodes to start with, like a cross between *Quantum Leap* and *The X-Files*, with an action movie homage thrown in.

Back to Nick:

How different would the show be without the Police Box, the English lead, the Home Counties landings? Well, very different in terms of production values I guess; I envision something akin to *ALIAS* in its look and target audience - a technologically-orientated show, perhaps, with young people very much the focus, and love stories and broken hearts aplenty.

As for the lead... in my mind, I've got Brendan Fraser running around the place in his *Inkheart* guise and get up: all bookish, actionish and romantic. I actually rather like this idea, but then again I rather like Fraser and he'd be my choice if we ever had an American lead. I think it's the McGann vibe he gives off in *Inkheart* that does it (and, indeed, McGann's 'eccentric Brit' costume is, for me, the most American thing about his sole outing, displaying the stereotypical notion of the Doctor as an antiquated eccentric British alien).

I digress. We'd have ourselves a very different show by necessity of location, which again shows us how something so basic in *Doctor Who* - the fact it is made in Britain - makes for a very different show when taken elsewhere. Something like *The Office*, as far as I am concerned, works equally well in its British and American versions, but I'm not sure *Doctor Who* would, or at least I think the changes made would be far greater than those made in something like *The Office*. That's not to say an American audience wouldn't appreciate or understand a hero like the Doctor: of course not; that would be a terribly patronizing view to take. It's more that the TV made in this genre Stateside tends to veer in very different directions to *Who*: that's not a bad thing, just an observation.

Icons aside, would we be looking at the standard twenty-two forty-five minute episodes for a season? Would that enable greater arcs *a la* shows such as *Veronica Mars*, *Buffy the Vampire Slayer*, and so on? Well, yes, of course it would, and I cannot see the show not doing this. Indeed, it's already doing it in its slimmer incarnation in reality.

I'm picturing a time travel-based *ALIAS* with Brendan Fraser overall though. I'm sure that America could produce a show like *Doctor Who* as it is produced over here, I'm just not sure they'd want to.

Hang on a minute though, what about the most pressing concern (for a fan, at least): what the hell would this do to established continuity?! We'd be buggered. Not even Lance Parkin could save us!

What if... it was strictly TV only?

A more implausible one this one I realize, but please, stick with me. What would our perceptions of certain Doctors be without the aid of the comics, books, audio adventures, and so on? Paul McGann for instance: without the above trinity of formats, what would any of us think about the eighth Doctor?

I only ask as, when asked recently who my favourite Doctor was, I was tempted to shove McGann high up there and watched the *TVM* soon afterwards to remind myself why. I watched it; I could not see why. Sixty-odd minutes of McGann being admittedly good is not the reason I like him so much. It's the countless Big Finish productions and the comics (*especially* the comics) that do, the books to a lesser extent as they vary greatly in quality and don't ever seem quite certain who the eighth Doctor is.

This is the most fannish 'what if' of them all I guess, but the idea of a Whoniverse minus Beep the Meep, *Spare Parts*, Colin Baker's blue costume, Izzy Sinclair and *Alien Bodies* is a far smaller and sadder world.

Now, *Doctor Who* thrives and belongs on TV primarily, I have no quibbles on that front, and you don't need to know of any of the spin-offs to enjoy the show either. Take, for example, *Star Wars*. I know the films, and that's enough for me: no books, comics, animations, or anything extra appear in my knowledge of the series, nor do I long to know about them, but - and this is the crucial thing, I suppose - the idea of the series *without* these additions is alien to me. I expect shows to have spin-off media. Hell, even *Primeval* has spin-off books and action figures!

For the old-school fan especially, the idea of a world minus Target novelisations or that *State of Decay* audiobook is a strange and not entirely welcoming one. What impact would that have had upon the older fans? I think we'd see a lot less love for Troughton, many having fallen for the second Doctor through the medium of the written word alone. I think RTD's era of the show would have been radically different: would we have had Rob Shearman's *Dalek*, Nicholas Briggs's voices, or half the writers we got? Possibly. Possibly not. I'm hedging my bets for the latter.

I think *Doctor Who Magazine* would be a very different beast, too, its comic being very much a staple part of the publication for years now. I think Doctors six, seven and eight would have far fewer fans going by their television performances alone, people still citing the audio adventures, books and comics and/or audio adventures respectively as housing the definitive versions of those latter day Doctors.

What if, indeed? It's hard to imagine. Bizarrely, I think this one has the greatest impact of them all so far.

What if... it was 'Doctor Who?' Instead of 'Doctor Who'?

It would solve a lot of tedious arguing over credits and names and so on. And there we have it. I'm just playing round the edges; there are far more interesting 'what if's to be done, I am sure. What if we had never had any of the Missing Episodes returned? What if the Pertwee era had carried on *a la* Season Seven? What if, what if, what if... such is the world of fandom; the 'what if's can go on forever, a lot like the show itself really. I told you they were cut from the same cloth.

I can see it, though: that darker amalgamation somewhere between Season Twelve and Thirteen where Tom Baker is replaced by Brendan Fraser between episodes to play the new Doctor Who/Doctor?/The Doctor/Who The Hell Is He Anyway, and no one writes anything bar the television series at all.

I take a step back from the threshold into the alternate. I'm very happy with what we've got instead.

Brax's Cutaway #4:

What if there was no *Doctor Who* TV series after those initial 13 weeks on telly, but instead the Peter Cushing Dalek films had continued as a British Institution, with a handful of movies every decade up to the present day? The Doctor would be recast a la James Bond, and the movies would change with the times, with the style of the sixties (after finding that it's Daleks behind things *At the Earth's Core*, naturally!) passing on to rival *Star Trek* in style (with Daleks instead of Klingons) in the seventies. The eighties could team Dr Who and his grandchildren / nieces up against a Dalek Empire a la *Star Wars* and *Battlestar Galactica* (with the survivors of an invasion of the colonies fleeing to Earth in a rag tag fleet of ships) passing into *X-Files* territory in the nineties: are the Daleks on Earth at the end of the twentieth century? Are the people who're starting to mutate and disappear turning into Daleks, or is the Government making their own loyal to Earth Dalek machines?

The noughties would go for a reboot/origin vibe, tackling things like who Dr. Who was and what the origins of the Daleks were. It might even follow the path of *Battlestar Galactica* and go for a complete re-imagining, where the Daleks are engineered-human deep-space agents who've decided they're better than their creators.

SEASON OF MISTS
by Paul Castle
Originally printed in Shooty Dog Thing #9 - Spring 2009

If you're a fan, you know what we're like when it comes to arguing about details that don't matter in the slightest. We're a broad church, and that brings a great deal of differing conceptions about the show. I think I understand now precisely what it means to have the devil in the detail. In fandom, just as it is in religion, it's the issues that are insignificant to the point of incomprehensibility to outsiders that cause the more bitter and vehemous arguments. But these arguments are getting old, and I'll scream next time I find myself drawn to another canon debate. What we need is something new to divide us.

One thing which is looking topical is that Steven Moffat apparently doesn't like the way his first series of *Doctor Who* is called Series 5, preferring Season 31. Yeah yeah, I know, old story - it's just the 'Season 27' debate five years on - and the easiest way to deal with it is to let people call their seasons of *Doctor Who* just what they want to.

But that isn't quite what I want to stir up. The thing is, we've all gotten used to the 'classic' series being divided up into 26 discrete seasons, with the first starting with the episode *An Unearthly Child* and ending with the final part of *The Reign of Terror*, and the last running from *Battlefield* to *Survival*. But it's not as simple as that. The whole concept of seasons is an eighties imposition on the past and does not always reflect how *Doctor Who* was made or broadcast. It's completely arbitrary but so well ingrained in our perceptions of the series that it's the one thing that we agree on. But we only agree on it because we never think about it.

Consider the following facts: Season 2 started a mere seven weeks after Season 1 finished, and Season 3 followed Season 2 by... Hang on, this is going to get confusing. Let's do a list of the gaps:

Prisoners of Conciergerie (Sept 12th) to *Planet of Giants* (Oct 31st 1964) = 7 weeks.

Checkmate (July 24th) to *Four Hundred Dawns* (Sept 11th 1965) = 7 weeks.

The War Machines 4 (July 16th) to *The Smugglers* 1 (Sept 10th 1966) = 8 weeks.

The Evil of the Daleks 7 (July 1st) to *The Tomb of the Cybermen* 1 (Sept 2nd 1967) = 9 weeks.

Yeah yeah, I know what you're thinking: Back in the sixties *Doctor Who* used to be on week in week out for pretty much the whole year, with season lengths running into the forties. But the main point I want to introduce here is that *Doctor Who* was not thought about in terms of seasons at that time, and it's more telling to think of them in production blocks, where the boundaries between our seasons are blurred (for instance, the first production block runs from *An Unearthly Child* up to *Flashpoint* (aka *The Dalek Invasion of Earth* 6) another runs from *The Invasion* to *The War Games*, and the first Tom Baker story is in the same production block as the one that started with *Invasion of the Dinosaurs* from Pertwee's final year. Stylistically, these groupings make sense.

The Wheel in Space 6 (June 1st) to *The Dominators* 1 (Aug 10th 1968) = 10 weeks.

The Mind Robber 5 (Oct 12th) to *The Invasion* 1 (Nov 2nd 1968) = 3 weeks.

Now, this is an interesting one. The so-called sixth season of *Doctor Who* kicked off with *The Dominators* ten weeks after the concluding episode of *The Wheel in Space*, but the actual gap between the two stories is only three weeks due to another showing of *The Evil of the Daleks*. This repeat is notable because it's led into by the same kind of cliff-hanger as was used to introduce the Macra at the end of *The Moonbase* a couple of years previously, and the first episode was modified to reinforce its place after *Wheel*, with the narrative device of the Doctor introducing the first episode to Zoe. At the start of *The Dominators*, Zoe asks if there was any danger of there being Daleks or Cybermen about. To all intents and purposes, the transmission break between Season 5 and Season 6 is the same length as the break between *The Mind Robber* and *The Invasion* ten weeks later, which are traditionally considered to be in the same season.

The War Games 10 (June 21st) to *Spearhead from Space* 1 (Jan 3rd 1970) = 28 weeks.

(The Pertwee years follow the same pattern as the above entry, give or take.)

Now, this is where it becomes more recognisably seasonal. After seven years, the programme is promoted to colour, and the season length is reduced by roughly 50% to pay for it. *Doctor Who* ceases to be a year-round mainstay of Saturday teatimes, instead running from the New Year to just before the Summer holidays. Oh what a long time the period of July thru December must have felt to those early fans! Well, they survived in the same way I did in the eighties: plenty more fish in the sea / absence makes the heart grow fonder / a change is as good as a rest etc etc! Oh, if only they'd give us a rest from *Eastenders* for half the year...

Revenge of the Cybermen 4 (May 10th) to *Terror of the Zygons* 1 (Aug 30th 1975) = 16 weeks.

Along comes Tom Baker, and although his first series is the shortest run of episodes so far, this is made up for by the change in term for his second series. *Doctor Who* moves to the scarier Autumn/Winter evenings slot, where the house is dark and spooky when you have to go to bed straight after. Brrrr!

The Android Invasion 4 (Dec 13th) to *The Brain of Morbius* 1 (Jan 3rd 1976) = 3 weeks.

The Seeds of Doom 6 (March 6th) to *The Masque of Mandragora* (Sept 4th 1976) = 26 weeks.

The Deadly Assassin 4 (Nov 20th) to *The Face of Evil* 1 (Jan 1st 1977) = 6 weeks.

The Talons of Weng-Chiang 6 (April 2nd) to *Horror of Fang Rock* 1 (Sept 3rd 1977) = 22 weeks.

The Sunmakers 4 (Dec 17th) to *Underworld* 1 (Jan 7th 1978) = 3 weeks.

And now we come to the main thrust of the argument that what we regard years later as discretely packaged 'seasons' is a construct invented by Jean Marc-Lofficier for his first *Doctor Who Programme Guide* in the early eighties. *The Brain of Morbius*, *The Face of Evil*, and *Underworld* were promoted by the *Radio Times* and the trailers on the telly as much of a New Series as the more 'traditional' openers *Terror of the Zygons*, *The Masque of Mandragora*, and *Horror of Fang Rock*. What makes the idea that *The Face of Evil* is the first in a new series absurd, despite the lengthy break for Christmas, the resumption on New

Year's Day (New Year, New Series!) and the introduction of a new companion, is purely because we're so accustomed to it being a direct continuation from the previous story in our much valued episode guides: it just goes to show what an influence the media can have on our lives without our even noticing.

The Invasion of Time 6 (March 11th) to *The Ribos Operation* 1 (Sept 2nd 1978) = 25 weeks.

The Armageddon Factor 6 (Feb 24th) to *Destiny of the Daleks* 1 (Sept 1st 1979) = 27 weeks.

The Horns of Nimon 4 (Jan 12th) to *The Leisure Hive* 1 (30th Aug 1980) = 33 weeks.

Hooray! *Doctor Who* no longer breaks for Christmas! Once more, as with the Pertwee years, the run of transmitted episodes corresponds to our idea of season.

State of Decay 4 (Dec 13th) to *Warriors' Gate* 1 (Jan 3rd 1981) = 3 weeks.

Well, aside from a brief blip, which comes a third of the way through what we've had marketed at us since its first video release as 'The E-Space Trilogy'. The whims of the schedulers, eh?

Logopolis 4 (March 21st) to *Castrovalva* 1 (Jan 4th 1982) = 42 weeks.

Time-Flight 4 (March 30th) to *Arc of Infinity* 1 (Jan 3rd 1983) = 40 weeks.

The King's Demons 2 (March 16th) to *The Five Doctors* (Nov 25th 1983) = 36 weeks.

Now shown twice weekly, the gap between series is immense! It's now a Spring-only series, *sob*. But you can see where the idea of discrete seasons of *Doctor Who* gets cemented in our minds. Coming at the end of a five year period of recognisably season-like series, the twentieth anniversary corresponds with the new official *Programme Guide*'s grouping together of the history of the series into twenty 'seasons'. The history of the series is finally authorised, filed, stamped, indexed, briefed, debriefed and numbered. The age of fandom had truly arrived.

The Five Doctors (Nov 25th) to *Warriors of the Deep* 1 (Jan 5th 1984) = 6 weeks.

Interestingly enough, despite there being 36 weeks between Season 20 and *The Five Doctors*, and only 6 weeks between *The Five Doctors* and Season 21, the anniversary special is always placed within Season 20 in the *Programme Guide*. Probably because '20th Anniversary' sounds more Season 20 than Season 21. The idea I'm trying to get across here is that it doesn't need to be in either.

The Twin Dilemma 4 (March 30th) to *Attack of the Cybermen* 1 (Jan 5th 1985) = 40 weeks.

Revelation of the Daleks 2 (Mar 30th) to The Trial of a Time Lord 1 (6th Sept 1986) = 75 weeks.

The oft decried 18 month hiatus was nothing more than a delay from a Spring transmission to an Autumn one. Oh what a massive fuss that was made!

The Trial of a Time Lord 14 (Dec 6th) to *Time and the Rani* 1 (Sept 7th 1987) = 39 weeks.

(The McCoy years follow the same pattern as the above entry, give or take.)

The final four years of the original 26 year run of *Doctor Who* found a home in the Autumn schedules. Though what it was scheduled against for the latter half of that effectively killed it, so it was taken into care and fostered out to publishing companies for years after.

And so we come to the new series, which started off a new run after 15 years absence from our screens (specials aside). There is no question that these are made in seasons, though to confuse the matter they're referred to as Series 1, Series 2 etc. So, things have settled down and it's easy now, huh? Nope. We've got the Christmas specials. Well, that's easy, those are simply regarded as part of the forthcoming series from the Spring. But then there's the 2009 specials, which are classed as part of the same series as the 2007 Christmas special thru the 2008 episodes, making a mockery of the very concept of series: the Series 4 DVD Boxed Set was out in the shops before they even finished writing the 2009 episodes, despite being in the same series officially.

Understand that I'm not writing this to provide any solution to the 'problem', my aim here is to point out the fundamental nonsensicality of using seasons and series to mean anything solid. These are purely constructs that have no more grounding in reality than geological timezones like the Permian, Cambrian, Jurassic etc. They're not anything that existed at the time, but are there to define eras into studyable - or indeed marketable - chunks.

But, turning this on its head, doesn't the idea of *Doctor Who* being split up into manageable groupings of stories help us keep track of things. It is, after all, far easier to recall what stories are in Season 5 than were broadcast in 1967, especially when things weren't as clear cut as that: 1967's *Doctor Who* starts halfway through Season 4's *The Highlanders* and ends a third of the way into Season 5's *The Enemy of the World*. It's obviously not helpful to think of the 1967 run in the same way than when considering the 1984 series.

Another argument for keeping the current season structure when thinking about the twentieth century series is that it's damn near universally accepted, and those who don't like it know it as well as everyone else. Changing things for the sake of a few quibblers like me would be like restructuring the entire English language to replace words like 'creature' with something with a more scientific and less religious root. But as that's simply absurd and smacks of the same sort of zealotry as the feminist opposition to any word with 'man' in it. But that does not mean that it's rational, or should be regarded as one of the laws of nature or anything. It's just shorthand for something which'll make day to day discussions bang-your-head-on-the-desk difficult if it suddenly popped out of existence. So, just for the sake of not being an arse, the season structure is here to stay without further noise from me. Well, not much, anyway.

Just remember: Season 5 doesn't actually mean anything in terms of transmission breaks between series of *Doctor Who*. Well, not much, anyway: it's just fans fudging it.

But, what else do we take for granted or on received wisdom without ever thinking about it? Question everything, respect nothing.

SHORT TRIPS: THE END OF THE ROAD
by Jon Arnold
Originally printed in Shooty Dog Thing #10 - Summer 2009

You might not have noticed it, or even thought about it if you had, but in May 2009 a long running era of *Doctor Who* quietly died. With relatively little fanfare Big Finish announced in April that the twenty-ninth *Short Trips* book, *Re:Collections*, would be a greatest hits collection that would mark the end of the six and a half year old series. And with it ended the last continuing strand of original written fiction based on the original run of *Doctor Who*. Eighteen years after the first *New Adventure*, thirty six after the Target books, there were no forthcoming books concerning the adventures of any of the first eight Doctors. And it passed with little comment bar discussions on who was filling the gaps in their *Short Trips* collection, and how many they needed to finish it. It might have been nostalgia (or N*A*stalgia) but there was part of me saddened by what had been one of the most creatively vibrant eras of *Doctor Who* ending. And part of me that cursed the audio adventures winning the ancient books vs audios arguments by default. Yeah, old loyalties die hard.

Short Trips, if we're honest, was always a pretty bland name for a book, never mind a range. It felt like a name given to a book as a placeholder until someone came up with a better, more exciting title. Except, of course, no-one ever did come up with a title with some excitement, a little zing. I might be well off course, but it seemed indicative of the fairly unimaginative and bland approach the BBC was taking towards *Doctor Who* fiction upon reclaiming the licence from Virgin. *Decalog* at least had a ring to it, but it was hard to get excited about something called *Short Trips*. Short trips are what you take to go to a local shop, or maybe visiting the next town over, a daytrip at best. Hardly the stuff of which thrilling escapades with a 900 year old alien renegade are made. Doesn't exactly fill your imagination with thoughts of *Doctor Who* at its exotic, adventurous best, does it? For that very reason Big Finish's initial announcement of having secured the short story licence back in 2002 was tinged with disappointment for me, although I assumed the BBC had insisted they use the BBC approved title for short story collections. And back then it was an after dinner mint to the main course that were the BBC Books (which were still relatively healthy, yet to feel the impact of the convoluted parallel universe eighth Doctor plot and halving of output), and rich desserts that were Telos' novellas. They were an optional extra in a crowded marketplace and, in critical terms, very much a distant third. Perhaps even a distant fourth if Big Finish's own audio plays were taken into account, maybe even fifth when the charity fanthologies which were still relatively common at the time of the *Short Trips* launch.

It seemed a little bizarre for Big Finish to start a range of printed *Who* fiction. There had been what seemed like a fairly aggressive push to position the audios as the real continuation of *Doctor Who* at the expense of the ongoing novel range. Book fans certainly seemed to feel hard done by with the prominent space accorded Big Finish's new releases in *Doctor Who Magazine* (although it should be noted that with, at most, only an author and editor to have their say, there's fewer people to interview regarding a book, therefore less potential to fill space). One more of fandom's minor schisms developed where the already small market (the subset of fans with enough interest and spare cash to keep up) was split, with fans championing their chosen medium. Of course, from the outside (and to a fair few on the inside) this looked ridiculous. With twice the opportunity to find a story they might enjoy, some fans found a way to spite themselves by halving their opportunities over some minor, pointless ideology. Think of it as the *Doctor Who* equivalent of *Life of Brian*'s Judean People's Front and People's Front of Judea and you have an idea how daft it is. A *Doctor Who* collection is richer for being able to include, for example, Paul Magrs and Lloyd Rose's books alongside Rob Shearman and Marc Platt's audios. And as that example points out fairly well, it's not as if either medium could claim superiority by having better writers as they mostly drew from the same pool. But with this new range who was going to buy them? The literary fans had developed a distaste for Big Finish and there was then the question of whether the audio buyers were loyal to Big Finish or the audio medium. Whatever the case, the target market had already been damaged over one of fandom's infamous in-fights.

Gradually though, the literary competition dropped away. Firstly Telos lost its licence amidst rumours of skulduggery. And then, in the wake of *Doctor Who*'s televisual revival, BBC Books brought its now 'classic *Who*' novel series to an end, understandably preferring to concentrate on novels based on the BBC Wales production which were more commercially successful than any previous range of *Doctor Who* novels by several orders of magnitude. With the publication of *Farewells* in March 2006, just over halfway through its lifespan, *Short Trips* was the last series standing. And as with the eventual passing, few remarked on it at the time. Most of us were too wrapped up in David Tennant's imminent first series, or too far behind with the mass of published *Who* related fiction, to even notice. But there still didn't seem to be any push for extra sales, not any publicity bar the quarterly advert and review in *DWM*. Maybe the sales were fairly consistent month on month, and an announcement sufficed to maintain the range's presence. Outpost Gallifrey quarantined the books in the Big Finish section, a move which meant that the *Short Trips* message traffic was dominated by those who snapped up any and all Big Finish products, unable to attract passing traffic from those interested enough to drop by the books section. So despite the best efforts of several authors, the only real spike in interest in coverage was during the open submission competition so successful that it ended up producing a whole book's worth of new writers for the range. One of the trademarks of the latter years of the range was an encouraging pursuit of writers new to *Who*, fresh voices and perspectives. *How the Doctor Changed My Life* was only the most obvious, and one of the best examples of that.

That the range is relatively neglected in terms of *Doctor Who* fiction isn't a disgrace, but there's a lot of good writing that doesn't deserve to be neglected because of publication in *Doctor Who*'s literary backwater. There are plenty of gems here, including several left out of the *Re:Collections* anthology. Many make the easy mistake of trying to tell a compressed *Doctor Who* adventure, but the better ones exploit the format to tell tales that wouldn't work at book length. Jonathan Morris' *The Thief of Sherwood* (in *Past Tense*) is a brilliant use of the format to detail a fictional lost Hartnell, Rob Shearman's *Teach Yourself Ballroom Dancing* in *The Muses* is quietly on a par with any of his audio work, Graeme Burk's *Reversal of Fortune* (in *Steel Skies*) makes literate use of a concept that Martin Amis demonstrated didn't really work when extended to book length, Simon Guerrier's *How You Get There* is a fine exploitation of the bits of a *Doctor Who* story you usually cut away from, in *Transmissions* Ian Mond finds an unusual way to tell a *Who* story in *Policy to Invade* ... there's a long list of stories worth a look, even if you occasionally have to work to sift them from the surrounding tales which don't work quite as well. For consistency though, it's difficult to beat Richard Salter's stunning *Transmissions*, where his experience editing the Canadian Doctor Who Information Network's *Myth Makers* short story fanzine is put to excellent use, with a strong theme thoroughly exploited by a well selected group of writers.

Perhaps my melancholia at the end of *Short Trips* is because there's now less opportunity than ever for new voices to break into *Doctor*

Who fiction, perhaps it's because of that ending to literature based on the classic series. Maybe though, just maybe it's the sense that, like the Virgin range, it hadn't exhausted itself creatively but was cut off at a point where it still had potential creatively, particularly with an enviable range of authors and editors ensuring it never felt as stagnant as the BBC range felt towards the end. Or maybe it's the thought that some gems of *Doctor Who* fiction, which played to a relatively small audience to begin with, will continue to be neglected.

6B OR NOT 6B

by Paul Castle
Originally printed in Shooty Dog Thing #10 - Summer 2009

As regular readers of *Shooty Dog Thing* will know, I have something of a soft spot for fan theories. The great granddaddy of them all I think is the Season 6b theory, which has its origins in the eighties following Patrick Troughton's reprisal of his role as the second Doctor for *The Five Doctors* and *The Two Doctors*. It's a theory that splits continuity lovers cleanly down the middle, and despite my bias in favour I'm going to attempt a reappraisal.

'The time has come for you to change your appearance'

The Doctor's life has come to an end many times over the last few decades, but the pointless 'because we've got to somehow' demises of the sixth and seventh incarnations aside, there's nothing quite as essentially arbitrary as the changeover between Patrick Troughton's second and Jon Pertwee's third Doctors. Don't get me wrong, I adore the end of *The War Games* and think that the second Doctor's sacrifice is as brave and selfless as Peter Davison's fifth. Story-wise, it works, but within the 'this is really happening' context of the mythos it sucks the big one.

The second Doctor doesn't 'die' because he's gotten old, or suffered fatal dosages of radiation, tarmac, poison, carrot juice, femme fatale surgeons, the time vortex, or schmaltz (as I'm sure will be the case with the tenth), he dies because he's being punished for caring about the universe and the people who live in it. Not only that, he's punished for a 'crime' that the people who've put him on trial admit

230

isn't such a bad thing because his sentence is exile to a place where his criminal activities could be put to the best use. That's like a burglar being given a job by the police to gather evidence they couldn't get otherwise and *still* being imprisoned for his full sentence. The sixth and seventh Doctors may have had their existences curtailed arbitrarily, but the second's life was ended unjustly. This whole sense of wrongness is what fuels the desire to see more adventures of the second Doctor following *The War Games*, and makes the Season 6b theory intriguing.

'I'm not exactly breaking the Laws of Time, but I am bending them a little'

Life is full of injustice, and the only way to remain both happy and sane is to get used to it. You simply focus on the sacrifice the second Doctor knowingly made to save all the people caught up in the eponymous war games and take solace in the fact that the Doctor's companions were returned home safely, even if the memories of their travels through time have been taken from them. It's not fair, but you get over it.

But then you get a couple of hints that things didn't end like that after all, that rather than being forcibly regenerated and exiled immediately the Doctor's allowed a brief time to do what he does best as one of the Time Lords' agents.

The first hint of this is when the second Doctor pops in to see his old friend the Brigadier at a UNIT reunion party in 1983's *The Five Doctors*. When he and the Brigadier are time-scooped to Gallifrey, he's not really surprised at the Time Lords' ability to find him easily (he admits that he shouldn't really be there) when prior to his trial he'd successfully eluded them. Physically he's a much older man, hinting that some time had passed since his official last moments as himself, but he's also knowledgeable about the events and consequences of his last story, as when they meet the phantom images of Jamie and Zoe he knows full well their fate after the events of his trial.

If it was the events of *The Five Doctors* alone where we meet a post *War Games* second Doctor that'd be enough evidence, but within eighteen months he's back on our screens, this time sharing screen time with Colin Baker's sixth Doctor in *The Two Doctors*. This second eighties reunion story builds on the idea of there being further adventures of the second Doctor. At a first glance it appears to be set at some point in season five, a long time before the trial. There's a reason given for Jamie being the Doctor's sole companion, when he was always up with one or two others in the sixties episodes. Victoria's absence is explained by her having been dropped off somewhere to study graphology. This argument doesn't hold water though. For starters, the TARDIS could never ever be directed and they always landed in random places. How then could the Doctor drop Victoria off anywhere with any hope of picking her up again? Secondly, there's no indication in *Fury from the Deep*, Victoria's final story, that she's ever been separated from the Doctor and Jamie before. Invoking the Victoria factor alone for placing *The Two Doctors* in season five ignores everything else we learn about the second Doctor and Jamie in this story.

For starters, there's the physical evidence. Both Jamie and the Doctor are considerably older. Jamie's a teenager in the sixties episodes, but here he's middle-aged. The Doctor's considerably greyer, even more noticeably so than his appearance in *The Five Doctors*. If this was the only evidence then you could charitably suspend your disbelief - actors get older as the decades pass - but the story itself treats the Doctor more like his exiled third incarnation: the TARDIS is sent on missions on the behalf of the Time Lords. For episodes 9 and 10 of *The War Games* to retain any dramatic credibility this has to be the first contact between the Doctor and his people since the Doctor went on the run with his granddaughter Susan. To come along and say that the Doctor had been doing a few jobs for them on the side makes a mockery of his final episode.

In addition to that, the second Doctor here has 'earned certain privileges' that the sixth Doctor had 'always wanted'. If the second Doctor's part of the story took place in an established part of the sixth Doctor's history, rather than somehow outside-of-time, then when presented with a Stattenheim Remote Control the sixth Doctor wouldn't have 'always wanted one of those' but would instead bemoan having lost it.

It's quite clear to me that the second Doctor we see in both his eighties reprises is from a point in his life some considerable time after *The War Games*.

Stuck in the middle with you

Season 6b is basically anything that happens to the Doctor between the last episode of Season 6 (*The War Games* #10, where we see a gurning Patrick Troughton being dragged into limbo) and the first episode of Season 7 (*Spearhead from Space* #1, where Jon Pertwee stumbles from the TARDIS and collapses into the undergrowth). Whilst the theory only really developed in the nineties, the idea that the second Doctor had a life after *The War Games* dates back to a mere nine days after the episode was broadcast.

TV Comic had presented us with the comic strip adventures of the Doctor almost as long as there'd been a TV series (kicking off with *The Klepton Parasites* on Monday 9th November 1964, two days after the broadcast of *Planet of Giants* #2), and had stayed with us week-in-week-out right up to the end of the second Doctor's era. They weren't going to let a simple matter of a few lines of dialogue put the comic on hold until the third Doctor was made available. The issue published on Monday 30th June 1969 kicked off a story called *Action in Exile!* and saw the second Doctor get, ahem, stuck into some action whilst in exile on Earth. For five months' worth of stories the second Doctor lived in a swanky hotel and had adventures with military types, concluding with the Time Lords' scarecrow representatives in *The Night Walkers* catching up with the Doctor in order to execute the second part of the Doctor's sentence and change his appearance. Seven weeks later, seventies *Who* is here and Jon Pertwee stumbles from the TARDIS in a daze and collapses, waking up a while later to have adventures with more military types.

In all honesty, these 21 installments of comic strip action aren't particularly great, but just as seventies *Battlestar Galactica* was reimagined for a noughties audience, this era of *Doctor Who* can be expanded and developed to take in and nurture the discontinuities of the second Doctor's eighties escapades.

Fantasy seasons

I'm rather glad I never did it now, but one idea I had for my fanzine *Eye of Orion* a decade ago was to devote an entire issue to a whole season of short stories, building up a framework in which the second Doctor could have more adventures with his friends. It was all very sad fanwanky stuff where the Doctor initially had adventures alone, building up some kudos with his people who eventually allowed him to pick up his young friends Jamie and Zoe again. Zoe only stayed for one story, choosing to return to her life, leaving Jamie and the Doctor to battle Cybermen and Quarks and giant wasps. They'd team up with other companions from the past from time to time, allowing plenty of room for Victoria's graphology course and the tenth anniversary *Radio Times* pictures of a seventies Ben and Polly being chased by Cybermen across the Norfolk broads. In the end, the Doctor and Jamie arrived in the eighteenth century highlands, where they battled the Yeti and set Jamie up as a local hero and laird. Now companionless, the Doctor found himself stuck on Earth for some action in exile...

Like I say, all very fanwanky, but hey, it was either that or write up lecture notes on sociology, geology, or statistical computing. The nineties was the decade of fanwank and short story fanthologies. There was no *Doctor Who* on television, and the uninspiring BBC Books range had replaced the *New Adventures*. There was a whole generation of *Doctor Who* readers that the innovative *NAs* had nourished, and we all felt like we owned the series. Some of us worked at it and got published, but most of us weren't anywhere near the entrance standard so we carved out little niches for ourselves. Mary-Sues, alternate universes, elaborate 'how we'd bring back the series' arcs etc etc. We all had toys to play with, and Season 6b was one of those toys.

'Canonised'

So you can imagine how we felt when the Season 6b theory was effectively 'canonised' by none other than Terrance Dicks, with the release of his novel *Players* in April 1999. I can't really speak for others, but reading this book I felt half endorsed, and half let down. It was encouraging that the theory was introduced into the continuity of the series, but disappointing that it was merely part of yet another retread of Terrance Dicks' past glories. *Players* came from the same toybox as *The War Games*, *Exodus*, and *The Eight Doctors*, and said toybox would be returned to with the publication of *Endgame* and *World Game* (the latter also set in Season 6b). It was essentially Season 6b being incorporated into Terrance Dicks' little slice of the cake rather than being used to open up new doors into unexplored realms. A good example of the way in which the concept could have been explored is with the not-named-as-such Season 23b, in which a whole new era for the sixth Doctor between the end of *The Trial of a Time Lord* and the future events shown in episodes 9-12 of the serial is opened up and explored thematically. Terrance's Season 6b, by contrast, is just window dressing for the same tired old rubbish.

Perhaps I'm being unfair to Terrance. *Doctor Who* is such a broad church that there's plenty of room for all of us. I fail to understand how people can dislike Paul Magrs' take on *Doctor Who*, for instance, or praise the dreadful Season 18 whilst damning the glorious Season 17. There's no such thing as canon, and nowadays with the return of the TV series worrying about such things seems insignificant to the point of ridiculousness. There's no point in getting het up about things you don't like when there's more than enough out there to please everyone, so you're free to ignore anything you don't rate. The only thing that matters is the quality of the writing, and by that criteria… sorry, there were Season 6b novels? Really? Gosh.

Season 6b turned up in a few of the *Short Trips* books, but as I've yet to sample many from that range I can't really comment how successful they've been. Nice to know they exist though.

The parting of the ways

I fear I pretty much forgot about the Season 6b theory after *Players*. I left university and got a job, and recreational reading time was drastically reduced. With that went my dabblings in fan-fic (mercifully so, it has to be said!) and aside from watching *The Five Doctors* and *The Two Doctors* as I got the DVDs, I thought about 6b no more.

And then suddenly, last year, I started thinking about it again. But I hadn't been watching Troughton DVDs, listening to any of the sixties audio episodes, reading any of the books or sampling any of the Big Finish *Companion Chronicles* or *Short Trips*. I was still enjoying the Hartnell episodes, and Season 6 was miles off. Nope, what sparked this off was last year's *Doctor Who* on telly, the stories with the tenth Doctor, Donna Noble, and crucially, the return of Rose Tyler.

That might sound like a bit of an odd connection to make, but to me *The War Games* and *Doomsday* are two peas in a pod, emotionally speaking. *The War Games* forcibly separates the Doctor from his companions, never to be reunited, and *Doomsday* separated the previously inseparable Doctor and Rose Tyler, never to be reunited.

Only trouble is, they brought back Rose Tyler in last year's *Doctor Who*. The build up was fantastic, the resolution was crass. In *Journey's End* Rose Tyler doesn't get her man, but she gets a carbon copy. The ending is a bit 'meh' when with *Doomsday* it was a hanky-wringing tragedy.

We got our happy ending, sort of, but rather than being a nice neat 1+1=2 it was a 1+1=2ish, remainder 1. The ending of the Doctor/Rose story was literally compromised.

So you see, I watched *Journey's End* and saw how it would compromise my enjoyment of *Doomsday*. I linked that into my desire years ago for the tragedy at the end of *The War Games* to be revisited and made better. What I learned from the last episode of the 2008 series of *Doctor Who* was that turning a tragedy into a happy ending is not necessarily a way of making something better.

So, where do I stand now? Do I reject the Season 6b theory? Do I go back to seeing the inconsistencies in the two eighties second Doctor stories as continuity errors? Do I start to regard the scene of Troughton's face being contorted at the end of the last sixties episode as his regeneration?

No, I don't think I need go that far.

Season 6b as a concept still makes a lot of sense to me, it's an elegant way of explaining all my previously covered 'problems' with *The Five Doctors* and *The Two Doctors*, and I fondly remember loving it. It's somewhere were we can tidy away the sixties comic strip adventures of the second Doctor and Jamie fighting Cybermen and Quarks, should we deem it necessary to tidy anything at all, and the idea of the *TV Comic* strips foreshadowing the television series with the Doctor's involvement with the military whilst in exile is a pleasing one. Not only that, having the second Doctor regenerating at the hands of scarecrows at the end of *The Night Walkers* is a far more arresting image than what we had onscreen.

So I think instead of discarding the theory, it should simply stay as it is. No more fantasy seasons, no more 'what if that picture of Ben and Polly from that *Radio Times* 10th Anniversary photoshoot is part of a story that could be told?' It should simply be what it is, with no additions or subtractions. It's no longer a going concern; shut down, cordoned off, finished.

Perhaps there is still a whole series of novels or comics or audios that can take place in Season 6b, exploring it fully. Perhaps the IDW comics with their reprints of the *DWM* strips and cameos in stories like *The Forgotten* will open up a range of stories that, for the second Doctor at least, fits in with the 6b concept quite naturally. Perhaps the loss of the printed fiction license at Big Finish means that the *Doctor Who* production team - Steven Moffat and Piers Wenger - have plans in place for a whole new era of past Doctor books where the second Doctor could find a new lease of life in 6b.

Perhaps, perhaps, perhaps.

But you know what? Maybe we should just let Season 6b exist without ever going there. Unexplored countries lose their mystique once they've been surveyed. Perhaps Season 6b only ever really worked as somewhere on a map of continuity marked *here be dragons*.

WHO COULD HAVE BEEN THE 456?
by Paul Castle
Originally printed in Shooty Dog Thing #10 - Summer 2009

I'm afraid I gave him a little stick for it, for reasons that'd become clear, but after the broadcast of the first episode of the superb *Torchwood* mini-series a friend of mine (I'll not name and shame him here, I'm here to poke fun at the idea, not pick on the guy) got all excited about who the 456 might be, convinced that the aliens had been in *Doctor Who* before. He noted in an article for Examiner.com things like information being encoded in intense bursts of radio, that the aliens had been to Earth and had dealings with the British government before, that they breathe air which is poisonous to us, and that they come to Earth and stay in an ambassadorial suite. This last bit especially led him to speculate that it's the creatures seen in 1970's *The Ambassadors of Death*.

To be fair to him, he does note that he may well be proven wrong the next day, but my mind boggles that anyone can take some really quite common science fiction staples and treat them as evidence that a long forgotten monster from decades ago is returning. It's the fannish equivalent of police rounding up some random black youths in hoodies after a crime :o)

So, I thought I'd turn back the clock in my mind to that Monday night and come up with my own ideas on who the 456 might have turned out to be if writers Russell T. Davies, James Moran, and John Fay hadn't had their own ideas.

The Nimon

The eponymous aliens from 1979's *The Horns of Nimon* were the first ones that jumped out at me. Another friend hadn't seen the *Children of Earth* episodes yet, warning me to be careful about spoilers, and I knee-jerk replied that it was the Nimon, a second later adding 'three Nimon!'. It was only later that I reflected that the Nimon are actually pretty close to the 456 in *modus operandi*, far closer than the unfairly named 'Ambassadors of Death' whose intent was peaceful. The Nimon are a little different in that they are basically invading parasites who travel from world to world (more akin to the Sky Ray creatures from *Planet of the Dead* in that they generate a wormhole; the Sky Ray do a *Superman the Movie* very very fast fly around the planet timewarp thing, whereas the Nimon artificially induce a black hole) whilst the 456 have a protection racket thing going. But the similarities between the Nimon and 456 are noteworthy: both require a Tribute of young humans, both keep themselves tucked away in the middle of a maze (all government buildings are labyrinthic), and the Tribute are chosen by the invaded peoples' representatives: in the case of Skonnos it's their defeated enemies the Anethians, whilst the leaders of Earth select the poorest inner-city kids (or their local alternative).

The Chameleons

The Chameleons from the 1967 story *The Faceless Ones* are also rather similar to the 456, but in a very different way. Again their prime interest is in the young people of our planet, kidnapping 18-30 type holidaymakers by employing a trick you could almost - but not quite - imagine seeing on *The Real Hustle*: the aeroplane the kids board is a convertible spaceship, and whisks them off into space. Postcards are sent home to the families from the holiday destination, and by the time the authorities investigate the disappearances Chameleon Tours have gone (or at least, they would have were it not for the arrival of the Doctor). The Chameleons need the bodies of the young humans to give them lives in some alien-psi-vampire-type manner.

The Ra'ashetani

'Who?!' you're probably exclaiming. These are Kate Orman's race of aliens from a *Brief Encounter* story from *DWM* (#206, 24th November 1993) called *One Minute Fourteen Seconds*. In this short story the alien Shiir'ha'ash from Ra'ashpep and his human (presumably governmental) colleague are guests on a chatshow. It's a very public *The Day the Earth Stood Still* situation, where the alien is offering to help clean up the planet in return for the commodity they trade in: food. The TARDIS materialises in the studio during the commercial break, and the Doctor approaches Shiir to ask if he's aware that the people of Earth wouldn't be told the full truth: that with the vegetables, confectionary, alcohol and meat, that human meat was part of the deal. Shiir is shocked that this would be a problem, having been led to believe that humans eat their own, and knowing who the Doctor is, thanks him for clarifying the situation and beams back to his ship: the deal off. The Doctor leaves the government agent alone on the guest sofa to answer the studio audience's questions of precisely which humans would have been part of the deal: refugees? Street kids?

So, my friend, if you must insist on choosing an obscure old alien you'd like to see return you've got to step up your game. For in just a piss-take filler piece I can out-fanboy you with three examples that make at least a little bit of sense, and not rely on similarities that come down to simple - not to mention generic sci-fi - tropes like 'they can communicate in a code that can easily be deciphered' and 'they breathe alien air'. The 456 are as akin to the 'Ambassadors of Death' as General Zod, Ursa and Non from *Superman II* are to the *Power Puff Girls*. Um, bad example?

MIRROR, MIRROR, ON THE WALL...

by Lee Catigen-Cooper

Original material for The Best of Shooty Dog Thing

Tell me, when you look in the mirror. What do you see?

I suppose that's something that all of us, at some point in our lives will ask, or be asked.

But what truly, is the answer? Obviously, we could quote a very famous sitcom and reply 'Me looking absolutely fabulous, naturally Darling' but is even that, or what it implies, the truth?

Do we, actually see, what everybody else sees? ... Is our reflection, really us?

Gay. Straight. Impaired.

All of these are titles that we, as living, breathing, human beings are forced to admit apply to us. Yes! That's me! I'm, one of the above!

Are you? Think about it. Are you truly one of the above? Or, are you, you?

Are those titles, in reality, just a part of who you are? Of course, all of them will apply to each of us in some way and will govern our lives respectively, and we should have no fear of embracing them, as that's what helps to make us the people we are.

But are you something more?

What, if you're something else?

What, if you're a *Doctor Who* fan?

Since the return of the BBC's flagship show, admitting to such a thing, isn't an issue, until you confess one other thing. 'I attend conventions.'

'Oh! ... You're an Anorak then?'

Are we? Obviously, we all have our favourite Doctor, Companion, and Story. That's what being a 'fan' of anything will entail, especially when the franchise catalogue is so extensive, but does that truly make us an anorak?

Don't non *Doctor Who* fans have their own appreciation of things? Of course they do.

Do you have a favourite band? 'Yes'.

Do you know the names of the band members? 'Yes'.

Do you have a favourite song? 'Yes'.

And do you know the lyrics to that song? 'Yes'.

'Oh! … You're an Anorak then?'

'No, I'm just a fan'.

Wonderful isn't it? …

Tell me, when you look in the mirror. What do you see?

Well? You're reading this, and it's in a book about *Doctor Who*, so there's a strong possibility you're a fan. And you may have attended conventions, so tell us.

Are you an anorak? Or, is being a *Doctor Who* fan and attending conventions, like all of the above titles just a part of whom you are?

Do you laugh and cry? Do you love and hate? Do you need and give? Are you, you?

If the answer is yes, and you have never, attended a convention. Then do so.

What! And become an anorak? No! It will not make you anything but what you already are, but it will make you feel something. Accepted.

Within this 'convention world' you can truly be who and what you are. Titles, no longer burden us. Gay. Straight. Impaired. It doesn't really matter; you're a fan, and one of us.

And I know this because … I'm a fan too … and I've been accepted.

Tell me, when you look in the mirror. What do you see?

IRIS WILDTHYME
AND THE CELESTIAL OMNIBUS
Reviewed by Jon Arnold
Originally printed in Shooty Dog Thing #10 - Summer 2009

For the connoisseur of *Doctor Who* related novels these have been dark times. The BBC's new series novels, occasionally good as they can be, are hamstrung by necessarily not being the vanguard of an ongoing series, as the literary tales of the seventh and eighth Doctors were. And they're certainly not aimed at the fans who bought the novels through the Great Telly Interregnum. Telos lost first the novella licence, then had to cancel their *Time Hunter* series due to poor sales. The future for *Faction Paradox* is, appropriately enough, unclear.

Big Finish has recently announced the end of their *Short Trips* range and, for the foreseeable future, look like they're down to one or two Benny books per year. Which all means that there's something of a gap in the market to sate those of us, mostly Target-*New Adventure*-EDA refugees, who craved a literary *Who* fix. And filling that hole is Obverse Books' debut release, *Iris Wildthyme and the Celestial Omnibus*.

Amongst *Who* fans Iris divides debate more sharply than even canon. On one hand there's those that find her an irritating old bat who's just a deliberate female photocopy of the Doctor. And on the other there are those who realise that's only part of it. A simple female photocopy of the Doctor simply wouldn't be able to carry an equal share of the novels and audios she's co-starred in. No, since striking out on her own it's fairly evident that the adventures of Iris Wildthyme are what you'd get if you strip the concept of *Doctor Who* back to bare essentials, losing all the unnecessary encrusted paraphernalia that's grown on the show like barnacles, then sprinkle them with everything you ever loved about *Doctor Who*, as well as a fair few things you didn't realise you did. Like much of the best *Doctor Who*, Iris stories are often camp as tits, shamelessly getting any genres that venture within bus range drunk and having their wicked way with them. This book will make you think that this is what *Doctor Who* could've been like if Williams and Adams had indulged Tom's mad ideas back in 1979 and found a way to make them work. And yet even that glorious possibility couldn't have been more fun than Iris currently is - where Tom wanted a talking cauliflower, Iris has acquired a sentient stuffed panda.

Reading this collection, or listening to the audios, you can't help but feel the same thing as you do about Season 17 - that everyone involved has had an absolute blast and hence given of their best. Most short story collections, particularly multi-authored ones, are something of a lucky dip, with each diamond of a story being balanced by one that's aspired to be a gem but somehow ended up as coal. That's emphatically not the case here. Even the stories that didn't dazzle, perhaps because they picked very obvious subjects or targets, have some laugh out loud funny jokes, killer lines, great ideas or the odd moment of quiet profundity.

The book opens with a devastating one-two punch which demonstrates the range of stories you can tell with Iris. Steve Lyons'

A Gamble with Wildthyme is short, sharp, intelligently funny and has a whale of a time playing with the basic concept of one of *Doctor Who's* most admired stories. That's just in the literary equivalent of the teaser sequence. It's perfectly contrasted with Mags Halliday's *Sovereign*, a beautifully realised homage to the fantasies of Susan Cooper and Alan Garner that children of the Seventies grew up on. It's proof that Iris can be at her best even when not being played for laughs and is, for me, the highlight of the collection.

But to simply call this a vehicle for Iris would be wrong (her bus is her vehicle for starters). While she's never upstaged by various strong personalities and camp icons such as Noel Coward, Marlene Dietrich and 'Mr Alucard', the stage is very much shared with her travelling companion.

Where most of the Doctor's literary companions have struggled to make an initial impression - aside from Benny perhaps only Fitz was consistently strongly written in his early days - Panda is not only a companion always recognisable from the description in the guidelines, but one with the vitality to transcend them (aided no doubt by David Benson's performances in the Big Finish audios). It's demonstrated best by co-editor Stuart Douglas' contribution, Panda's witty, often caustic narration enhancing a fast and funny tale that might otherwise lean a little too heavily on cheeky *Doctor Who* allusions.

It's also commendable that Obverse continues the tradition of *Doctor Who* publishers by offering authors a chance to see their work professionally published. Of these new contributors, simply for the splendidly bizarre concept and engagement with a foreign culture, Cody Schell's tale of Mexican wrestling, extradimensional mummies and the periodic table provides the highlight. The distinctive subject matter and colourful cultural perspective makes Schell an author worth looking out for in the future.

All this without even mentioning Paul Magrs and Phil Purser-Hallard's eloquent skewering of the inherent ridiculousness of *Torchwood* and the recently deceased *Battlestar Galactica* revival respectively, and Steve Cole's most affecting story, which is almost as eloquent about fans as *Love & Monsters*.

If you're one of those who believe that a story in whatever medium simply being dark makes it mature and deep then you're probably better off looking elsewhere. But if you're mature enough to realise that life's at least equally about having as much of a laugh as you can at life's absurdities while you're here, *Iris Wildthyme and the Celestial Omnibus* is a joyous technicolour party of a book that'll bring plenty of sunshine, and not a little gin, into your life.

N.B. Coming December 2009: *The Panda Book of Horror*
www.obversebooks.co.uk

WALLOWING IN
THE ICECANOS OF NOSTALGIA
by Paul Castle
Originally printed in Shooty Dog Thing #10 - Summer 2009

Did you catch *On the Outside it Looked Like an Old Fashioned Police Box* - Mark Gatiss' tribute to the age of the Target novelisations - on Radio 4 recently? If you did, I wonder if the same thing about it niggled you as much as it did me.

For the main part I enjoyed it, and was wallowing in the Icecanos of Nostalgia as much as the next fan (in this case, Jon Arnold, as evidenced by his Facebook status update at the time) as we heard from the likes of Uncle Terry and Chris Achilleos as Mark briefly took us through the origins and development of the range (if you're interested in learning more then you'll find David J. Howe's *The Target Book* a very fine read: buy it before it goes out of print!) taking full advantage of the audiobooks to illustrate why these books are loved by a generation of readers.

But the thing that niggled me was the way that Gatiss mourned the lack of novelisations today. Before you agree with him that it would be great to have 'Doctor Who And The Unquiet Dead by Terrance Dicks', let me explain myself. It wasn't his mourning of there not being such a range of novelisations, it was the way he made out that children are missing out on something that kids in the seventies and eighties had: *Doctor Who* books to read in the car whilst Mum and Dad were wandering round the garden centre.

The thing is, the modern day WhoKids *do* have this, you can even argue that they have something better! What kids today have is the TV series they love on DVD almost as soon as it's broadcast, and a constant run of repeats on BBC3, so I don't think there'd be a great market for straight novelisations. But the lack of 'Doctor Who And The Empty Child' doesn't mean today's little Mark sitting in the back of his parents' car isn't catered for, as Gatiss seems to think. What WhoKids have today is something far far better: they have brand new stories! They have something which is a halfway point between the Targets and the Virgin books I grew up with. Little Mark is far from deprived, where we had *Doctor Who and the Loch Ness Monster*, he's got *Shining Darkness*, where we had *Doctor Who and the Space War*, he's got *Only Human*.

So that was my niggle: simply that Mark Gatiss was painting a picture of children today not having *Doctor Who* they could carry around with them, to read on holiday or in the classroom as we did. Some things have changed, and some remain the same. But don't let nostalgia blind you into creating some sort of golden age, because as those of us who read *Doctor Who and the Dinosaur Invasion* as kids know where *that* can lead…

But do catch the programme if you can, for aside from that one minute or so right at the end it's an enjoyable half hour's diversion as you walk home or wash the dishes or whatever it is you do when listening to the radio. It's bound to be repeated on BBC7 or released on CD at some point.

One thing the Radio 4 programme made me consider was just how similar the Targets we had then are to the books the kids of today have. We might look back and see practically every story from every Doctor represented and think that the current climate of having novels released with just the current bloke on the cover, but looking at the lists in *The Target Book*, it was just the same back then, with Pertwee dominating the schedule from '73-'75, and Tom and Davison dominating their respective years. The chances are that if a book was new on the shelf, it was an adventure of the bloke currently on the telly, just like it is now. It makes me think of all the potential fans out there today whose first exposure to *Doctor Who* might be this autumn, catching the tail end of Tennant's run just as I caught the last days of Tom.

Might these new fans' primary exposure to Eccleston and Tennant be the novel adventures of the ninth and tenth Doctor from the local library, just as my early experiences of the third and fourth Doctors were the Targets? I would like to think so. But then, I'm ignoring the telly repeats on BBC3 and therefore just as guilty of bias as Mark Gatiss.

SUITS YOU SIR!
by Paul Castle
Originally printed in Shooty Dog Thing #10 - Summer 2009

The moment one first claps eyes on the official new costume for a new Doctor is a funny thing. I can't speak for anyone else, so please indulge me. The thing I have found, right from my very first glimpse of a new Doctor's costume at the tender age of six with the Doctor of the same designation, was sheer horror. Of course, such a reaction was pretty natural for anyone with both cones and rods in their eyes, but it wasn't just that first episode of *The Twin Dilemma* where I felt costume-shock. Amazing as it may seem, I grew to like both Colin's Doctor and his sense of sartorial elegance, and whilst I couldn't wait for the seventh Doctor to shed his predecessor's skin, and found myself echoing the Rani's impatience with his several costume changes in *Time and the Rani*, when he settled on his last one I called out 'no, not that one, try another!'

The next time we had a new Doctor though, the situation was very different. I was considerably older and was aware of breaking news and promo photoshoots. Here it was a different story: I immediately fell in love with the costume that Paul McGann wore for that initial announcement back in January 1996, and hated the Edwardian fancy dress he ended up in. I got used to it, and even started to like it in the *DWM* strip, but always wished that they'd stuck with the cropped hair, heavy dark overcoat and grey checked scarf.

Eccleston's leather jacket and Tennant's geek chic? Aside from an initial surprise, I have to say I loved them! They were just perfect for the actors, who looked natural in them.

But for Matt Smith, I knew from the second I saw those initial publicity images back in January that we were in trouble. You see, I simply adored the black jeans, dark jacket with close-knit woolly jumper underneath with the sleeves folded up over the jacket's cuffs. The second I saw it, I knew that they'd not be able to top that: it had the right level of understated eccentricity. It was something I'd be comfortable in myself, not as a dress up (no, just no!) but as normal clobber.

But then, filming for the 2010 series started on Monday 20th July and we got our first glimpse of the new Doctor (and the new TARDIS, but that's another ramble). I felt underwhelmed, disappointed that I'd been proven right. It looked far too eccentric for my modern NuWhu tastes. It looked, on that first in-passing glance as if they'd just dug out John Smith's suit from *Human Nature*.

But you sleep on it, and see a couple more pictures, and start to rationalise it. I remember saying online somewhere (probably to anyone who'd listen) back in 2004 that the 1950s Oxbridge professor look, all tweed and leather elbow patches, was the modern equivalent of Hartnell's Edwardian gentleman attire from the sixties: 2010 minus 1950 is equal to 1963 minus 1903.

Once I rationalised this as being given precisely the costume I was gunning for five years ago, when I had Giles from *Buffy the Vampire Slayer* as my model Doctor, I started to actually like it. I think it suits the old man in a young body look that Matt Smith has, and he seems to look comfy in it.

It took me 24 hours, but I'm very happy with the look of the eleventh Doctor. Now all they've got to do is stop putting Karen Gillan in baggy figure concealing jumpers and we're sorted.

DIMENSIONS 2009:
REVIEW OF A WHO CONVENTION
by Richard Parker
Original material for The Best of Shooty Dog Thing

Conventions, for me, are about bar prices. Seriously, whenever a convention moves to a new hotel, the first question on everyone's mind is 'what are the prices like at the bar?' Secondly, 'what are the staff like?'

Okay, so that's not the the first question on absolutely *everyone's* mind, but let me explain.

For years, I didn't know any other fans of *Doctor Who*. I was aware they were 'out there', somewhere. But the nearest I got to fandom was reading *Doctor Who Magazine*. Fair enough, but a few years ago I resolved to track down my nearest local group and to start attending conventions.

What I found was an incredible social circle, a multitude of long, boozy weekends and very little actual talk of *Doctor Who*.

Drinking until six in the morning, catching some disturbed sleep for a few hours and then heading back to the bar at eleven to try and ward off the hangover ... and this goes on for four days. Fairly regularly, someone will plonk food down in front of you, you'll manage to stagger to the toilet, you'll feel divorced from reality for four days and every so often you'll catch sight of someone you think you recognise from the seventies. Alzheimer's is probably not dissimilar.

There are only so many autograph queues to stand in, Q&A panels with guests to attend and merchandise dealers to avoid, so eventually everything comes back to the bar.

This was the fourth year in a row I've been to Dimensions. It is, I think, the longest running convention still around and it's not hard to see why. For the autograph hunters there was plenty of star talent about, topped by Colin Baker and Paul McGann. Katy Manning remembered me telling her of my adventures in Soho three years ago, before discussing science and rationality with me over coffee. Anneke Wills and Nick Briggs hung around outside cadging fags off the smokers. Rob Shearman sat in the bar on the Friday night, keeping me in stitches with his wicked and all-too-accurate impression of Terrance Dicks. ('And Barry said to me, 'what colour?' you see, and I said to Barry, 'Gween! The colour for monsters is Gween!)

There's the obligatory cabaret, of course. It's traditional for it to be awful. Imagine Richard Franklin dressed as a schoolboy, dancing around a stage while singing 'Daddy Wouldn't Buy Me a Bow Wow.' You can't, can you? Neither could we. Even when it was in front of us. McGann had hidden in his room by this point.

Then there was the - equally obligatory - disco. No one told me they were videoing the bloody thing, but I'm now stuck forever with the embarrassing atrocity that currently inhabits Facebook. 'Young Man', indeed.

A non-fan straight boy kept hugging me and told me I was his first 'man crush.' His friend thought he was confused. I thought he was pissed.

And rather cute.

The hotel manager being a fan helped, of course. His staff must have been instructed not to take the piss out of us nerds, and it has to be said we were all treated royally. And, the bar area was exclusively devoted to a live screening of *The Waters of Mars* on the Sunday evening. 100 fans, absolutely spellbound. McGann wandered down for a fag half-way through, stopped, looked around quizzically as if thinking 'What on earth are you all watching?' then realised, shrugged and disappeared outside in a wreath of smoke. The only moment of the whole weekend he could get out of his room without being pestered about what it's like to snog Daphne Ashbrook.

Monday mornings are always the worst. Home, and reality, beckon. Breakfast with Anneke. Checking the local rag to see how much of a hatchet job yesterday's journalists have done. Strong coffee and lots of it, then the pain as you sober up and realise by just how much you've blown your budget for the weekend. Then the long drive home.

Conventions: best weekends of your life.

Even the straight boy said so.

AFTERWORD
by Anneke Wills

In the past few years I have had the privilege of being invited to many conventions, run by the lovers of *Doctor Who*, and as Colin Baker once stated, 'God Bless the *Doctor Who* fans!' As well as being an actress from the early days of this unique series I am also proud to be part of its fandom. What an extraordinary and unique bunch of people we are. We come from all walks of life. There are judges, doctors, care-workers, architects, comedians, nurses, civil servants, writers and actors. And of course, since the show was brought back to our screens with such panache and power by such talented and dedicated fans, we now have lots more young people at the conventions, who have enthusiastically embraced the Doctor and his world to their heart, and who knows? Maybe some of children I meet will also become the writers and directors, Doctors and Dalek operators of future *Doctor Who*. There is a great sense of camaraderie among us, we have such fun at the conventions, putting the world to rights, getting to know each other, and occasionally gossiping about *Doctor Who* in the bar, we have shared inspired interviews with the stars of the show, listened to the Big Finish producers; there is always something new to hear and someone inspiring to meet. I often come away from an event having spent the entire weekend laughing. Over the past 3 years I have been to practically everything, signing my books, and I must say how very kind and supportive and generous and loving everyone has been - I feel very grateful for it all. When I first appeared in the series back in 1966, I had no idea that over 40 years later I would still be so much a part of *Doctor Who*. What do I put it down to? Magic! This is the power of the myth. We need mythological figures to inspire our imagination and the idea of the Time Lord, travelling through space is indeed, timeless magic, and it will endure. I'm so happy to be included in the vast group of people who delight in calling themselves *Doctor Who* Fans, but to me they are simply friends.

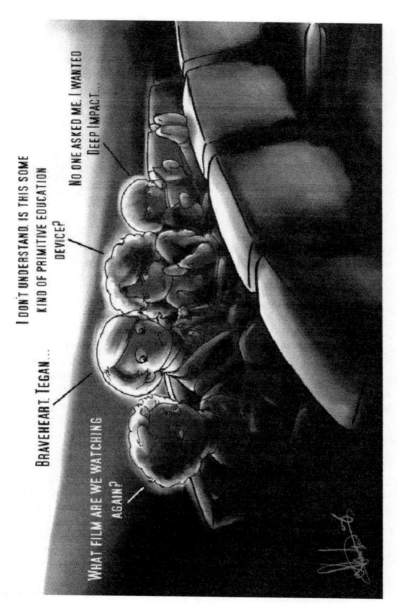

Art by Danielle Ellison, words by Paul Castle.

Also Available from Hirst Books

'Look Who's Talking' by Colin Baker

A compilation of articles from 15 years of his weekly newspaper column

He may be the sixth Doctor to us fans, but to the residents of South Buckinghamshire he is a weekly voice of sanity in a world that seems intent on confounding him. Marking the 15th anniversary of his regular feature in the Bucks Free Press, this compilation includes over 100 of his most entertaining columns, from 1995 to 2009, complete with new linking material. With fierce intelligence and a wicked sense of humour, Colin tackles everything from the absurdities of political correctness to the joys of being an actor, slipping in vivid childhood memories, international adventures and current affairs in a relentless rollercoaster of reflections, gripes and anecdotes. Pulling no punches, taking no prisoners and sparing no detail, the ups and downs of Colin's life are shared with panache, honesty and clarity, and they are every bit as entertaining and surreal as his trips in that famous police box... For a world that is bewildering, surprising and wondrous, one need look no further than modern Britain, and Colin Baker is here to help you make sense of it all, and to give you a good laugh along the way.

"Like all the best writing, this collection of Colin's columns is forthright, witty, verbose and manages the deft trick of being both stridently opinionated and charmingly self deprecating. His dextrous, even florid, vocabulary, makes for some wonderfully phrased observations that would have enlivened many an episode of Grumpy Old Men. His arguments are sometimes curmudgeonly (but never mean spirited), and often whimsical. He has you nodding vigorously or disagreeing passionately, and then he wrong-foots you by delivering a touching account about the dangers of cigarettes that would move even the most hardened smoker. If ever he tires of acting, writing could well prove to be this Baker's bread and butter."

- Toby Hadoke, Comedian

Also Available from Hirst Books

'Self Portrait & 'Naked' by Anneke Wills

One extraordinary life.
Two breathtaking books.
Countless Adventures.

Did you know that Anneke Wills once lived naked in a jungle? Or that she was a follower of a **notorious** spiritual leader? Maybe the fact that she was a **child actress** who in her late teens started a relationship with Anthony **Newley**, had passed you by. Of course, you know all about her time at the heart of **swinging sixties** London, her famous friends, like **Peter Cook**, and her turbulent marriage to **Michael Gough**. Don't You? Next you'll be saying you didn't know that she's descended from an **Elizabethan** hero or that she lived in **California, Canada** and **India**. You are of course aware that she was Doctor Who's first **glamour** girl, but did you know that she's appeared alongside six doctors? Or that **Doctor Who** has stayed with her for over 40 years? Did you know she climbed Sydney Harbour Bridge with Colin **Baker**, partied with Paul **McGann** in Vancouver and baffled Jon **Pertwee** at a BBC party? Did you know about the mysterious death of her brother, on the trail of the **Holy Grail**? Surely you've heard how she drove a huge truck across the **Rockies**, and how she and her friends took two double-decker buses across **Europe** and **Asia** to **India**? Oh, and then there's the other two marriages, and living on the remote Canadian island. Obviously you've seen at least **100 of her works of art** and personal photos, and no doubt you've experienced her warm, **intimate** storytelling style, and found yourself moved by her honesty, touched by her **sadness** and entertained by her wit. No? **You should probably buy the books.**